Digital Drawing **for Landscape Architecture**

Digital Drawing **for Landscape Architecture**
Contemporary Techniques and Tools for Digital Representation in Site Design

SECOND EDITION

Bradley Cantrell

Wes Michaels

Cover Design: Wiley

Cover Art: © Spackman Mossop Michaels

This book is printed on acid-free paper. ∞

For general information about our other products and services, please contact our Customer Care Department within the United States at (800) 762-2974, outside the United States at (317) 572-3993, or fax (317) 572-4002.

Wiley publishes in a variety of print and electronic formats and by print-on-demand. Some material included with standard print versions of this book may not be included in e-books or in print-on-demand. If this book refers to media such as a CD or DVD that is not included in the version you purchased, you may download this material at http://booksupport.wiley.com. For more information about Wiley products, visit www.wiley.com.

Library of Congress Cataloging-in-Publication Data:

Cantrell, Bradley.
 Digital drawing for landscape architecture : contemporary techniques and tools for digital representation in site design / Bradley Cantrell, Wes Michaels. — Second edition.
    pages cm
 Includes bibliographical references and index.
 ISBN 978-1-118-69318-6 (pbk.); ISBN 978-1-118-93308-4 (ebk); ISBN 978-1-118-93891-1 (ebk)
 1. Landscape architecture--Computer-aided design. 2. Landscape design—Data processing. I. Michaels, Wes. II. Title.
 SB475.9.D37C36 2015
 712.0285—dc23
                        2014011446

Printed in the United States of America

10 9 8 7 6 5 4 3 2 1

Contents

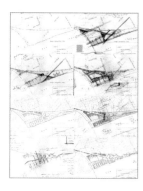

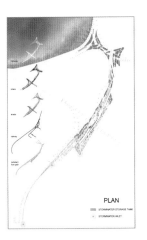

Foreword[1]

It is easy these days to assume everyone knows how to use new media. One probably imagines that by now new electronic media and image making are embedded in the DNA of everyone who uses a computer, personal device, or other digital tools. But the reality is that media and image making are an art form with learned techniques and protocols. There is always need for excellent tutorials that describe basic techniques and their application and I am pleased that *Digital Drawing for Landscape Architecture* is providing for a new generation of landscape architects training in contemporary digital media and its application as an emerging art form.

I come from the generation that learned manual graphic techniques came of age using digital applications as an extension of these traditional techniques. As a student, I remember learning photography by reading manuals and silk-screening from printmaking books. Skills like collage and montage were acquired much more intuitively, and other techniques such as press-on lettering were learned on the job in an office. It is interesting to me to see how much of the old methods are built into the new digital procedures. One of my favorite Photoshop filters is *pixelate-mezzotint*. From my knowledge of printmaking, this filter makes clear sense to me. Likewise *cut* and *paste* tools are basically collage techniques, and *dry brush* and *cross hatch*, etc., are based on traditional art processes. Expanded electronic techniques go beyond mere digital adaptation of the traditional to create new graphic and design possibilities that were difficult or even impossible to achieve before. Certain kinds of geometric distortions, such as stretching, bending and inversions, are not only transforming the representation of landscape design but also design itself as new forms and spatial relationships are pioneered in digital space. Combining techniques to create non-standard representation forms has emerging potential as well. This is clearly evident in today's contemporary art world where artists are creating new art which incorporates a vast array of new media in innovative ways to challenge our way of seeing and understanding the world. Today, my office uses an array of representation techniques ranging from drawing to physical model building to digital modeling, and all sorts of combinations of digital imaging and animations, all at a range of differing scales. Ultimately, the best design still results from thinking, designing and representing with multiple scales, views and methods.

This book will become a standard manual for students entering the profession and learning their craft, as well a valuable reference for those already in practice who need to keep current with emerging trends. Just as it was impossible to practice twenty-five years ago without knowledge of ozalid printing, letraset, zipatone and rapidiograph use, today it is unimaginable to practice in a world without Photoshop, Illustrator, 3DStudioMax, Rhino, SketchUp and CAD.

—Ken Smith

1. Originally published in the first edition.

Preface

Digital Drawing for Landscape Architecture: Contemporary Techniques and Tools for Digital Representation in Site Design is the product of many years of professional practice and teaching at the Louisiana State University Robert Reich School of Landscape Architecture. As designers, we attempted to create a book that focused on getting the job done. In this sense, each section tackles the basics of the subject matter and each chapter introduces a short background with an explanation of how to accomplish a phase of the representation process with current digital tools. Our inspiration comes from the books that introduced us to landscape architectural graphics, such as Grant Reid's *Landscape Graphics* and Chip Sullivan's *Drawing the Landscape*. Both books present the reader with techniques that are applicable to a specific topic with just enough background to explain how it fits within the larger profession. Our hope is that *Digital Drawing for Landscape Architecture* will serve as a contemporary, digital version of these books for landscape architecture professionals and students.

We come from a group of academics and professionals who did not take any formal digital media courses. Instead, we were taught analog mechanical drafting and drawing and then applied those skills to our interest in digital media. All of our skills come from exploration through trial and error. We learned that doing it the second or third time was always the most productive. Typically, we would jump into a project and begin to experiment. If we didn't understand a tool, we opened the Help file or just started using it to see what happened. This book outlines techniques, but we encourage you to experiment. There are an infinite number of ways to get to the same solution, and it is important that you find a way that works for you.

Digital Drawing for Landscape Architecture is a book about the moment, bridging analog and digital techniques. Digital landscape representation relies heavily on the past, and we attempt to tie past and present together. We are consistently amazed at the work our colleagues and students produce, and our hope is that by putting out defined techniques, individuals will question and evolve these practices. In the long run, landscape representation will eventually begin to leave the conventions of the mechanically drafted orthographic drawing in favor of parametric modeling and geographic information systems. While these systems exist, they currently do not address the needs of site designers as creative design tools.

It is always a risk to base any book on specific software, but when techniques are introduced it is almost impossible to be completely software agnostic. It is possible to create amazing work with any software, but we focused on the tools we use every day: Adobe Photoshop, Adobe Illustrator, 3ds Max, SketchUp, and Vectorworks or AutoCAD. These are not the only tools, but they are the ones we have evolved with over time and, therefore, feel the most comfortable using. While software does change, it has essentially been very consistent for the past 10 years. Features are added and refined, but the process has not been considerably altered through time. It is very easy to constantly chase the newest tools, but it is typically more productive to evolve our own processes with or in spite of the tools. You will find that most of the techniques discussed in this book will work in software versions that date back 5 to 10 years.

Digital Drawing for Landscape Architecture presents examples and techniques for each of the traditional design drawings: diagram, plan, section/elevation, and perspective. These drawings are the basis for all of our representation endeavors; and while we encourage experimentation in how these drawings evolve, it is important to recognize the need for measured drawings when working in digital media. The techniques also focus on speed and efficiency, which translates to getting a job done quickly, with the fewest mouse clicks, and being able to edit the drawing when necessary. You will find that almost every technique allows representation to be an iterative process, creating elements that we assume will be changed or modified. There is very little certainty within the design process and, therefore, it is essential that drawings remain flexible.

This book assumes that readers are versed in basic representation concepts and computing principles. The book spends a small amount of time discussing how computing affects the representation process and the basics of each piece of software, but it is not intended as an introduction to any particular piece of software. There are many great books that catalogue and explain each feature of the software. The software's Help file is a great resource to help you understand every tool and its effect. If you don't understand a concept in the Help file, use a search engine and find out more information on the Web. We are no longer working alone, and someone else may have already figured out or encountered many of the issues you will run into with the software.

This book is intended to highlight examples, explain techniques, and provide context for how we use digital media as designers. Feel free to start at the beginning or jump around to areas of interest; either method is suitable to take advantage of the information. We hope you will take away something new and contribute back to others with new and interesting techniques.

Acknowledgments

We were pleasantly surprised at the strong reception the first edition of the book received from both the professional and academic landscape architecture communities. Our aim was to write a book that was useful to students as they enter the profession, and working professionals looking for new ways to work with digital media. The majority of the work for this book comes directly out of the courses we have taught at the Robert Reich School of Landscape Architecture at Louisiana State University over the past 10 years, so the first set of acknowledgments should go to the long list of students we have worked with at LSU. With all the new student work collected for the second edition, the students are too numerous to name individually here. I think it is safe to say they have taught us as much as we have taught them over the years.

In particular, we would like to thank Keely Rizzato and Peter Summerlin, recent graduates from our program at LSU, for their help putting together this new edition of the book. Both Keely and Peter helped us in almost every aspect of the second edition, but they also played a large role in writing new material for the book. Keely helped with Chapters 3 and 13, while Peter worked on Chapter 9 and all of the chapters in Part 4. Thanks for all of your hard work.

We would like to thank our colleagues for all of their feedback from the first edition and encouragement to continue the work. Thank you for contributing your work to the book and all of the suggestions you had for how to improve the second edition. Finally, we would like to thank our families for all of their support.

swamp

marsh

mississippi

louisiana

Part 1
Concepts

Chapter 1
Introduction/Overview

Digital Drawing for Landscape Architecture: Contemporary Techniques and Tools for Digital Representation in Site Design provides professionals and students with a clear guide to understanding the digital representation process for a variety of design drawings. Each chapter highlights a specific technique by examining its role in the digital media and landscape representation process through methods available in current software. This provides the reader with tangible tools to explore digital media in the creation of design drawings.

The professions of landscape architecture and urban planning have a strong tradition of representation that has evolved with the professions. During the last hundred years, this has been dominated by analog representation—primarily pencil (graphite), pen (ink), markers (pigment), and watercolor (pigment). The aforementioned analog representation techniques have focused on creating a variety of design drawings such as functional and operational diagrams, orthographic plans, section/elevations, isometrics, and perspective renderings.

The content in this book intends to bridge a fundamental gap between the analog and digital tools used to represent landscape architecture and urban planning projects. The gap has formed in representation methods with the introduction of digital tools that have been adopted despite a generation of designers who are versed in analog methods. *Digital Drawing for Landscape Architecture* aims to fill this gap by pulling from the methods of analog representation and applying these concepts to digital media. Examining individual working methods and applying the content of this book to enhance the current design and representation processes are essential to this goal.

A misnomer that many designers intend to embrace when moving to digital representation methods is that the past can be left behind; nothing could be further from the truth. Knowledge of analog representation plays a vital role in understanding the application of digital tools and techniques. Tools such as Adobe Illustrator and Photoshop are born directly from analog processes and tools defined by their physical counterparts. The Paint Bucket tool is used to pour paint into areas, and the PaintBrush tool applies paint to a virtual canvas. This language is intentional and builds on our current knowledge of illustration, avoiding the creation of a new digital tool that has no context in the physical world. It would be confusing and the learning curve would be that much steeper if the Photoshop Paint Brush tool was called the Pixel Application tool and the canvas was called the pixel grid.

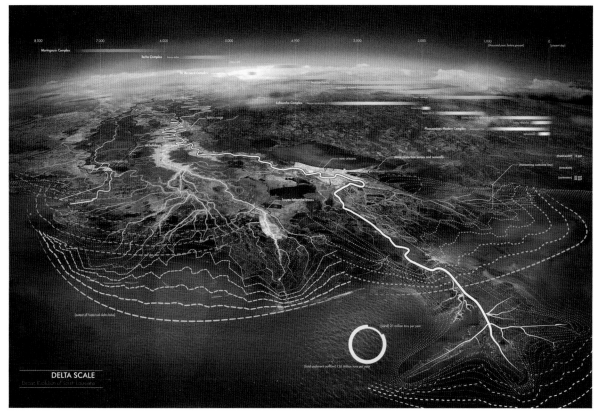

Figure 1.1. Delta scale lobe building visualization. *LSU Coastal Sustainability Studio, Ian Miller, MLA 2014, Louisiana State University Robert Reich School of Landscape Architecture*

   The connections between analog and digital modes go beyond naming conventions into techniques and processes. Current digital rendering processes vary greatly between individuals and firms, as well as across a range of software. It is commonly said that there are an infinite variety of ways to accomplish the same task in image- or vector-editing software. The versatility of most software packages comes from the variety of tools and the options for combining those tools to complete a specific task. This versatility allows the software to be used across a variety of professions from photography to technical illustration. Because of the depth and versatility of the software, the learning curve is typically steep for new users. Similar to using a pencil and pen, there is no way to automatically generate a section, plan, or elevation. Instead, a combination of tools and methods come together through a proven process to generate the desired results. Digital media provides efficiencies in some areas but does not provide a shortcut to learning the fundamentals of drawing and illustration.

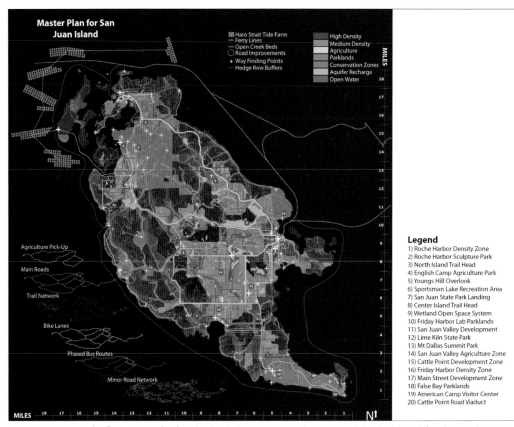

Figure 1.2. Master plan for San Juan Island. *Joshua Brooks, BLA 2012, Louisiana State University Robert Reich School of Landscape Architecture*

Understanding the fundamentals of drawing is essential, but it is not exclusive to either medium. The contemporary design world fully embraces both mediums as valid methods to represent projects and explore design ideas. It is possible to understand the fundamentals of composition, lineweight, texture, color, and/or atmosphere with a pencil or with Photoshop. The physical processes may be different, but conceptually the rules and ideas are similar.

Conceptually, each designer must embrace digital media as a tool with analytic, performative, and representational possibilities. Many designers view the computer as a rival that must be conquered in order to accomplish each task. It is important to reverse that role. In order to do this, the designer should have a general understanding of how a computer and operating system function. This environment of hardware and software is where most processes occur; therefore, taking the time to become familiar with your surroundings is very useful. Typically, this is a low priority for designers; we are not computer engineers and, therefore, we often overlook or even overcomplicate basic hardware and software functions.

Figure 1.3. Atchafalaya Basin section perspective. *Joshua Brooks, Kim Nguyen, Devon Boutte, Martin Moser, Responsive Systems Studio, Fall 2011, Louisiana State University Robert Reich School of Landscape Architecture*

Software

Software typically describes code or computer programs that perform a specific task within a computer system. Although there are many types of software, designers are typically concerned with specific types of applications for pixel/raster editing, vector editing, three-dimensional modeling, and video/motion graphics editing. Each type of application plays a different role in the representation process but also interacts with and utilizes the hardware in different ways. Beyond applications, it is also important to understand the role of the operating system because it is at the core of any hardware/software relationship.

Operating System

The operating system handles the intricacies of the interaction between the user and the hardware. Generally, nearly all of the computing devices we use from desktop computers to video game consoles use some type of operating system that we interact with using a graphical user interface (GUI). The two prominent operating systems for design professionals are Microsoft Windows and Apple OS X. For architects and landscape architects, Windows has traditionally been the dominant operating system because Autodesk AutoCAD runs exclusively in Windows. This is slowly changing as compatibility increases. Many offices work in either operating system and exchange information between them seamlessly.

OS X and Windows are different types of operating systems created by the companies Apple and Microsoft, respectively. OS X will only run on Apple hardware (laptops and workstations), but Windows will run on any compatible hardware including Apple hardware. This makes it possible to use Apple hardware to boot into either OS X or Windows when necessary. This method is accomplished by creating two separate partitions on the computer's hard drive and then choosing which system to boot into when restarting the computer. Either OS X or Windows must be chosen while booting up the computer; it is not possible to work in both systems simultaneously.

Another method for running an operating system is *virtualization,* which creates "virtual" hardware on which the operating system then runs. This allows an operating system such as OS X to host or virtualize an operating system such as Windows, which means both can run simultaneously and have access to similar resources. This is an ideal working situation, but it falls short on performance—specifically when using resource-intensive applications such as Photoshop or AutoCAD. Virtualization works best when using applications for word processing or project management, or when accessing the Windows partition in order to do quick edits in CAD.

Applications

Applications represent a broad range of software created to accomplish specific tasks such as word processing, image editing, or financial management. When considering the representation of design drawings, typically we will use a range of applications to edit photos, create CAD linework, and build virtual models. Excluding applications for programming and word processing, the main types of applications designers will use are image editors (Photoshop, GIMP), vector editors (CAD, Illustrator), three-dimensional modelers (3ds Max, Maya, Blender), and video/motion graphics editors (Final Cut, Premiere, After Effects). Using each application, it is possible to find crossover or even repetition between the functions of one piece of software and another. For example, Photoshop and Illustrator share many of the same vector-editing tools to control pen paths. This crossover makes it easy to attempt to use one piece of software to accomplish everything, but it is important to understand the strengths and weaknesses of each application in order to efficiently use both pieces of software.

Image Editing

Image-editing software refers to a broad range of applications that are used to manipulate pixels for tasks such as adjusting photographs, editing illustrations, and/or altering image sizes. Pixel-based imagery is also referred to as *raster images*. Image-editing applications typically use three paradigms that are specifically useful for design representation: layers, selections, and brushes. Methods that combine these three types of tools can typically perform all of the tasks necessary to manipulate pixels. Layers are used to organize pixels in order to edit specific pixels separately from other pixels, overlay pixels on top of one another, or apply effects or adjustments to specific layers.

Selections are used to select pixels on layers or multiple layers and can range from simple shapes, such as a square or circle, to complex shapes with multiple selection percentages per pixel. Selections can be made based on shape, the color or value of pixels, vector paths, and/or existing pixels on layers. A selection typically works as a range represented by a range of grays from unselected (0, black) to fully selected (255, white). This creates a selection using 256 values, so that edits or effects can be applied as a ramp or gradient. If an area is selected, it is possible to then edit those pixels. This creates an area in which to apply the edits based on the values in the selection. For example, if an image had a rectangular selection that was fully selected, then filling it with red would create a red rectangle. If the selection were rectangular but went from fully selected on the left to unselected on the right, then filling that rectangle would create a red box that slowly faded away from left to right.

Brushes are the third component that is typical in most image-editing applications, and they are used to apply or erase pixels. Brushes consist of a brush-tip shape and controls for the dynamics of how the tip creates a stroke. This allows brushes to carefully mimic real-world brushes or create all new brushes for specific needs. Brushes can apply a single color, a range of colors, or a pattern; they even transfer pixels from one side of an image to another. All of these tasks, either applying or erasing pixels, are accomplished with a selected brush, giving the artist many options to adjust the desired effect.

Figure 1.4. Master plan illustrated to scale. *Spackman Mossop+Michaels*

Figure 1.5. Conceptual image board. *Joshua Brooks, BLA 2012, Louisiana State University Robert Reich School of Landscape Architecture*

Vector Editing

Vector-editing software refers to the use of points, lines, and shapes in order to represent imagery. To accomplish this, mathematical equations are used to represent the location of points, the direction of lines, and the fill-in to create shapes. There are two main types of vector-editing software for designers: illustration software such as Adobe Illustrator and drafting software such as Autodesk AutoCAD. The main difference between these types of software is that CAD applications focus on precision, and illustration applications focus on effects and appearance. In both types of vector-editing application, the tools and results are slowly becoming more congruent, as AutoCAD provides more tools to adjust style and appearance and Illustrator has third-party applications that increase the range of drafting tools.

The tools for vector editing focus on selection, transformation, and stroke/fill manipulation. Selections are typically accomplished in three scales in vector-editing applications: multiple objects, single objects, or subobjects. A single object is typically defined as a series of points, lines, and fills that create an object such as a rectangle (four points, four strokes, and a fill). It is possible then to select a group of rectangles, the rectangle itself, or a single point or line. Once an object or subobject has been selected, it is then possible to transform the element with typical transformations such as move, rotate, or scale. Depending on the application, it may be possible to perform many other types of transformations with a variety of tools. Transformations can typically be applied interactively or by entering values for more precision.

Three-Dimensional Modeling

Similar to vector-editing applications, three-dimensional modeling applications create wireframe representations of objects using points (vertices), edges, curves, and triangles. The most common type of three-dimensional modeling is polygon modeling, which creates representations of a model through a shell or surface. Other types of modeling include solid modeling, which creates accurate representations of an object's volume and is typically used in medical or engineering simulations. NURBS modeling, or nonuniform rational B-spline, creates surfaces from curves, creating precise freeform models. A fourth type of modeling is called subdivision modeling, which is similar to polygon modeling but uses a series of refinements on the initial mesh in order to create a smooth object. In most applications, each modeling type can be converted from more complex models, NURBS, and subdivisions to simpler polygon models.

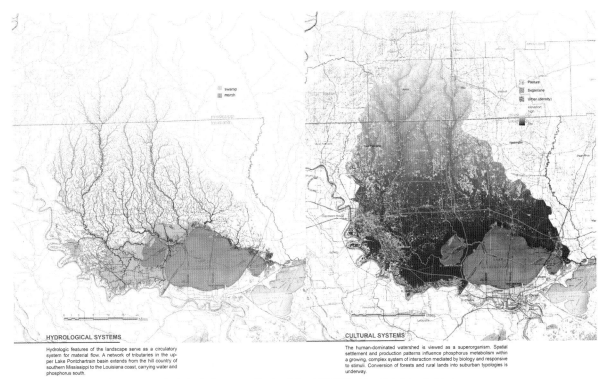

HYDROLOGICAL SYSTEMS

Hydrologic features of the landscape serve as a circulatory system for material flow. A network of tributaries in the upper Lake Pontchartrain basin extends from the hill country of southern Mississippi to the Louisiana coast, carrying water and phosphorus south.

CULTURAL SYSTEMS

The human-dominated watershed is viewed as a superorganism. Spatial settlement and production patterns influence phosphorus metabolism within a growing, complex system of interaction mediated by biology and responsive to stimuli. Conversion of forests and rural lands into suburban typologies is underway.

Figure 1.6. Lake Pontchartrain Basin hydrological systems. *Matthew Seibert, MLA 2013, Louisiana State University Robert Reich School of Landscape Architecture*

Three-dimensional models are viewed in two ways: *real time* (allowing a user to move around the world interactively) and *rendered* (creating an image or animation with preselected lighting, materials, and movements). Real-time viewing typically occurs within the application viewport as the model is created or edited. It is also possible to create real-time models that can be explored in third-party viewers or applications and perform similar to first-person video games. Real-time viewing is ideal, but it is limited by the power of a computer's graphics card. In most cases, the graphics card cannot render the model, materials, and lighting at cinematic quality, which requires drawing 30 to 40 frames every second. A rendered view or animation is created from a three-dimensional scene after the models are built, materials are applied, and the animation is planned. The computer will then calculate the complex interaction between the light and objects with the ability to create extremely complex imagery. The user can choose to render a single image or a series of images in order to create an animation.

Video Editing and Motion Graphics

Animations and movies require applications specifically suited to sequencing, modifying, and compositing a series of inline images. Two types of applications are specifically suited for this task: video-editing software such as Adobe Premiere or Apple Final Cut Pro, and motion-graphics software such as Adobe After Effects or Apple Motion. Both types of software have specific uses, but there are many overlaps between them. Video-editing software excels at placing clips and sound within a timeline in order to edit sequences and create transitions. There is a huge range of video-editing software from high-end professional packages such as the aforementioned Final Cut Pro to entry-level applications such as Apple iMovie or Windows Movie Maker. Many tasks can be accomplished in the entry-level software, but the output and refining process will be extremely limited.

Motion-graphics software excels at compositing or layering multiple images and movie clips within a timeline. Software such as After Effects can do basic movie-clip sequencing, but the tools are typically limited compared to the professional video-editing software. Motion-graphics software uses layers and keyframing to animate layers of film, allowing the user to separate areas with masking. Most motion-graphics applications use a three-dimensional environment that makes it possible to build simple geometry with planes that can contain other movies or images. This creates a diorama-like environment that can be used to create film sets, special effects, or even complex animated diagrams.

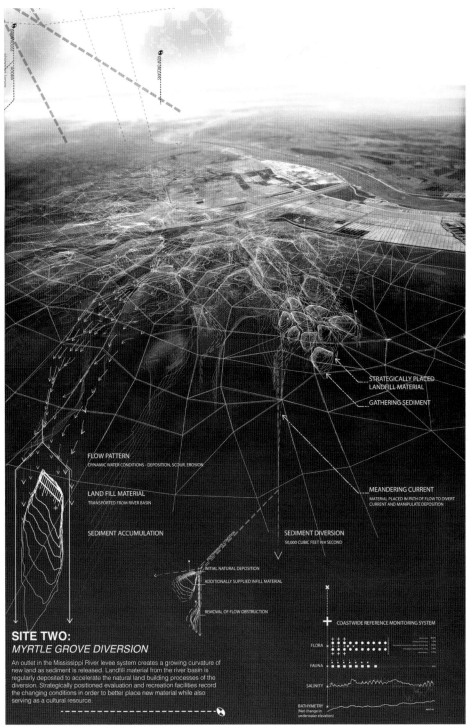

STRATEGICALLY PLACED
LANDFILL MATERIAL

GATHERING SEDIMENT

FLOW PATTERN
DYNAMIC WATER CONDITIONS - DEPOSITION, SCOUR, EROSION

LAND FILL MATERIAL
TRANSPORTED FROM RIVER BASIN

MEANDERING CURRENT
MATERIAL PLACED IN PATH OF FLOW TO DIVERT
CURRENT AND MANIPULATE DEPOSITION

SEDIMENT ACCUMULATION

SEDIMENT DIVERSION
50,000 CUBIC FEET PER SECOND

INITIAL NATURAL DEPOSITION

ADDITIONALLY SUPPLIED INFILL MATERIAL

REMOVAL OF FLOW OBSTRUCTION

COASTWIDE REFERENCE MONITORING SYSTEM

FLORA

FAUNA

SALINITY

BATHYMETRY
(Net change in
underwater elevation)

SITE TWO:
MYRTLE GROVE DIVERSION

An outlet in the Mississippi River levee system creates a growing curvature of
new land as sediment is released. Landfill material from the river basin is
regularly deposited to accelerate the natural land building processes of the
diversion. Strategically positioned evaluation and recreation facilities record
the changing conditions in order to better place new material while also
serving as a cultural resource.

Figure 1.7. Myrtle Grove diversion perspective. *LSU Coastal Sustainability Studio, Bradley Cantrell, Jeffrey Carney, Matthew Seibert, Elizabeth Williams, Louisiana State University Robert Reich School of Landscape Architecture*

Workspace

The space that we create for ourselves when creating drawings is particularly important for designers. This is no different when we are working with digital media. The most important aspects of any workspace are efficiency and comfort. When working with digital media, we need to consider two workspaces: the physical as well as the virtual environment. There is no formula for what a workspace should be because it differs greatly for each individual. Some users prefer a space devoid of distractions, while others relish multiple activities occurring around them. Both types of spaces can provide creative inspiration for different individuals. Because we spend many hours working on drawings, the physical space we occupy must be comfortable for us as individuals. The space should provide room for a computer and all of the peripherals, as well as space for other design explorations such as drawing and modeling.

The computing environment consists of the operating system and application interface, as well as the input devices used to control them. Typically, the input devices will be a keyboard to enter commands and a mouse to interact with elements of the user interface or drawing. The best way to use this combination of devices is to keep one hand on the mouse and the other hand on the keyboard. Maintaining a consistent relationship between the position of the hands and the input devices allows the individual to quickly select hotkeys on the keyboard while maintaining the position of the cursor on the screen. This will allow an individual to look at the keyboard very little and maintain their focus on the screen in order to see feedback from the application.

When working in any application, the user will need to perform many repetitive tasks; therefore, it is important to minimize the amount of effort required to perform each task. If instantiating a command to draw a line requires the mouse to move up to a toolbar in order to select the Line tool, the designer will waste a good portion of his or her time simply moving the mouse away from the drawing area. If the designer needs to pick up a drafting pencil, draw a line, put down the pencil at the top of the drafting table, and then pick up the same pencil again in order to draw the next line, the extra step of putting down and picking up the pencil will add hours to the drafting time. However, this is what many users do when they use the applications, constantly clicking a button to draw a line.

The easiest way to speed up repetitive tasks is to use hotkeys or key combinations in order to instantiate commands. In an application like AutoCAD, every command can be entered through the command line. In Photoshop, hotkeys exist for nearly every tool and menu item. It is possible to also create custom hotkeys for most applications, but depending on the working environment, it is advisable to use the defaults as much as possible. Using the defaults makes it much easier to use another computer that may not have the same hotkey customization. Depending on the user, it may be helpful to create a quick reference card in order to quickly see the default hotkeys for the application they are using. In most applications, the hotkeys will also be visible within the menus and as tooltips when the mouse rolls over a button. All designers should make it a priority to learn the hotkeys in order to efficiently use the application in which they are currently working.

Most applications are used for a range of design purposes. For example, Photoshop can be used to render a plan or adjust photographs. This means that there is a huge range of tools for many different purposes, and the interface can often get cluttered and hard to navigate. It is advisable to only turn on or display the features that are necessary in order to minimize the onscreen clutter. This will also give more space to the drawing area than to tools, palettes, and dialog boxes. It would be silly to put every pencil, marker, and paintbrush on the workdesk, and the same holds true in a virtual workspace. Open and display only the tools necessary to accomplish the job at hand. Depending on the application, it is usually possible to save multiple user interface configurations that can be customized for different tasks.

It is important to understand that specific hardware and software are not necessary to create beautiful digital drawings. Amazing work has been created by the humblest of applications and hardware, while thoughtless, poorly crafted work can just as easily come from the best applications running on a high-end workstation. The goal for designers is to find a combination of hardware and software that functions reliably and comfortably for a specific design environment and user.

Chapter 2
Analog and Digital Rendering Comparisons

It can be argued that analog rendering and sketching is quicker and more natural than using digital media. The lack of a "natural" feeling is specifically attributed to the hardware and software that mediates our ability to directly manipulate the drawing surface and/or media using our hands. The main advantage of digital media is its editability and efficiency, but these are things that must be considered during all phases of the representation process. A drawing created digitally is no more editable or efficient than an analog drawing unless the tools are used correctly. This requires the designer to use a process that is both systematic and natural. It is important to define what is meant by the terms *editability* and *efficiency*.

Editability and Efficiency

Editability refers to the ability to alter, change, or update various aspects of a drawing in order to maintain flexibility as the design process progresses. Typically, a drawing that is completely editable will be a larger file in terms of data, therefore taking up more hard drive space, and will be slower to work with during the representation process. It is important to find a middle ground where the image maintains enough flexibility in editability options, element organization, and file size. Each designer will have his or her own method of organization to enhance editability, and often this will change for each phase of a project. For example, on a large site plan the shading and texturing that represents the roadways may be grouped as layers and exported (to be retrieved later when needed), allowing that portion to be flattened into a single image. This minimizes the overhead as hundreds of street trees and vegetation are placed throughout the rendering. It is not necessary to have access to all of the shading at this phase of the process, so there is no need to have those layers or effects available.

Efficiency can be enhanced in several ways: automation, portability, replication, and transformation. Digital media, based in computing, creates a paradigm that embraces the reuse of drawings and symbols through scaling, rotating, and effects. Most repetitive tasks can be automated when working with digital media. An easily understandable example of this is the resizing of images for a PowerPoint presentation. In most cases, large images should be resized in order to optimize the presentation. This can be accomplished using **File > Scripts > Image processor** in order to automate the resizing of the vertical or horizontal pixel dimension for each image. This task would take a very long time and would be maddeningly boring if done manually, but luckily we can hand that task to the hardware and software.

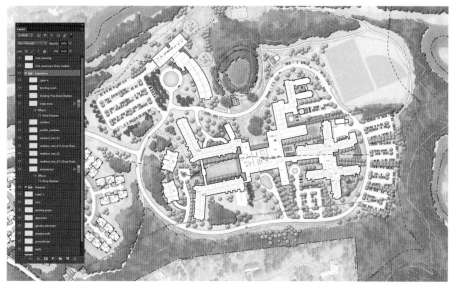

Figure 2.1. The ability to maintain and edit layers adds to the flexibility and editability of digital drawings. *Geller DeVellis, Inc.*

Portability addresses the ability of drawings to be translated across software packages and presentation formats. This is a huge advantage of digital media, but a few things must be considered before a drawing is started in order to make it as flexible as possible. When working with raster images, they should be created at the highest resolution necessary because it is always possible to make an image smaller, but it is more difficult and sometimes impossible to make an image larger. It is also important to think about the overall color and aesthetics of the drawings in advance in order to create a cohesive series of drawings. This includes lineweights, fonts, symbols, and color palettes that are similar between drawings in order to create a comprehensive package that can be used as a set or individually.

Replication and transformation are two other important paradigms in digital media that must be embraced in order to fully take advantage of the software. The idea that symbols, textures, and layers can be easily replicated and altered is a huge departure from analog media. Cutting, copying, and pasting happen with relative ease using digital media, which becomes apparent in renderings unless steps are taken to transform and edit the copies. When a copy is created using analog media either through transfers or tracing, there are typically small differences in each copy—whereas with digital media, each copy is an exact copy. Small changes in transforms (rotating, scaling), color, and masking can add enough change that each copy won't appear to be exact duplicates.

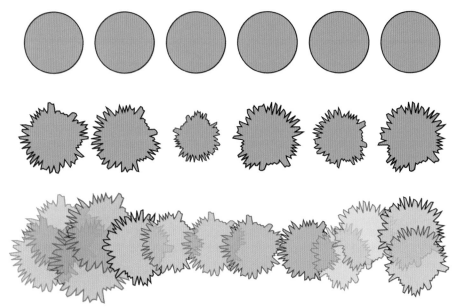

Figure 2.2. Duplication and replication is very easy with digital media. Copies of the same objects; instances with basic transformations applied; and instances with screening, tinting, and transformations applied.

Commonalities and Parallels

Although digital media differs in some ways from analog media, there are many overlaps that should be observed and taken into consideration, including drafted linework, texturing, and layering of media. The basis for almost every rendering starts with a well-drafted measured drawing with good lineweights and high-fidelity linework. This is true in both analog and digital media and cannot be overlooked; not only is it the basis for understanding design/spatial relationships but it is also the framework for the representation process. Similar to mechanical drafting, digital linework should have a consistent hierarchy that can render depth or emphasize importance and weight within a site.

Texturing in analog media can come from the interaction of media such as graphite on Canson paper or the technique in which media is applied, such as pen and ink stippling. The technique and media of an analog rendering produces a discernible aesthetic in an illustration and defines aspects of how a site is represented. This fact creates unique and compelling drawings that are products of the artist, media, and technique. In digital media, many of these aspects are flattened due to similar application of color, brushes, and effects without enough variation. When creating digital drawings, it is important to create interesting and unique interactions between the canvas, layers, and effects.

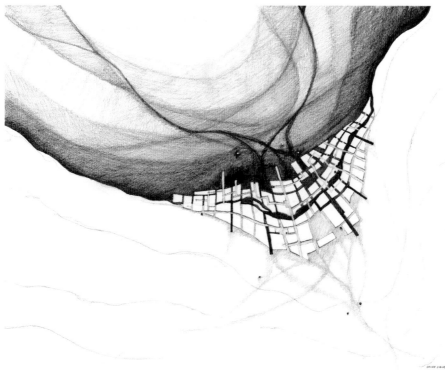

Figure 2.3. Graphite provides a range of tones that are products of the pressure, texture of the paper, and the softness of the lead. Maintaining a similar range of tones when working in digital media is important. *Louise Cheetham, MLA 2010, Louisiana State University Robert Reich School of Landscape Architecture*

Layering in analog media typically occurs when media is applied successively in multiple passes, creating an interaction between colors or textures. Often, this occurs on one canvas but can be separated through sheets of vellum or mylar with a base of color overlaid with the texturing of a finer media. Digital media provides many more options for layering, but the effects and interactions are very similar. Layers are typical components of any image-editing software. They can be used to organize drawings, but more importantly to create a series of layers with the topmost layers interacting with the layers below through transparency and screening.

Hybrid Techniques

Because there are many similarities between analog and digital media and most designers are versed or experimenting with both, hybrids are very common. An analog/digital *hybrid* refers to a drawing that may incorporate one aspect of analog media, such as a sketch, and another aspect of digital media, such as Photoshop shading and coloring. Creating hybrid drawings is an excellent way for an individual versed in analog media to explore digital techniques (and vice versa) because it allows one expertise to serve as the framework.

Figure 2.4. Linework is drafted by hand with texture, entourage, and context assembled in Photoshop. *Matthew Seibert, MLA 2013, Louisiana State University Robert Reich School of Landscape Architecture*

When CAD was first introduced, it was typical for designers to draft on the computer and print to bond, mylar, or vellum. If the print was on bond, markers or colored pencils could be used to add color and shading. However, this type of rendering is often limited by the quality of the bond paper, and the linework needs to be enhanced with pen and ink. If the linework is printed to mylar or vellum, designers can create a blueprint reproduction, which is similar to bond, or the image can be rendered directly on the back side of the mylar or vellum. Rendering on the back side of mylar or vellum leaves linework that is very well defined and tones down the color overall. Neither of these examples represents a real relationship between digital and analog media, but instead isolates aspects of the representation process within each medium.

Many other creative relationships truly integrate both media rather than isolating one from the other. It is possible to print directly to watercolor, rice, Canson, or other types of paper to create a textured interaction between the printed image or linework and the paper surface. The final output can be anything that is created on the computer from imagery to CAD linework. After printing, most inks from an inkjet plotter are able to be manipulated with brush and water. This interaction between media and manipulation of one media by another provides many rich possibilities when creating design drawings.

CAD/CAM devices, such as laser cutters or 3D printers, can perform another interaction between analog and digital media. A laser cutter enables a direct relationship between two-dimensional (2D) CAD linework and a physical material such as chipboard, wood, or acrylic. The CAD linework is used to either cut or etch the surface of the material in order to create components of a three-dimensional (3D) model.

Figure 2.5. Digital painting applied in Photoshop with hand-drawn perspective. *Kossen Miller, MLA 2014, Louisiana State University Robert Reich School of Landscape Architecture*

Figure 2.6. Geographical Information System (GIS) data is used to build a regional base plan that is assembled by 3D printed and laser-cut models. *Directed by Bradley Cantrell, Advanced Digital Representation, Louisiana State University Robert Reich School of Landscape Architecture*

Chapter 3
Basic Overview of Digital Concepts

Two common modes are used for storing graphic data: raster and vector. Photoshop is the primary *raster-based* program used in digital rendering. Programs like Illustrator and AutoCAD are primarily *vector-based,* although there are elements of both raster and vector tools in all of the programs.

Raster-Based Programs

Raster images are stored in a file as a set of pixels, with each pixel representing a single area of color in the drawing.

The *pixel* is the smallest unit in an image, and it cannot be subdivided. The overall image is created by the combination of a large number of pixels. When an image is printed or displayed on a screen at normal resolution, the individual pixels are so small that they are not noticeable to the human eye. When the pixels are small enough, the illusion of a continuous image is created.

Figure 3.1. Image at full resolution.

Figure 3.2. Area shown in detail in Figure 3.3. This is an area of 20 × 20 pixels.

Figure 3.3. The full-resolution image is composed of individual pixels. Each pixel represents a single color and cannot be sub-divided. It is the smallest unit in a raster image.

The number of pixels in an image determines the overall size of the raster image. If an image is said to be 1200 × 800 pixels, it means that there are 1,200 pixels across and 800 pixels from top to bottom.

Resolution in Raster Images

When a raster image is printed, the quality of the final image is determined by the resolution of the image. In terms of printing, *resolution* refers to the number of pixels per inch on the printed paper. If the number of pixels per inch (ppi) is too low, you will be able to see the individual pixels when the image is printed. This kind of image is often referred to as a *pixelated* image.

The resolution determines the size of each individual pixel on the printed page, as well as the overall size of the image: the higher the resolution, the smaller each individual pixel and the smaller the overall image. For example, if an image that is 100 pixels wide by 100 pixels high is printed at a resolution of 10 pixels per inch, the final size of the printed image would be 10 inches wide by 10 inches tall, approximately the size of a standard piece of paper.

Each pixel in this image would be 1/10 of an inch tall by 1/10 of an inch wide. At this resolution, the image is pixelated: the pixels are large enough to be seen individually by the human eye. If, however, the image is printed at a higher resolution of 100 pixels per inch, the overall size of the image would be 1 inch and each individual pixel would be 1/100 of an inch wide by 1/100 of an

Figure 3.4. If individual pixels are visible in the printed image, the image is said to be *pixelated*. The original image shown in Figure 3.1 is 2500 pixels × 1875 pixels. This image has only 200 pixels × 150 pixels and therefore it appears pixelated.

10 point text at 120ppi
12 point text at 120ppi
14 point text at 120ppi
18 point text at 120ppi
24 point text at 120ppi

Figure 3.5. Larger fonts read from farther away on large images can be acceptable for presentation. Smaller fonts at 120 ppi are usually unacceptable.

inch tall. This resolution would be referred to as 100 pixels per inch, or 100 ppi. One hundred pixels per inch is typically the minimum resolution needed to create the illusion of a continuous image, or a *nonpixelated* image.

For a printed page, you would need a minimum of 150 ppi to avoid pixelating the image. In practical applications, however, the minimum resolution required to create a nonpixelated image differs according to how the printed image is being displayed. Images that are going to be viewed up close, such as images in a book or on an 11-inch × 17-inch sheet of paper, need a higher resolution than images that are printed in a large format. Large format images that are viewed from farther away may need fewer pixels per inch to create a nonpixelated image.

Higher resolution leads to a higher-quality image. However, frequently an image is not large enough to be printed at a high resolution and at the size needed for presentation. To print an image as large as possible without resorting to upsampling, which can reduce image quality, it is important to understand what resolution is needed to print images that do not look pixelated. Here are some general guidelines for the minimum resolution that can be used without causing pixelation.

Table 3.1. Minimum Resolution Guidelines

IMAGE SIZE	LOWEST ACCEPTABLE RESOLUTION	OPTIMUM RESOLUTION
11 × 17 or smaller	200 ppi	300 ppi or greater
24 × 36 or smaller	150 ppi	200 ppi or greater
larger than 24 × 36	120 ppi	150 ppi or greater

This assumes that the larger printed images will be viewed from a distance and not meant to be read from up close. At 120 ppi, fonts smaller than 14 point will be fuzzy. At 100 ppi, fonts smaller than 22 point will likely be fuzzy.

Upsampling and Downsampling

Upsampling increases the number of pixels in an image, and *downsampling* decreases the number of pixels in an image. It is important to make a distinction between *image size*, which is the number of pixels in an image, and *resolution*, which is related to the printing of an image. An image of the same "image size" can be printed on 11 inch × 17 inch paper or on a 4 inch × 6 inch paper, depending on the resolution. The size of the print is not the same as the size of the image. Typically, these issues become important when images are too small for the desired output. An image that is sharp at 4 inches × 6 inches may be pixelated if printed at 11 inches × 17 inches. If the image needs to be printed at 11 inches × 17 inches, there are two choices: lower the resolution and risk pixelation, or increase the image size through upsampling and risk a fuzzy image.

Figure 3.6. This is the original image at full resolution of 2500 × 1875 pixels.

If you want to increase the output size of the image beyond the limits of the resolution, you can upsample the image. *Upsampling* means adding more pixels to an image so that you can print a larger image at a resolution that does not cause pixelation. However, upsampling an image often causes a loss of quality in the image. As you saw in the previous section, simply enlarging the size of the drawing by lowering the resolution will cause the image to appear pixelated. Upsampling actually increases the number of pixels in the image. Several algorithms are used to upsample an image, but they all work in basically the same way. Upsampling spreads out the existing pixels and then attempts to create new pixels to fill in the gaps.

Figure 3.7. This shows the original image downsampled to 200 × 150 pixels. Many of the pixels that created the detail in the original image were discarded during the downsampling.

The problem with upsampling is that when the program fills in these new pixels, they do not always perfectly match the existing pixels. It is extremely difficult for the software to create new pixels that make sense within the overall image, because the software does not know what the image represents. After an image is upsampled, it is typical for the image to be fuzzier and linework to have a halo or echo effect.

Figure 3.8. The upsampled image shows the effects of adding pixels to an image. The pixels that were lost during the downsampling are approximated in the upsampling process. Upsampling generally causes fuzziness and ghosting in the image.

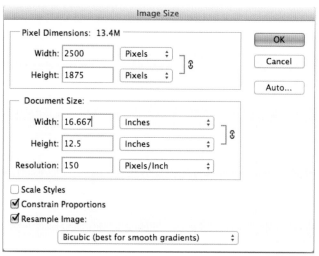

Figure 3.9. The Image Size dialog box.

If an image is not large enough to use in a project, upsampling can often be an acceptable technique for increasing the image size to avoid pixelization. Despite the limitations, sometimes the degradation of the image is negligible and it is worth testing the results. The easiest way to upsample an image is to adjust the image size from within Photoshop. Photoshop has several upsampling algorithms built into the software, so it is worth testing the different algorithms to see which one is the most effective for a particular image. To upsample an image, using Photoshop:

1. **Image > Image Size, from the menu.**
2. Choose the Bicubic algorithm, or one of the other algorithms provided in the drop-down menu.
3. To resize the image and increase/decrease the number of pixels in the image, choose the Resample Image option.
4. To keep the same proportions for the image, choose the Constrain Proportions option. If this option is not checked, the image may be stretched horizontally or vertically.

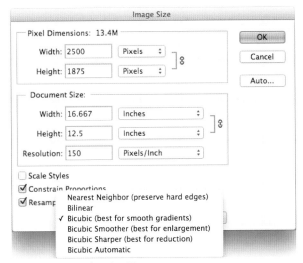

Figure 3.10. Sampling algorithms.

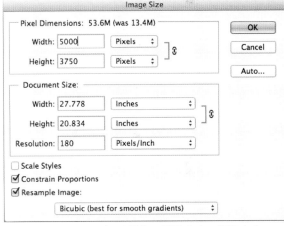

Figure 3.11. Increasing the width from 2500 pixels to 5000 pixels quadruples the size of the file.

As the image size changes, the file size also changes.

You will notice that doubling the size of the image increases the file size by a factor of 4. This increase is less of a factor as computers become faster and storage media becomes less expensive, but it is still an issue to be aware of—especially if the files are being transferred via email or uploaded to an FTP site.

Downsampling is the process of removing pixels from an image to make the image smaller. Downsampling does not have the same issues with image degradation as upsampling. It can be accomplished using the same Image Size dialog box in Photoshop. Instead of increasing the number of pixels, reduce the number of pixels.

Vector Images

Vector images contain different data to describe a drawing than raster images contain. Vector images use a series of coordinates and formulas to describe the image that are independent of the scale of the drawing. In vector graphics, a formula behind each piece of the image describes how it is to be drawn. Compared to raster images, this has the advantage of allowing documents to be printed at almost any scale without the loss of image quality. It also typically results in smaller file sizes compared to raster images. This is a simplified example of how a vector-based program might describe a line:

Draw Line from point 2,2 to point 7,7; Color Red; Thickness .01 inch.

A vector-based program has the ability to draw that line at any size and scale the thickness, depending on the desired output size. Unlike raster-based programs, there is no need for upsampling to increase the size of the print.

Vector linework is also editable in a way that raster images are not. In a raster representation of a line, the line is constructed of pixels that when seen together form the illusion of a smooth line. However, the line cannot be selected in the same way as a vector line.

Using Raster Images in Vector-Based Programs

Many different graphics techniques, such as importing a base map into Illustrator, use raster images in vector-based programs. Although vector-based linework created in programs such as Illustrator can be scaled to any size, the raster images imported to these programs are subject to the same issues of image size and resolution as discussed in the raster section. The raster image must be properly sized for the final output before being imported into the vector-based program. If a vector-based file is increased in scale, the raster image will suffer from the effects of upsampling just as if it were in a raster-based program.

Conversely, there are often times when vector-based linework will be imported into a raster-based program such as Photoshop. This technique is most often used when creating plan renderings that use AutoCAD linework as the basis for the plan. When the vector linework is imported into Photoshop, it is *rasterized* or converted from an editable vector line into pixels.

Color

When a designer begins to illustrate, his or her first step after creating the base linework is to begin adding color and develop an overall color scheme. Before adding color, it is important to have a basic understanding of color theory in order to develop an illustration that has the effect. The basic tool for combining colors is the color wheel, which consists of 12 colors based on the RYB color model. The RYB color wheel consists of three primary, three secondary, and

Figure 3.12. The color wheel.

six tertiary colors. The primary colors are red, yellow, and blue; these three colors can be mixed to create the three secondary colors green, orange, and purple. The six tertiary colors can be created by mixing combinations of primary and secondary colors.

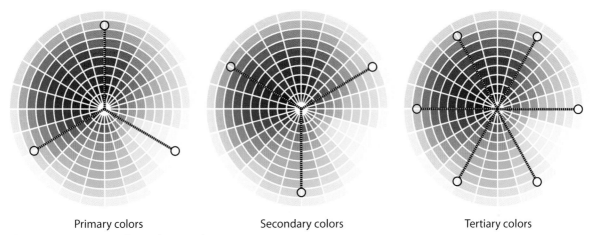

Primary colors   Secondary colors   Tertiary colors

Figure 3.13. Primary, secondary, and tertiary colors.

Each color can be referred to in terms of tint, shade, and tone. *Tint* refers to taking any pure hue and adding white to make it lighter. If you add black to make any pure hue darker it is called a *shade*. Adding gray to any pure *hue* creates a *tone*.

Tint

Shade

Figure 3.14. Swatches palette displaying tint, shade, and hue.

The color wheel can identify several color harmonies that consist of two or more colors from points on the color wheel. *Complementary color* refers to colors that are opposite one another on the color wheel. The most common are red and green, which create a vibrant color scheme. Complementary color schemes can be very strong, especially at full saturation, and should be used sparingly. Complementary schemes work well when it is important to make objects stand out. A variation is the split-complementary scheme, which uses a base color and the two colors adjacent to the complement. In general terms, the split-complementary scheme has the same contrast as a normal complementary scheme, without being as strong.

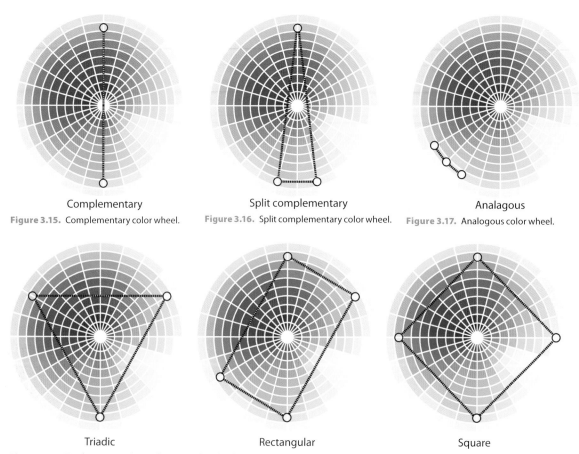

Complementary

Figure 3.15. Complementary color wheel.

Split complementary

Figure 3.16. Split complementary color wheel.

Analagous

Figure 3.17. Analogous color wheel.

Triadic

Rectangular

Square

Figure 3.18. Triadic, rectangular, and square color wheels.

An analogous color scheme uses colors that sit next to each other on the color wheel. This typically produces a subdued color scheme that maintains an equal hierarchy between the colors. It is common for plan renderings to use an analogous scheme with complementary colors to highlight specific elements. Three other common schemes are the triadic, rectangular, and square color arrangements. *Triadic* uses colors evenly spaced around the color wheel, *rectangular* uses two pairs of complementary colors, and *square* also uses two pairs but they are evenly spaced around the wheel. Each of these three schemes works best if one color is dominant and the other colors are used as accents.

It is important to continually evolve illustrations and, therefore, it is worthwhile to sample color palettes from old drawings. Doing so is a common starting point for many illustrations and, therefore, it is appropriate to start from a defined color palette. It is also important to experiment and evolve the work, but there is no need to start from scratch every time. Another available resource is Adobe's Kuler website (kuler.adobe.com), which allows you to save and share your color palettes and user-defined color palettes with other artists. You can also use tools to develop color palettes based on the previously mentioned schemes.

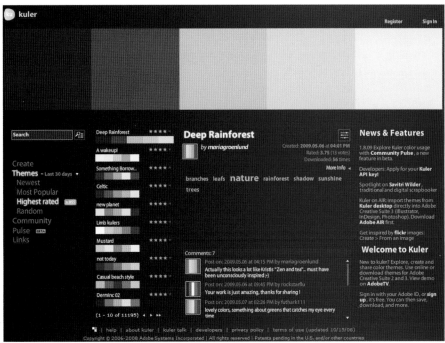

Figure 3.19. The Adobe Kuler website (http://kuler.adobe.com) provides an excellent starting point to test color combinations.

Adjustment Layers

Image Adjustments

The original method of making changes to images is by image adjustments by choosing **Image > Adjustments**. These permanent and destructive edits give you only one opportunity to adjust settings. Once the image adjustment has been applied it cannot be undone without using the history panel, or Ctrl+Z. The same exact adjustments are available as adjustment layers with the exception of two specific options, Shadows/Highlights and HDR Toning.

Adjustment Layers Overview

Adjustment layers provide us with simplified editing techniques that are convenient and flexible. They may infinitely refine image edits because they are nondestructive. You can adjust the intensity to see the extreme or minimal effects of an adjustment until you find the proper balanced effect you are looking for. The adjustment layer will appear in the layers panel with a specific icon according to the kind of adjustment.

There are two methods of creating an adjustment layer, the black and white circle icon in the layers panel or from the layer menu **Layer > New Adjustment Layer**.

Figure 3.20. The adjustment layer will appear in the layers panel with a specific icon according to the kind of adjustment.

Figure 3.21. Creating an adjustment layer from the layers panel.

29

Solid Color

This adjustment layer will fill the entire document with a solid color. It is a great short cut for creating a background color. Solid color becomes more useful when it is applied in combination with a mask.

Gradient Fill

The gradient fill adjustment layer applies a gradient across the entire image with all of the standard gradient options. You can specify the color, style, angle, and scale of the gradient fill.

Pattern

The pattern fill adjustment will fill the entire document with a pattern. You can customize the scale and use all of the patterns in your pattern library.

Brightness/Contrast

One of the most commonly used adjustments is Brightness/Contrast because you can lighten and darken the image and also specify the level of contrast. There is an Auto option; however, it will not always produce the best results but many times can be a good place to start.

Levels

Levels are associated with a histogram that represents a map of black, white, and midtones in an image.

You can customize the range of tones by shifting the triangle pointers; if you hold the Alt key while clicking on the pointer Photoshop will show you the pixels with black tones or pixels with white tones. The gradient bar below the graph can add more white or black to the image; reversing the pointers will invert the image. Three eyedroppers representing black, midtones, and white can be used to tell Photoshop which colors should be sampled. There are also several timesaving presets that may be used to simplify the process of adjusting levels.

Figure 3.22. The Levels histogram represents grayscale tones.

Curves

Curves go further than levels, allowing you to *manipulate* the tones of an image. In the Curves dialog box you can see the levels histogram imposed below the curves grid.

The best way to modify curves is to place several points on the sloped line using the default Select Points tool. You can also draw a custom curve and smooth out the curve values. Just like Levels, Curves contains three eyedroppers to sample black, midtones, and white values in the image.

Vibrance

Vibrance adjustment gives you two similar aspects to control, vibrance and saturation. Saturation equally affects pixels across the entire image, but Vibrance is a more selective version that determines which pixels require more or less color adjustment. This can be particularly helpful when adjusting images with skin tones, as Vibrance is more intuitive and can sense that skin tones should be preserved.

Figure 3.23. The Levels histogram is imposed below the Curves grid.

Hue/Saturation

This image adjustment gives you the most control over colors in an image allowing you to customize hue, saturation, and lightness. In the bottom of the dialog box you will see two identical rainbow strips; the bottom strip will shift when you adjust the hue value to represent which color is replacing the original. There is a Master option, which allows you to specify the specific color. Brackets will appear between the two rainbow strips; these brackets can also be adjusted. These are useful presets.

Color Balance

Although color balance adjustment is somewhat similar to hue adjustment, it allows you more control over color combination and overall composition. It can be very useful for correcting white balance. Color balance adjustment gives you control to change the shadows, midtones, and highlights of an image.

Black and White

The black and white adjustment is more nuanced than simple black and white, giving you control over the contrast range for each color value. Customizing the contrast produces an image with greater depth and interest. You can also add a uniform tint of color to an image using the black and white adjustment.

Photo Filter

This adjustment is useful for correcting unintentional color washes that occur when a digital camera picks up on a certain tone or light. Photo filter allows you to make subtle changes to color balance and temperature while preserving luminosity.

Channel Mixer

The channel mixer adjustment is able to take information from one channel and apply it to another.

Color Lookup

This new addition to CS6 creates different looks by remapping colors based on technology used in the film industry. It contains several interesting default effects and can be enhanced by loading additional lookup tables.

Invert

This adjustment layer does not contain any options for you to specify. It will automatically invert all colors on the layer making each color its exact opposite. This adjustment is often combined with other adjustments to create more interesting effects.

Posterize

The posterize adjustment layer flattens the colors of the image and allows you to specify the number of color levels to be applied, giving the photo an illustrated effect.

Threshold

The threshold adjustment has only one value to customize, the threshold level. Any tone that is darker than the threshold level is represented by black pixels and any tone that is lighter than the threshold level is represented by white pixels essentially reducing your image to only two colors, either 100% black or 100% white.

Gradient Map

This adjustment layer is a fun yet controllable color correction tool. Photoshop will map the colors of a gradient to the luminance values of an image.

Editing Adjustment Layers

Adjustment layers are always created with a mask, the method for applying adjustments to specific selections of the image. If you decide you would like to make a change to the adjustment layer you can edit by double-clicking on the adjustment layers thumbnail in the layers palette. Photoshop will display the settings in the Adjustment Layers dialog box under the Properties panel. Adjustment layers apply to all

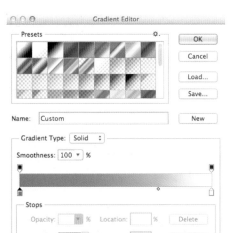

Figure 3.24. The gradient map can be customized through the gradient editor.

layers beneath them so their order in the Layers panel is extremely important if you are combining multiple adjustments. Stacking order of adjustment layers and regular layers becomes complicated with an increasing number of layers.

This adjustment affects all layers below (click to clip to layer)

Figure 3.25. Clipping the adjustment layer to affect only the layer below can be done in the Adjustment Layers dialog box.

When the adjustment layer is properly clipped to the layer beneath, a small down arrow will appear next to the thumbnail. With the adjustments complete you can always flatten by merging layers to simplify the Layers panel.

Masks and Channels

Masks

Overview

Masking is a powerful tool that will greatly enhance your efficiency in Photoshop. Masks allow us to continually edit and make adjustments to a specific area. As the complexity of your Photoshop document builds, it becomes increasingly important to preserve pixel data in a flexible way. Masks are nondestructive editing techniques that do not affect the original data. Photoshop offers five different types of masks to be used for varying scenarios, but fundamentally all masks behave the same. A specific portion of the document is "masked" while the other portions are left "unmasked." Black covers the area of the image to be unaffected, making it transparent so any layers beneath are visible. The white portion of the mask is revealed and remains visible. Masks can be thought of as another way of making selections without corrupting potential useful data.

Pixel Masks

The most commonly used type of mask is a pixel mask.

Pixel masks are easily modified, but when scaled, can cause unwanted artifacts or blurriness due to their raster format. To create a pixel mask, select the layer and click the Add Layer Mask option at the bottom of the Layers palette.

A second thumbnail will be added to the layer, giving a preview of the mask. By default the mask will be entirely white, however, if you have an active selection when creating the mask, the selection will be used to determine the mask's visibility.

Figure 3.26. The pixel mask is based on raster pixels and determines opacity on a grayscale from 1 to 100 that directly corresponds to opacity values.

Add layer mask

Figure 3.27. The pixel mask can be quickly found at the bottom of the Layers panel.

Figure 3.28. Photoshop will use the active selection for the mask.

Once the mask has been created it can be edited by Alt+clicking on the mask's thumbnail. Completely masked pixels are represented by black, completely revealed areas are represented as white, and partially selected pixels are represented as shades of gray. The lighter the gray, the "more selected" the pixel. Darker grays are "less selected" and will allow less transparency revealed while lighter grays allow greater transparency.

Vector Masks

Vector Masks are created by using paths, and provide a superior level of precision ideal for defining shapes with crisp, clean lines. A disadvantage of using Vector Masks is that they are not capable of varying pixel opacity in the way of Pixel Masks. A Vector Mask can be made from an active path by Command+clicking the mask icon. **Layer > Vector Mask > Current Path** can be used only when a *saved path* is currently selected. Once a Vector Mask has been made, paths can be added or subtracted by selecting the mask's thumbnail and painting black or white to conceal or reveal pixel data. A Vector Mask can also be created using the Shape tool and Shape layers. This is useful for creating buttons or other elements that need to be resized without interpolating data.

Sometimes it is necessary to get creative by using a Vector Mask to define a solid edge in conjunction with a Pixel Mask for more complex areas with varied opacities. You can effectively achieve a flexible, refined product by combining the abilities of these two different masks.

TIP	Masks can be toggled on and off by Shift+clicking the mask's thumbnail. A red X will appear over the layer thumbnail.

Quick Masks

Quick Mask mode is a type of Photoshop Mask that is more comparable to "painting on the mask" rather than using the standard selection tools. This method can be helpful in creating a mask that varies in transparency. Clicking on the "Quick Mask Mode" on the Tools palette changes to Quick Masks mode.

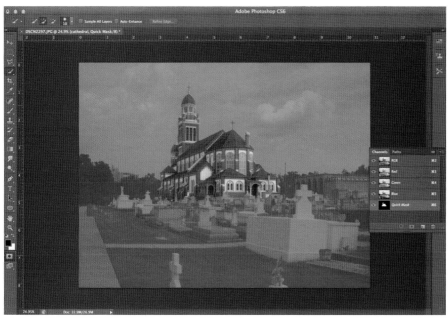

Figure 3.29. Quick Masks mode is found on the Tools palette.

Note this is different from the method used to create Pixel and Vector Masks. The hotkey to access Quick Mask is Q. The options for this mask allow you to change how the Quick Mask is viewed, by double clicking the "Quick Mask Mode" icon you can set the color and opacity, as well as whether color indicates the masked area or the selected area. After refining your Quick Mask, it can be saved by going to **Select > Save Selection**. It will then be stored in the Channels palette with access to the mask to make a selection from it any time.

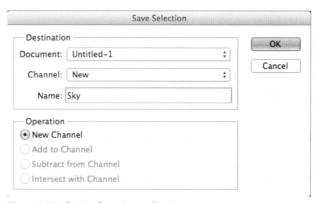

Figure 3.30. Options for saving a selection.

Clipping Masks

Clipping Masks can be a time saver when you encounter many layers that require the same mask. Clipping Masks are especially helpful when using adjustment layers because you are able to "clip" adjustment layers to a single layer without affecting layers below. You can press Command+Option+G to clip a layer to the one below it.

Figure 3.31. Blur applied selectively.

Clipping Paths

Figure 3.32. The Mask palette.

The final type of mask is called a Clipping Path. It is similar to a Vector Mask in that it requires a path to be made, however, the important difference is a Clipping Path applies to the entire document rather than one layer. This type of mask is useful when the document requires a specifically shaped crisp edge, most often applied for print and graphic designs. To create a Clipping Path you must first have a path saved. After the working path has been saved you are able to choose "Clipping Path" from the options menu. Although the document's appearance does not change, if you were to import the Photoshop document into Illustrator, it would be clipped to the Clipping Path.

Masks Palette

All of these masks can be created and refined using the very helpful Masks palette found in CS6 under the Properties panel.

Here you can set the mask density to determine the strength of the mask and affect the overall transparency of what is being masked. At 100%, fully masked areas will be completely transparent. When density is set to 50%, those same areas would be only 50% transparent. Also in the Mask palette, you can adjust the pixel feather count after a mask has already been created without altering the original data.

Mask Edge refinement is invaluable when making selections with tricky artifacts. Smooth, Feather, Contrast, and or Contract/Expand should be used to further refine a mask's perimeter.

Channels

When using Masks, another concept you should be familiar with is Channels. Each time a layer containing a mask is selected, a temporary channel is stored in the Channels palette. Here you can save the selection as a channel for later use by clicking the "Create New Channel" button at the bottom of the Channels palette. In the Channels palette are the Red, Green, and Blue channels in an RGB document. In some cases, depending on the contrast of the image, these channels can provide a built-in selection. If the channel has a high enough contrast between the objects you want to select and the background, you can Command+click it to create a selection and apply a new mask.

Channels are extremely useful working with .tiff files of digital models because .tiff files have the unique ability to store channels, meaning if you applied a reflection or shadows in your render, they will be included as channels.

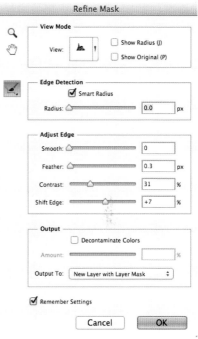

Figure 3.33. The Mask Refinement palette.

Smart Objects

Overview

Smart Objects are layers that contain data from raster or vector images. What sets them apart from layers is that they preserve an image's source content for reference.

Smart Objects enable you to edit in Photoshop nondestructively, that is, the changes you make to the image remain editable and do not affect the actual image pixels because they are preserved. This tool gives you greater flexibility than you normally get with a standard layer. Regardless of how often you scale, rotate, skew, or otherwise transform a Smart Object, it retains its sharp, precise edges because the entire original layer is stored as a reference.

You may have discovered that the Free Transform command is a destructive tool; Photoshop discards the pixel information when the transform is applied. This can be avoided by converting the layer into a Smart Object before making large changes in scale.

Figure 3.34. You can identify a Smart Object in the Layers panel by the icon that appears on the thumbnail.

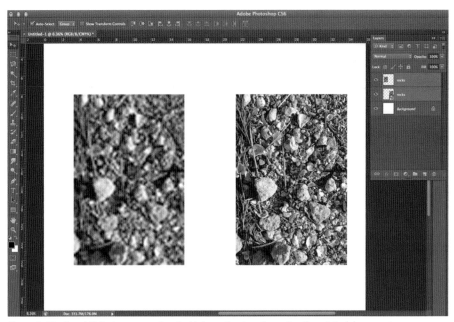

Figure 3.35. Smart Objects preserve the pixel information by referencing the original document.

Creating Smart Objects

To create a Smart Object simply right click the layer in the Layers panel and choose "Convert to Smart Object," or **Layer > Smart Object > Convert to Smart Object**. By converting the layer into a Smart Object you are indicating to Photoshop to save the layer as a separate embedded file within the .psd file.

Importing and Editing Smart Objects

You can also import vector objects from Illustrator as Smart Objects using **File > Place**. If you are placing a PDF or .ai file the Place PDF dialog box will appear. The major advantage of using Smart Objects in Photoshop is the fact that you can edit the contents, or source data. If you edit the original vector data in Illustrator, the changes will be reflected in the placed Smart Object in your Photoshop image file. If the source content is raster-based, the file opens in Photoshop. In order to edit the contents of a Smart Object, choose **Layer > Smart Objects > Edit Contents**. Also, you can simply double-click the Smart Objects thumbnail in the Layers panel; a dialog box will appear instructing you to save the file in the same location when edits are complete. This guarantees Photoshop will know where to look when referencing the image data so that all instances of the Smart Object are updated.

Smart Filters

Creating Smart Filters

Select a Smart Object layer, choose a filter, and then set Filter Options; applying a filter to a Smart Object converts it into a Smart Filter.

After you apply a Smart Filter, you can adjust, reorder, or delete it. It is possible to edit or remove a Smart Filter at any time because they are nondestructive. You can apply multiple filters to the same Smart Object with very clean and organized appearance in the Layers panel below the Smart Object layer to which they are applied. To expand or collapse the view of Smart Filters, click the triangle next to the Smart Filter icon, displayed to the right of the Smart Object layer in the Layers panel. Hide individual filters while keeping others visible by using the eye icon, and move or copy filters from one Smart Object to another. Additionally, you can also edit the Filter Mask, which is created automatically. One creative advantage is you are able to change the stacking order of the filters, creating unique combinations. All of this is possible while still maintaining the integrity of the original pixels of the Smart Object. Smart Filters are a powerful tool in Photoshop CS6 and capabilities have been expanded to include the Liquefy tool.

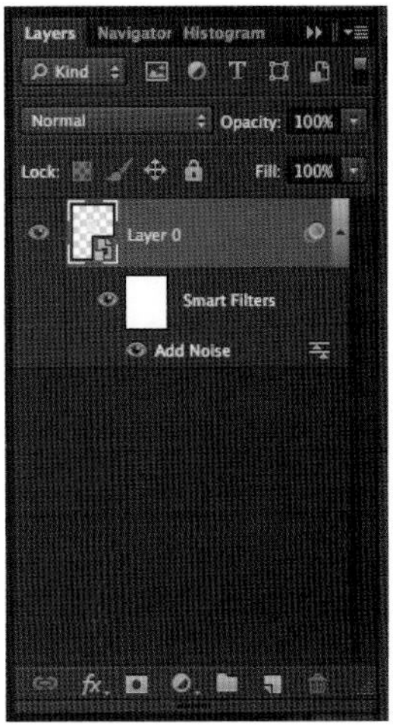

Figure 3.36. Smart Filters can be affected through the Layers panel.

Editing Smart Filters

Smart Filters are easily edited by double clicking on the Smart Filter layer in the Layers panel or by right clicking and choosing "Edit Smart Filter." The option to affect the Blending Mode of each Smart Filter is available through the Layers panel, allowing you to customize the Mode and Opacity of the Smart Filter.

> **TIP**
>
> When you edit a Smart Filter, you can't preview filters stacked above it. After you finish editing the Smart Filter, Photoshop again displays the filters stacked above it.

Masking Smart Filters

When you apply a Smart Filter to a Smart Object, Photoshop displays an empty (white) mask thumbnail on the Smart Filters line in the Layers panel. By default, this mask shows the entire filter effect. If there was an active selection before applying the Smart Filter, Photoshop will apply the mask on the Smart Filters line in the Layers panel. Using filter masks to selectively mask Smart Filters allows you to affect only a portion of an image. It is important to note, however, when you mask Smart Filters, the masking applies to all Smart Filters—you can't mask individual Smart Filters unless you create a separate Smart Object copy. Filter Masks work similarly to Layer Masks, and several of the same techniques can be applied. Like Layer Masks, you can paint on a Filter Mask and continue to edit even in retrospect. Use the controls in the Masks panel to change the Filter Mask density, add feathering to the edges of the mask, or invert the mask.

Blending Modes

Overview

It may be helpful to think of blending modes by first examining how opacity works. Changing the percent opacity makes the pixels of the active layer translucent, revealing the layers beneath. Blending modes operate in a similar manner, except Photoshop uses different mathematical calculations to determine the behavior of the active layer. Pixels of the blended layer are displayed in combination with pixels beneath, giving us different layer interactions. Blending modes are nondestructive and can be infinitely readjusted making them easy to use. They allow you to quickly combine images with minimal effort and create layered complexity. Blending modes are essential for compositing images and can be used in combination with Layer Masks. The best way to understand them is to experiment!

Blending Modes

Blending modes are most commonly used in the Layers panel to determine layer mode. Layer blending modes can be specified in the drop-down menu.

It should be noted that the Painting and Editing tools in the Tool panel also have their own blending mode. This includes painting with the Brush tool, where you can determine in what mode pixels are applied to the canvas. The options of blending modes are more or less the same for all of these tools, with the Brush and Shape tools having the largest selection of modes to choose from.

Opacity versus Fill

When using blending modes it becomes important to distinguish the difference between opacity and fill. For many other tools the opacity and fill percentage seem to be identical, but one important way opacity and fill differ is how they perform when used in conjunction with blending modes. There are eight blending modes that behave differently when changing fill rather than opacity; they are color burn, linear burn, color dodge, linear dodge, vivid light, linear light, hard mix, and difference.

Figure 3.37. Blending modes can be found in the drop-down menu on the Layers panel.

Normal Modes

The default mode of Normal requires no mathematical equation and displays as original pixels. Dissolve Mode acts on partial and transparent pixels to apply a diffusion dither pattern, breaking up hard edges. Used in combination with different brush strokes, Dissolve provides additional texture.

Figure 3.38. The effects of Dissolve Blending Mode on pixels applied with the Brush tool.

Darken Modes

Darken Mode only blends tones and colors where the active layer is darker, keeping all of the dark pixels and replacing the light pixels with the pixels of the layer below. Multiply is possibly the most useful of the darkening modes, ideal for creating shadows and easily removing light colors. The color of the base pixel is multiplied by the blend color.

Multiplying any color with black produces black; multiplying any color with white leaves the color unchanged. Multiply Mode can be a valuable time saver when working with black and white linework because it automatically removes all white pixels and keeps the black.

Color Burn Mode has a more intensely dark effect, as does Linear Burn Mode, which uses less saturation. Darker Color Mode operates using the composite channel rather than RGB as separate channels, as darken uses.

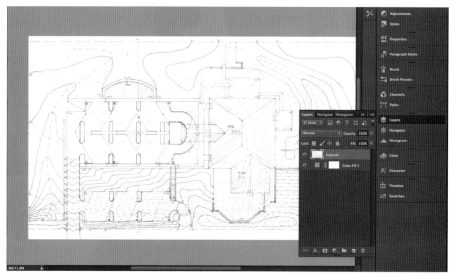

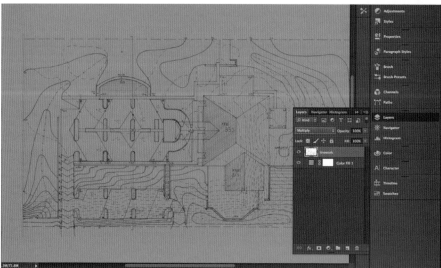

Figure 3.39. Multiply Mode multiplies each overlayed pixel.

Lighten Modes

This group of Blend Modes can provide nuanced effects to bring light source consistency to renderings. Lighten Mode is the opposite of Darken Mode, and will only blend tones where the blended layer is lighter, keeping all of the light pixels and replacing the darker pixels with the tones of pixels beneath. Screen Mode removes more of the dark pixels creating a brighter effect. It is essentially the inverse of Multiply, a great method for eliminating dark pixels and preserving lighter ones. The Color Dodge Mode is more intense with contrasting saturated midtones and exaggerated highlights. Linear Dodge is brighter even than Color Dodge but results in less saturation. Lastly, Lighter Color Mode works nearly identically, but it operates using the composite channel rather than RGB as separate channels.

Contrast Modes

The fourth and largest group always adds contrast by combining a complementary Lighten Mode and Darken Mode. Overlay uses a combination of Screen and Multiply; it is unique because it determines calculations based on layers beneath the active layer rather than the active layer itself like other contrast Blend Modes. A great technique to create custom shadows and highlights is using a layer that's been filled with 50% gray pixels set to Overlay Blend Mode. You can paint with a black brush to burn in dark tones and white brush to lighten midtones and highlights, changing the opacity to control the depth of the effect. Soft Light Mode has an effect similar to shining a diffused spotlight over an image with subtle highlights and shadows.

Figure 3.40. Soft Light is ideal for adding subtle texture.

Hard Light Mode uses a combination of Multiply and Screen modes for an effect similar to shining a harsh spotlight on the image, creating an intense and harsher result. Hard Light is perfect for creating shadows that can be adjusted with the fill percentage. Vivid Light Mode uses a combination of Color Dodge and Color Burn. Linear Light Mode combines the effects of Linear Dodge and Linear Burn for a more extreme effect. Pin Light Mode uses Lighten and Darken; the effects can be quite dramatic or result in large areas of noise or completely removed midtones. Last in the group of lightening modes, Hard Mix provides extreme contrast and benefits from adjusting the fill percentage.

Comparative Modes

Comparative Modes work by either inversion or exclusion. Difference works by subtracting pixels on the active layer from equivalent pixels in the layers beneath. This can be very useful when compositing overlapping aerial imagery because similar colors cancel each other. Where the overlapping portion of the imagery is perfectly aligned it results in a solid black.

Exclusion Mode is identical to Difference Mode except when similar colors cancel out the resulting color is gray instead of black. Subtract Mode works by subtracting pixels on the active layer from the composite of pixels beneath except black does not have an effect and white pixels are converted to black, and similar colors cancel each other out with a resulting color of black. Divide Mode divides pixels of the active layer by equivalent pixels on the layers beneath. Similar colors turn to white, which often results in extreme highlights.

HSL Modes

The final group of Blend Modes begins with Hue. This mode combines the hue of the blend layer with the brightness and saturation of base layers, allowing you to have the

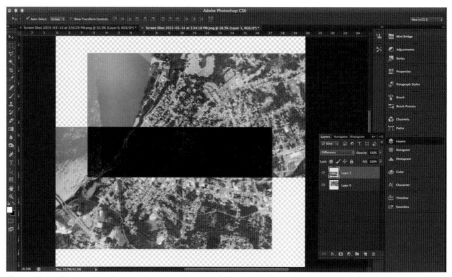

Figure 3.41. The overlapping portion of the imagery is perfectly aligned out resulting in black.

image of the underlying layers with only the colors of the active layer. Saturation Mode maintains the saturation of the active layer and blends the luminosity and hue of underlying layers. Saturation Mode is an excellent method of isolating colors and dulling the rest of the image. Select by color range the color you would like to isolate and fill the inverse area with 50% gray. When you set the gray layer to Saturation Mode it will remove saturation from everywhere except the chosen color.

Figure 3.42. Set the gray layer to Saturation Mode to remove saturation from everywhere except the chosen color.

Color Mode keeps the color of the active layer while blending hue and saturation of the active layer with the luminescence of underlying layers. This can be a time-saving method to change the overall color of an image. Luminosity Mode creates a blend with the luminance of the blend layer and the hue and saturation of the base layer.

Group Blending Modes

When layers are combined into a folder to form a group the Blending Mode will default to Pass Through. In this mode, Photoshop will act as if there isn't a group and will perform the blending in the usual order. If the mode of the group is changed from Pass Through the result is essentially changing the order in which layers are processed.

Blending Options

In addition to the Blending Mode drop-down menu in the Layers panel, Blending Modes can be adjusted in the Layer Style's dialog box under Blending Options.

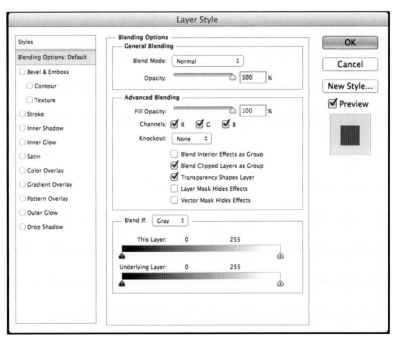

Figure 3.43. Layer Style's dialog box.

Part 2
Workflows

Chapter 4
Digital Drawings in the Design Process

Because both hardware and software tools are used to create digital representations of the landscape, it is important to understand how to apply them. Why would someone use a vector-editing application for one task and a raster application for another task? There are many answers to this question, and every designer has different opinions, but it is possible to discuss some specific cases that may shed light on this topic.

Applications for Specific Tasks

When any orthographic, measured drawing is being created, it is necessary to use vector-based drafting software. Typically, a CAD application such as Autodesk AutoCAD, Nemetschek Vectorworks, or Graphisoft ArchiCAD can be used. CAD applications are tailored drafting tools that are engineered for accuracy, which is required when representing design proposals that are intended for construction. The measured drawing, whether it is a site plan or section/elevation, is the basis for all subsequent work and must be created with CAD or something equally accurate. Equivalent results can be hand-drafted drawings or scaled drawings created with a vector illustration software package such as Illustrator. A measured/drafted drawing should never be attempted using raster-based software such as Photoshop; the result would be inaccurate linework.

A rendered plan or section/elevation can be developed in many different software applications, based on an accurate, drafted plan. Depending on the final product, vector software and raster software are best suited to perform specific tasks. Raster-based image-editing software, such as Adobe Photoshop or GIMP, excels when creating richly textured and blended illustrations using tools that are similar to analog brushes and pencils. Brush tools allow designers to quickly represent complex landscape surfaces with ambiguous edges. Other tools make it possible to quickly integrate textures or context from photographs as well as make adjustments across an entire canvas within multiple layers. The downside is that when a raster drawing is started, the final output size needs to be determined in order to avoid pixelation. If the images being worked with are large, file size also becomes an issue with raster images. It is very easy to create an image that is over 1.5GB when working on an illustration that is 36 inches × 48 inches at 120 dpi. File size is becoming less of an issue because Photoshop CS4 has transitioned to 64-bit (Windows only) and can use over 4GB of system RAM.

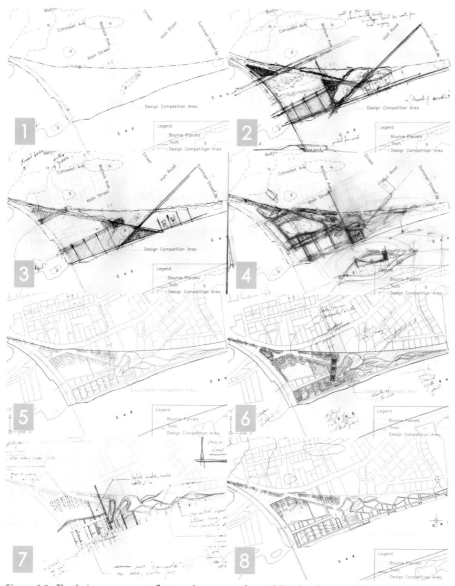

Figure 4.1. The design process must fluctuate between analog and digital techniques. This sequence of images shows the evolution of a site design through iterative analog and digital representations.
Bridge Park Competition Submission, Cantrell Michaels

Vector illustration software, such as Adobe Illustrator, excels at tasks that require precision and flexibility in the final image size. You can use it to make small refinements and adjustments to CAD linework, including minor drafting or lineweight changes. Typically, most text, labels, and leaders can be created with vector-editing tools because of the crispness that vector software provides. Text and leaders are also easier to edit in vector software, allowing labels to be quickly moved or changed and leader lines to be readjusted as elements are added or subtracted. If your drawing-size requirements change, you can scale vector elements up without worrying about pixelation. The downside to vector-based applications is that everything is represented as objects; therefore, oddly formed elements are difficult to blend together. Vector drawings can also be difficult to organize due to the large number of objects required to create complex illustrations.

Moving between Analog and Digital Techniques

Generally, analog drawings are static, representing stages of design. The static nature of analog drawings is expanded through layering and reproduction, creating new drawings from remnants of the past. Each reproduction is slightly altered or changed, creating small or large evolutions in successive stages of a drawing. For the most part, this changes when the process becomes digital, where reproduction occurs with exacting tolerances and revisions are compiled within a single file. This relationship is important to consider as drawings move back and forth between analog and digital environments.

Typically, drawings are created in analog and move toward digital as they are refined. For example, many design concepts will start with sketches, progress to CAD alternatives, and then are refined and rendered for client presentations. This process has formed due to the representational skills of senior design professionals and young designers. In most cases, the senior designer will feel more comfortable with analog processes and will sketch or draw ideas that are then passed to junior designers who are more facile with computer technologies. In many cases, the process of digital representation transcribes the analog and then slowly refines itself through phases of the design process. This process relegates either medium to a confined portion of the design process and does not promote a rich interaction between a design team's hierarchy.

On a smaller scale, it is also possible to use digital data, such as a CAD model as the framework for a hand-rendered drawing. The CAD model can be a simple massing to explore volumetric relationships or may be a detailed building model. This process requires the composition to be completed digitally and then printed or projected to complete an analog drawing. The detail of the digital information affects this process; less detail allows the analog rendering to make inferences; the opposite holds true when a more-refined digital model is used. This process is typically efficient, as it utilizes the strengths of each medium and the designer but tends to forgo a real relationship between digital and analog processes.

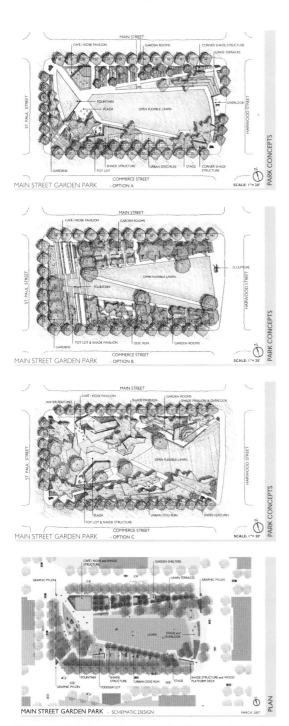

Figure 4.2. Early design sketches may begin in an analog medium and progress to a digital version generated by CAD linework.

Dallas Main Street Park, Thomas Balsley Associates, Inc.

Ideally, digital and analog media find a middle ground, where an exchange of information can occur. As a designer, you need to understand how drawings inform one another in order to make decisions at each stage of the representation process. The final result for either medium is to create drawings that accurately represent design ideas, evoke the experiences being designed, and contribute to the design process.

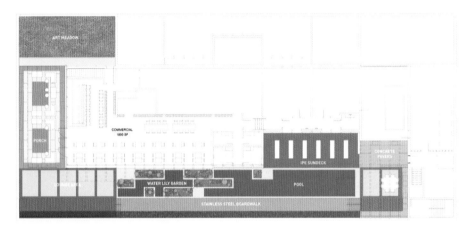

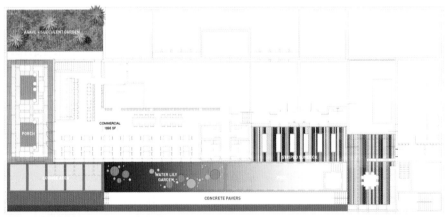

Figure 4.3. Design sketches can be combined with plan view to illustrate concepts. *Spackman Mossop+Michaels*

Chapter 5
Setting up the Document

In the world of digital media, the word "document" is an ambiguous term used to describe the AutoCAD workspace, the Photoshop canvas, and the Illustrator artboards. Nearly every digital media application requires the user to define the document setup during the initial stage of the creation process. When designers first embark to create an illustration, they must carefully consider the type of surface on which the final product will appear—whether it is a physical canvas, watercolor paper, or a sheet of vellum. Through experience, a designer learns how to plan the final output and predict how different formats will translate between different media.

When first setting up a drawing in a digital media application, many novice users assume that anything can happen. They simply start to work, thinking the image can be printed at any size or scale desired. This is not always true, especially when dealing with raster images or vector layouts with raster image links. Typically, it is possible to change or modify the document setup, but there are limitations that must be considered before proceeding.

Drawings at Multiple Sizes

Setting up the document to be flexible is key to creating a fluid digital workflow. One of the first things to consider when setting up a document is what the final output is likely to be for the drawings. In contemporary practice, a single drawing is likely to be presented in many different formats: as a printed document on a presentation board at 24 inches × 36 inches or larger, as an image in a bound document at 8.5 inches × 11 inches, as a slide in a public presentation on a digital projector, or as an image on a webpage. Thinking about how all of these images will be created from a single set of drawings is critical to producing efficient and effective drawings.

The basic rule is to create the drawing at the largest size likely to be needed, especially if the drawing is brought into Photoshop at an early stage in the process. As discussed in the section "Raster-Based Programs" in Chapter 3, the size to which a raster image can be enlarged is limited. For example, if a plan is set up for an output of 11 inches × 17 inches and rendered in Photoshop for that output size, it will be difficult to use the same drawing for a 24 inch × 36 inch print if the need arises later. However, a 24 inch × 36 inch drawing can easily be printed at 11 inches × 17 inches.

How Drawings Move through the Digital Workflow

Another issue to consider is how the drawing data will be transferred from one program to another. As discussed previously, drawings will move between several software applications before they are completed. Just how this movement occurs depends on how the drawing is set up in the beginning. There is usually more than one way to sequence the movement of the drawing through the software to get the same result.

For example, to complete a drawing you could:

1. Start with an aerial photograph in Photoshop.
2. Add existing CAD data (contour lines or property lines) to the aerial image in Photoshop.
3. Link the Photoshop file into Illustrator and draw a diagram over the aerial/CAD information.
4. Label and print the drawing from Illustrator.

Alternatively, to get the same results you could:

1. Import the CAD data into Illustrator.
2. Draw and label the diagrams in Illustrator using the CAD data as a base.
3. Import the aerial image from Photoshop as an underlay.

As discussed in Chapter 1, certain programs are better for certain tasks. Thinking about these issues in advance will prevent situations where you are forced to lose drawing flexibility or degrade your image through multiple rasterizations or color mode changes.

Setting the Image Size

One of the key issues in setting up your document is to reduce the amount of upsampling you must do to create images at all of the sizes you need for output. The simplest rule is to set up your images at the largest size you expect to output. This is obviously more critical for raster images that you will be using in Photoshop. The issues of resolution and the difference between raster and vector drawings were discussed in Chapter 3. If you are working solely in Illustrator or CAD, with no aerial images imported from Photoshop, you do not need to worry about the document size at the beginning of the process, as Illustrator and CAD are vector-based programs. As previously discussed in Chapter 1 in the section "Software," vector-based programs can easily be scaled up or down with no loss of quality. However, if you import vector linework into Photoshop, you will need to consider these issues. Anytime you move your drawing into a raster-based program, such as Photoshop, you should consider the setup size of the drawing.

For example, if you think you will print an image at 24 inches × 36 inches for a presentation, you should set your drawing to be 3600 × 5400 pixels wide, or 24 inches × 36 inches at 150 pixels per inch. When a new document is created by selecting **File > New,** the dialog box shown here is used to set the size of the document.

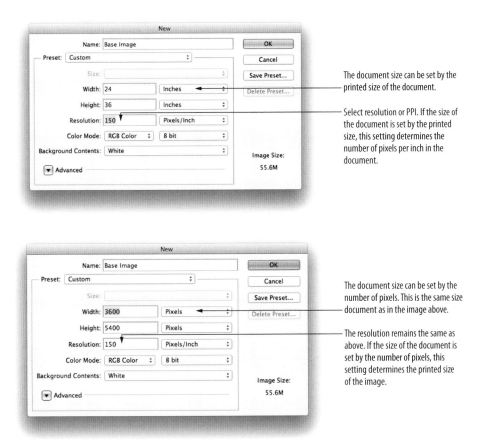

The document size can be set by the printed size of the document.

Select resolution or PPI. If the size of the document is set by the printed size, this setting determines the number of pixels per inch in the document.

The document size can be set by the number of pixels. This is the same size document as in the image above.

The resolution remains the same as above. If the size of the document is set by the number of pixels, this setting determines the printed size of the image.

Figure 5.1. There are two ways to establish the size of a new document.

By setting the document to the largest size likely to be printed, the image is less likely to need to be upsampled later in the process, which would likely degrade the quality of the image. The relationship between the pixel dimensions and the resolution can be seen once the document is created by selecting **Image > Image Size**.

The one issue that might cause you to limit the size of your document is the speed of your hardware. If your drawing is extremely large and your hardware has limited capacity, your computer may slow down so much that it is not feasible to work at the maximum size of your final output. If this is the case, and you cannot move to a faster computer, there are a couple of techniques that you might use to speed up your working process.

The first is to create the drawing at the smallest possible size needed to get a good-quality, nonpixelated image. For example, you could set the resolution of your 24 inch × 36 inch image to 120 ppi instead of 150 ppi. As we discussed in the section "Raster-Based Programs" in Chapter 3, an image at this resolution is sharp enough to be acceptable for use in most situations. The savings in terms of file size between 120 ppi and 150 ppi is almost 40%. A 24 inch × 36 inch file at 150 ppi requires 55MB, while the same file at 120 ppi requires 35MB.

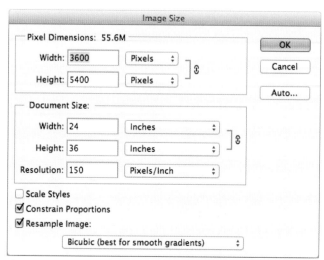

Figure 5.2. Once the document is created, the Image > Image Size dialog box shows the relationship between the Pixel Dimensions and the Resolution.

However, a Photoshop file with only one layer is rarely too large for hardware to handle. The 55MB file is not likely to cause problems. Usually, a file only becomes too large for a system after multiple layers are added. There are several techniques that can be used to work with large, multilayered files while maintaining a high-resolution image. In most cases, it is better to keep the file at the desired resolution and use some of these techniques than it is to work with a smaller image. We discuss techniques within Photoshop for working with large files in Chapter 8.

Chapter 6
Base Imagery and Scaling

Typically, digital illustration begins with some form of aerial photography, linework, or site photos. When a designer is working with any orthographically projected drawing, such as a plan or section/elevation, having the base imagery at a known scale is critical. It is not possible to use drawings that are not to scale for any serious design decisions. Without a scale, the images and linework have no relationship to the "real world." This holds true in both analog and digital media.

Two types of photographs are typically used as base images in design projects: aerial and site. Aerial photographs provide an overview of site conditions and are typically recorded at a specific resolution, making it possible to scale based on pixels or through known measurements between elements on the photograph. When scaling is based on the distances in an aerial photo, the results are not extremely accurate; this inaccuracy must be taken into consideration as a project moves forward. Pixelation, earth curvature (in large images), and lens distortion can make it difficult to create an accurate base plan. A CAD plan traced from an aerial photograph is no substitute for a properly acquired site survey. Multiple aerial photographs (quads or tiles) can be assembled to create high-resolution images of a large area or to serve as the context for further design and representation work.

Site photographs are another important method of obtaining base imagery for an illustration. Site photography is typically used to create context for sections/elevations or textures in plan renderings. It is important to remember that site photographs are not orthographic images and, therefore, cannot be scaled unless compared to another orthographic drawing. For example, CAD linework for an

Figure 6.1. An aerial photograph altered in Photoshop to desaturate the image, combined with contour lines created in AutoCAD and water bodies on the site drawn in Illustrator. *Mossop+Michaels*

elevation can be used to align existing context; often doing so may require stretching the site photos in order to fit them to an orthographic projection.

Aerial Photography

Aerial photography is a common base for large-scale site design projects. The rise of online databases such as TerraServer, Google Earth, and GlobeXplorer (which offer easy access to aerial photography) has made the use of aerial photographs a key component in the early stages of most large-scale design projects. One of the reasons aerial photography is often used at the beginning of a project, or in a speculative project such as a competition, is that you can start work immediately before a site survey is completed.

For academic or speculative projects, a CAD base is often created from an aerial photograph due to the lack of survey information. Aerial photography can be used in conjunction with Illustrator at the beginning of a project as a diagrammatic tool to show site boundaries, site analysis/ inventory, and initial design concepts.

Or, an aerial image can be used with a project to provide context to the site plan.

Obtaining the Aerial Photograph

Several sources for aerial photography are available on the Web. The U.S. Geological Survey (USGS) has a large database of aerial photography that can be viewed for free from the Internet via the TerraServer website; use of this material is subject to copyright restrictions. Google Earth has an ever-evolving set of data, also subject to copyright restrictions, that can be used for projects. For most long-term projects, high-resolution aerial images will need to be purchased from commercial courses such as GlobeXplorer or provided by the client.

Tiling Aerial Photographs in Photoshop

Several different methods are used for tiling together separate photographic images. If a site is large and a high-resolution base image is needed, several high-resolution aerial images may need to be tiled together. The technique of tiling images together is used most frequently to create panoramic photographs.

Figure 6.2. The same aerial photograph used as a background image for the site plan.

Figure 6.3. Several photographs can be tiled together to create a panoramic image of a site. A similar technique can be used to tile together several aerial images to make a composite aerial to use as a base.

The separate images can be tiled *by hand* or tiled automatically using software. Photoshop's Photomerge tool automates the tiling of separate images, and several other standalone software packages will perform the same task. Our discussion here explains the process used to tile together several aerial images, but the process works the same for tiling site photographs into a panoramic image.

Manual Method

The manual method involves lining up each separate image by registering common areas on both images. This method is referred to as "manual" because the images are assembled using the mouse and the Move tool in Photoshop. Although there are automated methods for tiling photographs, the manual method is useful for adding aerial images to the base material midway through a project. For example, if the drawing is mostly completed and the base needs to be expanded to include a new part of the site, it is often easier to insert the new aerial images manually rather than reassemble the base material using Photomerge.

For the images to be tiled by hand in Photoshop, the individual images need to have some overlapping areas or common edges with which to register the images. The following steps provide an example for tiling images by hand:

1. Place the two images to be tiled on separate layers in the drawing. Make the upper layer active.
2. Reduce the Transparency of the image on the upper layer to 50%.
3. Use the Move tool to register the two images. Once the images are close to being in the correct positions, use the arrow keys to nudge the image into place.
4. Return the Transparency of the upper layer to 100%.
5. Select both layers by holding down the Cmd/Ctrl key and clicking on the layers in the Layers palette.

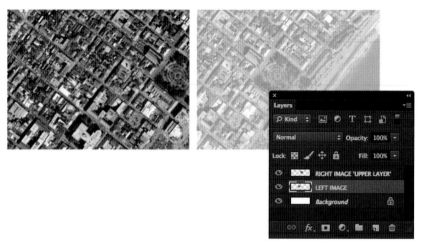

Figure 6.4. The two images to be merged should be on separate layers. The image on the upper layer has a reduced opacity to facilitate its registration with the lower image. To register an image, find a landmark in both images and move one image over the other. In these images of New Orleans, Jackson Square is present in both images and can be used as a registration mark.

Figure 6.5. Use the Move tool to register the images. Once the images are in close proximity, the arrow keys on the keyboard can be used to move the image in small increments to fine-tune the registration.

6. Right-click the layers and select Merge Layers to create a single layer from the two images. Merging these two layers is not necessary if the layers need to be kept separate for future editing. Merging the layers has the advantage of creating a less cluttered Layers palette.

7. Additional images can be added at any point in the project. However, the size of the canvas may need to be increased to add them. This can be done using the **Image > Canvas Size**, which will open the Canvas Size dialog box. Increasing the canvas size differs from increasing the image size because it does not affect the resolution of the image.

Figure 6.6. Merging the layers makes the Layers palette less cluttered. The individual images could also be collected in a Group in the Layers palette if the images need to be edited again later.

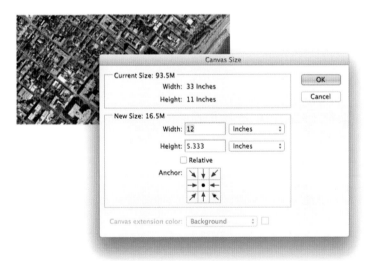

Figure 6.7. If another image needs to be added to the right side of the current image, the canvas size needs to be increased to accommodate the additional image.

Tiling Photographs with Photomerge

Several software applications are available to automate the process of tiling separate images into a single image. Photomerge in Photoshop is one of the most readily available tools for merging photos, but other third-party applications work in a similar way.

The steps shown here provide an example for tiling images using Photomerge:

1. The images that will be tiled should be saved as separate files and placed in a folder on the hard drive. Each image must overlap the images that will be adjacent.

Figure 6.8. All downloaded images to be tiled must have areas of overlap with the adjacent images. This example has 10 images to be tiled.

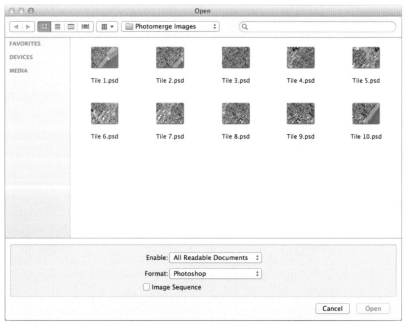

Figure 6.9. The images can be put in a single folder to facilitate the Photomerge operation.

2. Open the Photomerge operation from the **File > Automate > Photomerge** menu. Using the Browse option, load the files to be tiled. If the files are in a single folder, select the Folder option from the drop-down menu. The Photomerge dialog box offers several options for tiling the images. For a set of aerial images, the Reposition Only option is the correct choice. If the images being tiled are panoramic

photographs with varying perspectives, the Auto or Perspective option is the most effective. The Interactive Layout option is useful for images that do not easily arrange themselves on the first pass. This option allows the images to be manually repositioned before the final compositing.

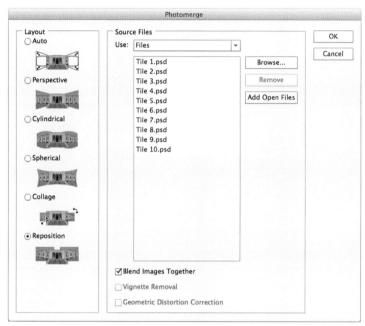

Figure 6.10. Using the Browse option, load the files that will be used for the tiled images into the Photomerge dialog box. For aerial images, use the Reposition Only option to tile the images without changing their proportions. For panoramic photos, the Auto option and the Perspective option offer the best choices.

3. The result of the Photomerge operation is a new file with all of the tiled images arranged on separate layers with a Layer Mask attached. These layers can be kept separate or merged into a single image.

Figure 6.11. The result of the Photomerge operation is a new file with each image on a separate layer.

Scaling the Aerial Photograph

Getting the correct scale is one of the most critical issues for importing an aerial image into a project. Geographical Information System (GIS) packages, such as ArcGIS, offer other methods for scaling the images; however, they are beyond the scope of this book. This book presents methods for scaling images that are not geo-coded, using only Photoshop, CAD, and/or Illustrator. There are three primary methods for scaling images in Photoshop and Illustrator: the Calculator method, the Scale by Reference method, and the Pixel Conversion method.

Calculator Method

The Calculator method uses conversion calculations to determine scale by referencing a known distance on the aerial image. There are simpler, more automated techniques to scale drawings in many software packages. However, this method is extremely useful as a fundamental technique for scaling drawings. It can be used with almost any software package that has a measurement tool. This method can also be used on a standalone photocopier or scanner with the ability to scale by percentages.

Similar to the Scale by Reference method, which will be discussed later, the Calculator method requires knowledge of at least one linear distance on the image, such as the length of a building or the distance from one point to another on the site. If this information is not available from a survey of the site, measuring devices are available in Google Earth and other online geography websites to determine a distance. This method is not as accurate as a professionally commissioned survey; but depending on the project, it is typically accurate within an acceptable range for diagrammatic work and creating a base for plan drawings.

The Calculator method relies on finding the difference between the current scale of the drawing and the desired scale of the drawing. That difference is used as a multiplier to scale the drawing. This is a simple example of this method to demonstrate the concept.

If a drawing is at 1 inch to 20 feet (current scale) and the desired scale is 1 inch = 10 feet, the drawing would need to be increased in scale by 2 times, or by 200%. In this example, the Scale Factor is 2 and the Scale Percentage is 200. The simple calculation is:

Current Scale/Desired Scale = Scale Factor (multiply by 100 to get Scale Percentage)

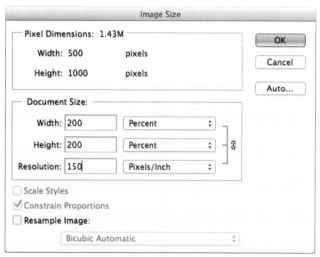

Figure 6.12. The image will be scaled by the percent value in the Image Size dialog box. Uncheck the Resample box to prevent upsampling.

The calculation and scaling operation in Photoshop would proceed in this fashion:

1. The current scale of the drawing is 1 inch = 20 feet or (20).
2. Divide that by the desired scale, which is 1 inch = 10 feet or (10).
3. The calculation is 20/10 = 2.
4. The Scale Factor is 2, and the Scale Percentage is 200.
5. To change the scale of the drawing in Photoshop, **select Image > Image Size**.
6. Change the drop-down menu to Percent, and increase the size of the drawing by 200%.
7. Make sure the Resample box is unchecked to prevent upsampling.

In practice, the current scale of the aerial image is not usually known. To scale an image that is at an unknown scale, at least one real-world dimension from the site must be determined. This could be the length of a road or the width of a building. Longer dimensions are more likely to result in more accurate scaling than shorter dimensions, because the chance for measurement error increases with shorter distances. This method requires a slightly more complex set of calculations to complete the scaling operation. It basically adds one critical step, determining the current scale of the image. After the current scale is determined, the same calculations used previously are used to find by what percentage the drawing needs to be increased or decreased to reach the desired scale.

The steps outlined here give an example of how to determine the current scale of the drawing:

1. Find a real-world distance measurement to use in the scaling operation. For this example, the length of the site will be the measurement. The length of this site is approximately 3,400 feet, based on a measurement using Google Earth.
2. Determine the desired scale. For this example, the desired scale is 1 inch = 500 feet on an 8.5 inch × 11 inch sheet.

Figure 6.13. Real-world distances can be determined by a number of methods. Surveys, onsite measurements, and online resources are among the many methods for finding measurements. This example shows the measurement obtained using Google Earth. *Image from Google Earth*

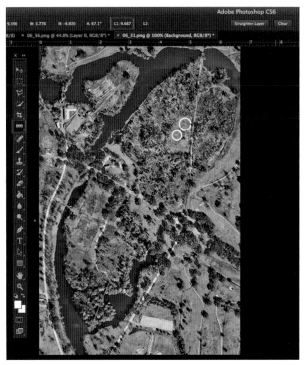

Figure 6.14. Use the Ruler tool to measure the same real-world distance on the aerial image. Uncheck the Use Measurement Scale box.

3. Determine the same distance, which can be referred to as the *image distance*, on the aerial in Photoshop. With the Use Measurement Scale box unchecked, use the Ruler tool to click and drag a measurement over the same distance that was used to determine the real-world distance. In this example, the image distance is approximately 8.5 inches long.

4. To determine the current scale of the Photoshop drawing, divide the real-world distance measurement by the image distance. In this example, divide 3,400 by 8.5 to get 400.

5. The current scale of the aerial image is 1 inch = 400 feet. The calculations to convert the image to the desired scale of 1 inch = 500 feet are the same as in the first simple example. Divide the current scale by the desired scale, or 400/500, which provides a Scale Factor of .8, or a Percentage Scale of 80%.

This technique works the same in Illustrator with two small differences. The Info palette is used to make the measurement of the image distance. An example of the different technique is shown here:

1. Using the Pen tool, draw a line that is the distance to be measured.

2. Select the line and bring the Info palette to the screen (Window > Info).

3. The length of the line will be displayed in the Info palette.
4. To change the scale of the objects in the drawing, select the objects, **select Object > Transform > Scale**, and enter the Percentage Scale in the dialog box.

Scale by Reference Method

The Scale by Reference method is an automated technique for scaling base material. Similar to the Calculator method, this method assumes that one dimension in the drawing, the real-world distance, is known. The difference is that the software will perform the calculations for you. SketchUp and AutoCAD are two commonly used programs with an automated Scale by Reference method built into the software. Typically, software that draws in "real world" units, such as SketchUp, AutoCAD, and most other 3D modeling packages, will use the Scale by Reference method. We will look at how to scale the image in SketchUp as an example.

1. Import the aerial image and place it on the model.
2. In this example, the real-world distance is the same as in the previous examples, approximately 3,400 feet.

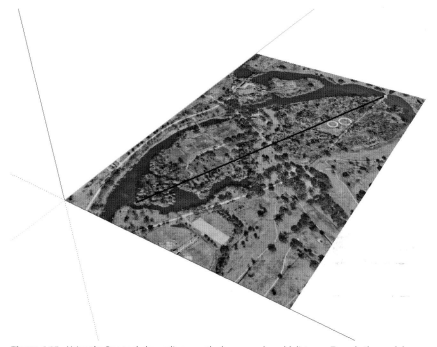

Figure 6.15. Using the Pen tool, draw a line over the known real-world distance. To scale the model, use the Tape Measure tool and click on each endpoint of the line, enter the real-world distance (3,400 feet), and press Enter.

3. Using the Pencil tool, draw a line over the real-world distance.
4. Using the Tape Measure tool, click on the two endpoints of the line.
5. Type in the new length, the real-world distance (3,400 feet), and press Enter.

Figure 6.16. After you press Enter, a dialog box confirms the operation. After you accept the transformation, the model will be resized according to the reference length.

6. A dialog box will appear to confirm the operation. Click Yes.
7. The software will scale the model to the appropriate size.

Pixel Conversion Method

The third way to obtain the correct scale uses the Pixel Conversion method. To use this method, you need to know the feet/meters-to-pixel ratio of an image before you scale it. This information is predetermined, and sometimes it is located on the documents that are downloaded with the image. Typical resolutions for this method are 1 foot = 1 pixel, 2 feet = 1 pixel, and 1 meter = 1 pixel, although there are many other ratios. The *feet/meter-to-pixel ratio* is the distance represented by one pixel of the image. For example, if the feet per pixel resolution of an image is 1 foot = 1 pixel and the image is 2,000 pixels wide by 1,000 pixels high, the distance across the top of the image is 2,000 feet. If you were to print the drawing at a resolution of 200 pixels per inch, the image would be 20 inches wide by 10 inches high and the scale would be 1 inch = 100 feet.

Adjusting the Hue, Saturation, and Lightness of Base Imagery

Photoshop is usually used to make adjustments to aerial photographs. A standard technique for adjusting an aerial image is to *desaturate* the image if it is in color. This removes the color from an image, offering more contrast to the linework that is added over the image. A fully desaturated image consists of only shades of gray, plus black and white; however, sometimes a small amount of color is retained, depending on the desired outcome. To desaturate an aerial image using Photoshop, follow these steps:

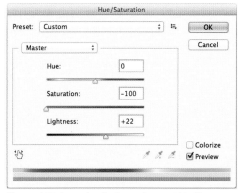

Figure 6.17. Lowering the Saturation to –100 will remove all color from the image.

1. Go to Image > Adjustments > Hue and Saturation.
2. The Hue/Saturation dialog box will appear. Lower the Saturation value to desaturate the image. Lowering the Saturation to –100 will create an image with no color.
3. Lowering the Lightness of the image will create a lighter image that often provides better contrast with the linework to be added to the drawing later.

Figure 6.18. Original aerial image in full color. *Image from Google Earth*

Figure 6.19. Image with Saturation set to –100. *Image from Google Earth*

Figure 6.20. Aerial image lightened to increase contrast with linework to be added later. *Image from Google Earth*

Another technique that achieves the same results, but which is much more flexible in the drawing workflow, is to use an *adjustment layer* to alter the hue and saturation rather than an image adjustment. An adjustment layer offers the same capabilities as an image adjustment, but with the ability to edit the adjustment at any time in the drawing process. Once an image adjustment is completed, the image cannot be reverted to its previous state except through History (or Undo) operations. An adjustment layer resides in the Layers palette and can be adjusted or completely removed at any time. Adjustment layers are saved with the drawing, just like normal layers, so the flexibility to undo or alter the adjustment always exists.

Many of the same adjustments can be made in both the **Image** > **Adjustments** menu item and the adjustment layers.

New adjustment layers can also be created from the Layers palette.

Figure 6.21. The adjustments that are available from the **Image** > **Adjustments** menu are similar to the adjustments available as adjustment layers

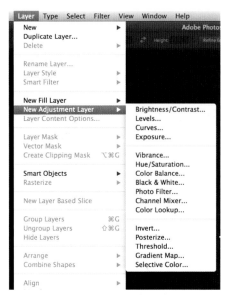

Figure 6.22. Adjustment layers have the added advantage of remaining editable throughout the life of the drawing.

Figure 6.23. New adjustment layers can be created from the Layers palette.

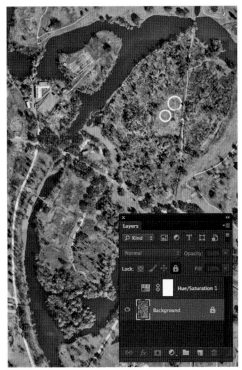

Figure 6.24. When the adjustment layer is turned off, the adjustment does not affect the image.

Figure 6.25. When the adjustment layer is turned on, the adjustments affect all layers below it in the Layers palette.

Double-click on the icon in the adjustment layer to bring up the Hue/Saturation dialog.

Figure 6.26. To make more adjustments, double-click the icon in the adjustment layer so that the dialog box will reappear.

To alter the adjustment, double-click on the adjustment layer so that the Hue/Saturation dialog box appears. By altering the values in this dialog box, more adjustments can be made to the image.

The layer order in the adjustment layers affects how an image is adjusted. Adjustment layers affect only the layers that are below them in the Layer palette. If a layer is placed above the adjustment layer, it will not be affected by the adjustment.

If an adjustment layer is placed above another layer, the adjustment will affect that layer.

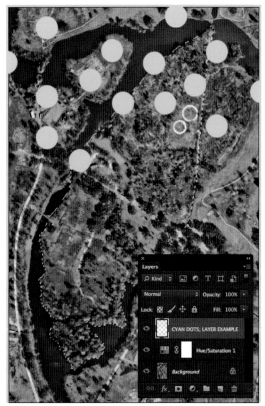

Figure 6.27. The adjustment layer affects only the layers below it in the Layers palette.

Figure 6.28. If the Cyan Dots layer is moved below the Hue/Saturation layer, it will be affected by the Hue/Saturation adjustment.

Figure 6.29. Select the areas that will be used for the mask. When a new adjustment layer is created, the selected areas are automatically converted to a mask and used in the adjustment layer.

Adjustment layers can also be used with a *mask* so that only a portion of an image is affected on the layers below it in the Layers palette. *Masking* is a powerful concept in Photoshop, and mastering the use of masks will increase your efficiency with Photoshop. A more detailed explanation of masks is found in Chapter 2. The technique used here uses masks in combination with adjustment layers to desaturate a portion of the image while the remainder of the image remains in color.

1. Create a selection around the area that will remain in color.
2. Invert the selection using **Select > Invert**.
3. With the selection active, create a new Hue/Saturation Adjustment layer.
4. The new adjustment layer will automatically have a mask attached to the layer. The outline of the selection will be visible in the Mask icon on the adjustment layer. The areas in white on the mask will be affected by the Hue/Saturation adjustment, while the areas in black are masked.

Figure 6.30. The Mask icon shows the areas where the adjustments will be masked. Areas that are white will be adjusted; the areas in black will be masked from the adjustment.

73

5. When the Hue/Saturation is adjusted, only the areas of the image that are not masked are affected.

Figure 6.31. The adjustment layer does not affect the area that is masked.

Using CAD Linework as a Base

Existing CAD linework can also serve as a context base for projects. The CAD linework can be used alone or combined with an aerial image to create the base. This section presents a simple technique for importing CAD linework into Photoshop as a base for diagrams, as well as techniques for altering the color of the linework and the background. Using CAD linework as the basis for a plan rendering is discussed in detail in Chapter 18.

Exporting the CAD Linework as a PDF

The linework should be set up in AutoCAD to be printed at the scale and paper size required for the final image. If the desired size/scale of the printed image is 24 inches × 36 inches at 1 inch = 100 feet, a Paper Space tab with the correct paper size, scale, and lineweights should be created in AutoCAD. This Paper Space tab should then be printed or exported as a PDF to be imported into Photoshop. For a more detailed discussion of this technique, see Chapter 18.

Importing the Linework into Photoshop

The advantage of importing the linework into Photoshop is that it gives you the opportunity to use the image-adjustment tools. Several different techniques can be used to change the appearance of the linework, including adjusting the color and transparency of the lines. If the linework is too light, it can be copied in place to make it darker. To copy the linework in place, simply drag the linework layer and drop it on the New Layer icon on the Layers palette. If the linework is too dark, the brightness can be adjusted using **the Image > Adjustment > Contrast and Brightness** command. The lines can be changed to white using **the Image > Adjustments > Invert** command. Here is an example of how to alter the linework in Photoshop:

1. Import the PDF created from the AutoCAD linework by opening the PDF directly in Photoshop. A dialog box will offer several choices for importing the PDF. Choose Bleed Box for the Crop To: option. The Image Size should be the same size as the page size created in the Paper Space tab in AutoCAD. Photoshop will rasterize the vector-based PDF linework at the Resolution selected in the dialog box. The resulting file in Photoshop will be the same size/scale as the Paper Space tab created in AutoCAD.

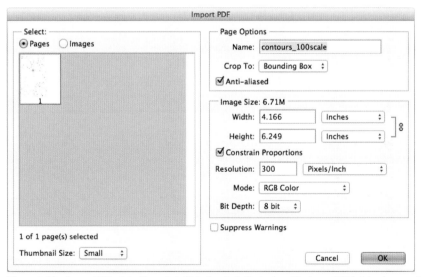

Figure 6.32. Open a PDF printed from AutoCAD directly in Photoshop. The Import PDF dialog box provides options for rasterizing the PDF. Choose Bleed Box to preserve the scale of the PDF.

2. The PDF will typically import with a transparent background. To create a solid color for the background of the image, create a Solid Color adjustment layer. The Color Picker will open to allow any color to be chosen as a background.

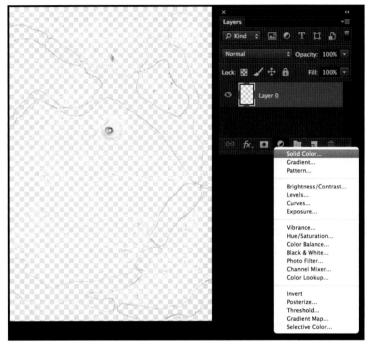

Figure 6.33. The Solid Color adjustment layer can be selected from the New Fill Layer menu.

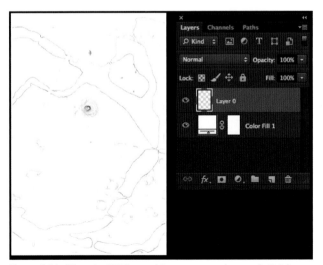

Figure 6.34. When the CAD linework is set up on one layer and a Solid Color adjustment layer is below it, many options are available for altering the appearance of the linework and background color.

3. This setup offers several alternatives for the appearance of the linework and image background. To create a black background with white linework, double-click the Solid Color Adjustment Layer icon and choose black as the background color from the Color Picker. To create white lines, select the linework layer and choose Image > Adjustment > Invert.

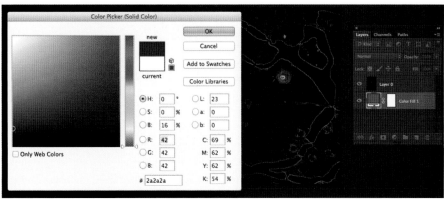

Figure 6.35. Double-click the Solid Color Adjustment Layer icon to recall the Color Picker. Any color can be chosen for the background and adjusted at a later time.

4. Another technique that is possible with this setup is to create a colored background with colored linework. In this example, a sepia background with sepia linework is created by again altering the Solid Color adjustment layer as in steps 1 through 3.
5. To create the colored lines, Cmd/Ctrl+click the icon in the linework layer to select all of the pixels on that layer. Create a new layer and hide the original linework layer. Select the color for the new linework using the Color Picker. Using the Paint Bucket tool, uncheck the Contiguous and Sample All Layers box in the options bar at the top of the screen, and click inside the selected area in the drawing. For more information on using the Paint Bucket tool, see Chapter 19.

Figure 6.36. Select the layer with the linework and then choose Image > Adjustments > Inverse to change the black lines to white. Another technique is to use the Image > Adjustments> Brightness/Contrast dialog box to adjust the value of the lines.

Chapter 7
Source Imagery/Entourage

Compiling a collection of people, plants, and textures to populate your drawings is an important element of successful drawings. These elements that are put into a drawing are often called the *entourage* of the drawing—the surrounding elements that add to the overall image. The difference between drawings that look pasted together and ones that accurately express the design idea often comes down to the quality of the entourage.

There are two main ways to obtain your entourage: make it yourself or purchase it. For some applications, purchased entourage is acceptable. Good collections of people and cars that fit most situations are available. However, it is important to understand how to create your own entourage, as most premade plant images look too much like brand-new nursery stock trees to create evocative sections and perspectives. Collecting images of vegetation from the actual site of a project for use in the drawings is the preferred method.

Frequently, unique elements that cannot be purchased are needed for an image—for example, a monument on the site or a bridge in the background. Although such elements are not strictly considered entourage, the same techniques are used to separate them from their backgrounds.

Selections

Understanding how to make selections is one of the key skills when working with raster images. Separating one set of pixels (for example, the pixels that create the image of a tree) from another set of pixels (everything else in the image) requires an understanding of the different tools Photoshop uses to select pixels. There are two basic ways to make selections in Photoshop: by hand and by pixel. The By Hand method uses the mouse to

Figure 7.1. Most of the trees for this image were created from images of trees on the actual site. Finding pre-made images of trees that express the character of the planting design is difficult. *Spackman Mossop+Michaels*

directly select the pixels. The By Pixel method uses the color or value of the pixels to make selections. The two most common tools used for the By Hand method are the Marquee tool and the Lasso tool. The two most common tools used for the By Pixel method are the Magic Wand tool and the Color Range selection. The following text shows some techniques that use these tools to select entourage for use in design drawings.

Manual Methods

There are several manual methods for selecting pixels. The simplest is to use the common Marquee tool. To use this tool to select pixels, click the mouse and drag a box over the pixels to be included in the selection. A similar, but more nimble selection tool is the Lasso tool. This tool draws a freeform shape with the mouse around the pixels required for the selection. The Polygonal Lasso works in much the same way, but clicking from point to point around the pixels makes the selection. In all three of these selection methods, the pixels are either inside the selection or outside the selection. Each pixel is 100% selected or 0% selected. There are other selection methods that allow a pixel to be "partially selected." Understanding how to use partial selections is key to a number of techniques used in the book.

Partial Selections

Pixels in Photoshop can be partially selected. This is a very powerful concept in Photoshop, and understanding it is critical to making advanced selections. Most people are familiar with the *marching ants* selection box in Photoshop.

In this type of selection, the pixels inside the box are selected, while pixels outside the box are not. There are no partially selected pixels in a standard Marquee selection. To see the difference between a *fully selected* pixel and a *partially selected* pixel, consider the following example:

1. In a blank 500 × 500 pixel document, make a selection using the Rectangular Marquee tool.
2. Using the Paint Brush tool, paint a color over the selection. All of the pixels inside the selection are painted 100% black, and none of the pixels outside the selection receive any paint at all.

"Marching Ants" designating an area that is selected.

Figure 7.2. To select pixels using the Rectangular Marquee tool, click and drag over the pixels to be included in the selection.

Figure 7.3. A standard selection with the Rectangular Marquee tool accepts color from the Paint Brush tool within the entire selection. All pixels are fully selected.

3. Make another selection using the Rectangular Marquee tool.

4. From the menu, choose **Select > Modify > Feather**. Choose 10 as the number of pixels to feather the selection. Feather will create a series of partially selected pixels at the edge of the selection. In practice, this is used to create selections that blend with other parts of a drawing. For this exercise, it will simply serve to demonstrate the effect of a partially selected pixel.

5. Paint a color over the new selection. The pixels at the edge of the selection, where the feather was applied, accept only a portion of the paint from the Paint Brush tool. These pixels are selected, because they accept paint from the Paint Brush tool, but obviously they are not fully selected.

Figure 7.4. To create a series of partially selected pixels along the edge of a standard Marquee selection, choose the Feather option. This will make a gradient of partially selected pixels along the edge of the selection.

Figure 7.5. When color is applied over the feathered selection, the effects of partially selected pixels are apparent. Where fully selected pixels receive all of the paint and unselected pixels receive no paint, partially selected pixels receive a percentage of the paint according to the percentage of the pixel that is selected. For example, a 50% selected pixel would be 50% gray if painted over with a black brush.

Masks

To understand how partial selections work, it helps to understand the concept of *masks*. Masks are simply a different way of seeing a selection. Consider the following analogy using a printed photograph and a piece of cardboard (or a mask). Imagine that the piece of cardboard is taped over the photograph. A hole is cut in the piece of cardboard to make visible a portion of the photograph. Cutting a hole in the cardboard, or the mask, is the equivalent of making a Marquee selection. If a paint brush is used to cover the image, the paint will affect the image only in the areas where the cardboard has been cut away. On the other parts of the image, the cardboard would *mask* the image.

Photoshop provides a simple way to view selections as masks instead of as standard selections, which is what the marching ants selections are called. Quick Mask mode is used to see the selection as a mask. Switching to Quick Mask mode does not alter the selection; it simply provides another way of viewing the same selection. To see how to switch between Standard Selection mode and Quick Mask mode in Photoshop, consider the following example:

1. To switch back and forth between Standard Selection mode and Quick Mask mode, click the Quick Mask icon in the Tools palette. If the Quick Mask icon is clicked again, the view toggles back to Standard Selection mode. Switching back and forth between the two views does not affect the selection itself. It is simply two different

Figure 7.6. Clicking the Quick Mask icon toggles back and forth between Standard Selection mode and Quick Mask mode.

Figure 7.7. In Quick Mask mode, the covered areas represent the masked areas, and the areas that are open to the image below represent the selection.

ways of looking at the same selection. However, to work on an image, the document must be in Standard Selection mode. As explained later in this section, if a change is made while in Quick Mask mode (for example, when using the Paint Brush tool), the mask will be altered, not the image.

2. In Quick Mask mode, the selection is represented as a colored area for the masked areas (in this example, the areas in black) and an open area that shows the image below for the selected area. In terms of the previous analogy, the black area is the "cardboard" covering the image, and the clear area is the portion of the mask that is cut away.

3. To make Quick Mask mode easier to use, Photoshop has provided a method to control the appearance of the mask. When the Quick Mask mode icon in the Tools palette is double-clicked, a dialog box appears that adjusts the colors of the mask. It is important to understand that the color or transparency of the "view" of the mask does not affect the mask itself. In this example, the mask has been colored black and the Opacity has been set to 100%. This more accurately represents how the mask operates and is useful for this demonstration. However, in practice it is usually easier to use the Quick Mask mode if the image below is visible, even in areas where it is completely covered by the mask. For that reason, Photoshop provides a way to alter the appearance of the Quick Mask mode.

Figure 7.8. Create a selection using the Rectangle Marquee tool.

Figure 7.9. In Quick Mask mode, the area of the selection should be clear and the masked area should be a color.

Although adjusting the appearance of the Quick Mask does not affect the selection, the selection can be altered using Quick Mask. This is really the main reason Photoshop includes a Quick Mask mode. Quick Mask mode can be used to paint selections onto the mask. While in Quick Mask mode, painting with white removes the mask and painting with black restores the mask. To revisit the photograph/cardboard analogy, in Quick Mask mode painting with white is similar to cutting away a part of the cardboard to reveal the photograph underneath; and painting with black puts the cut-away cardboard pieces back on top of the photograph. Here's another way to think about altering masks: painting with white in Quick Mask mode selects pixels and painting with black deselects pixels. To see how this operates within Photoshop, consider the following example:

1. Open an image in Photoshop and make a selection using the Marquee tool. This Marquee selection is just to aid in the demonstration of the concept.
2. Switch to Quick Mask mode. If the covered areas in Quick Mask mode are not black, double-click the Quick Mask mode icon to change the appearance of the Quick Mask. For this demonstration, these settings have been chosen because masks are most often represented as a black, white, and gray image in other areas of Photoshop.

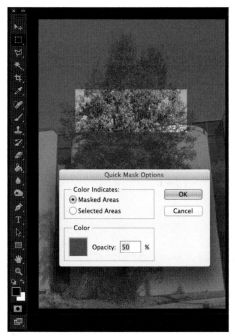

Figure 7.10. To see how quick masks operate, change the appearance of the mask to black at 100% Opacity rather than the default color of blue at 50% Opacity. To change this setting, double-click the Quick Mask icon in the Tools palette.

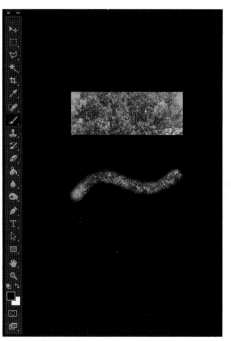

Figure 7.11. Painting the mask white removes the mask or selects the pixels. Painting the mask black restores the mask or deselects the pixels.

3. Notice that the colors in the Color Picker have changed to grayscale colors. This is because only grayscale colors are typically used to alter the mask. To alter the selection, choose white as the foreground color, select the Paint Brush tool, and paint an area of the mask white. The area that is painted white will reveal the image below the mask.

4. The area painted white has been removed from the mask—or put another way, the area painted white has been selected. To see the selection, click the Quick Mask mode icon to switch back to Standard Selection mode. The area that was painted white shows as a selection in this view.

Figure 7.12. Areas that were painted white in Quick Mask mode appear as selections in Standard Selection mode.

Up to this point in the examples, the Quick Mask has allowed only two types of selections for the pixels below: completely deselected or completely selected. The mask has either black or white. In terms of the analogy used earlier, the cardboard is either covering the image or it is not there at all. Imagine that the cardboard covering the image could let some of the paint through and keep some out. The cardboard is really more like a screen than a solid cardboard. Where the screen has larger holes, more of the paint gets through; where the screen has smaller holes, less of the paint gets through. The screen can still be completely open to allow all the paint through or closed to completely block all paint from affecting the image below. The area where the screen is partially open represents partially selected pixels in Photoshop. In a mask, these areas are represented by shades of gray. If a completely covered area is represented as black, and a completely open (or selected) area is represented as white, a partially selected pixel is represented as a shade of gray. The lighter the gray, the "more selected" the pixel. Darker grays will allow less paint through to the image below; lighter grays will allow more.

To partially select a pixel in Quick Mask mode, consider the following example:

5. Starting where the previous example left off, click the Quick Mask icon in the Tools palette to return to Quick Mask mode.

6. Choose the Paint Brush tool and click on the Color Picker. Choose a shade of gray from the top half of the grayscale, a lighter gray.

7. Paint an area of the mask this shade of gray. At this point, the paint is affecting only the mask, not the image below.
8. Return to the Color Picker and choose a shade of gray from the lower half of the grayscale.
9. Paint an area of the mask this darker shade of gray.

Shades of gray greater than 50% show up in the Standard Selection

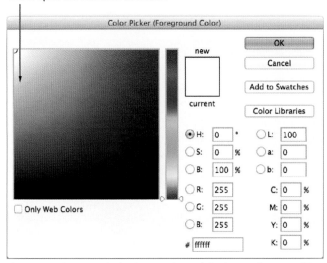

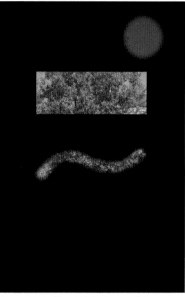

Figure 7.13. Painting a shade of gray on the mask that is more than 50% white will show up in the Standard Selection mode.

Figure 7.14. The circle in the top-right corner was painted with a light shade of gray.

Shades of gray darker than 50% do not show up in the Standard Selection

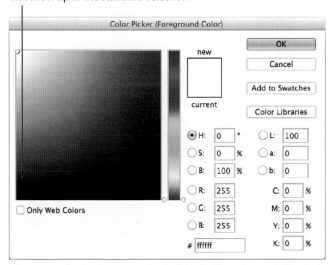

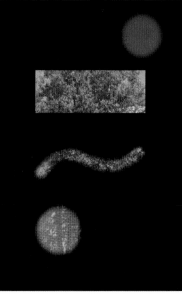

Figure 7.15. Shades of gray more than 50% black will not show up in Standard Selection mode. However, these pixels are still partially selected, even if they do not have the "marching ants" surrounding them.

Figure 7.16. The circle in the lower-left corner is painted with a dark shade of gray. This selection will not show up in Standard Selection mode, but these pixels are still partially selected.

10. Switch back to Standard Selection mode by clicking the Quick Mask icon in the Tools palette to see the results. Notice that the area in the upper-right corner that was painted with the lighter shade of gray has marching ants around it, while the other area in the lower-left corner does not. This is because in Standard Selection mode, the marching ants highlight only areas of the drawing that are more than 50% selected. An area painted a darker gray will not show up in Standard Selection mode. However, this does not mean these pixels are not partially selected.

Figure 7.17. The areas of the mask that are painted with a light gray show up in the Standard Selection mode; those that are painted with dark gray do not.

Figure 7.18. Painting over the entire image shows that selected areas that were painted dark gray in Quick Mask mode, but do not appear in Standard Selection mode, will still accept some of the paint from the Paint Brush tool.

11. While in Standard Selection mode, choose the Paint Brush tool and choose red as the foreground color. Paint over the entire drawing. The area painted dark gray in Quick Mask mode allows some of the paint to come through, even though it does not have marching ants around it. In the rest of the drawing, you can see the areas that are completely masked and allow no paint to pass. Areas that are partially masked allow some of the paint through.

The concepts of masks and partial selections are fundamental to many advanced techniques in Photoshop. The previous examples are intended to demonstrate the concept. Examples of techniques that use these concepts will be demonstrated throughout the book.

Creating Entourage

Understanding the advanced selection tools introduced in Chapter 3 and the concept of masks presented in this section will increase your ability to create advanced entourage selections. However, not all entourages need to use these advanced selection techniques. The simplest way to create entourage is to use the Lasso tool to trace an outline around the entourage element. This technique requires some patience, and the results are often a bit choppy. This is fine if the images are meant for the background or will be mixed in with other images, such as in a forest.

If you are going to use the image in the foreground, it is often better to use a more advanced technique than the Lasso tool. Advanced selections rarely use only one tool, however. It is better to use the Magic Wand or Color Range selections in areas where there are small, dispersed pixels, such as the edge of a tree, and the Lasso tool where the outline is easy to distinguish, such as the trunk of a tree. In the following example, the Lasso tool is used in areas that do not have enough contrast to use the Magic Wand or Color Selection tools. Consider the following example that uses both the By Pixel and By Hand methods for selection:

1. To select the tree from the background for use as entourage, choose the proper method for selection. The distributed or "fuzzy" portion of the image, the area with the canopy, is against a solid background. This will make it easier to select this part of the tree using one of the By Pixel methods. The lower portion of the image, where the ground plane has a color similar to the trunk of the tree, will require a By Hand method for selection.

2. Using the Color Range Selection tool, select the middle of the blue sky. In this example, the Fuzziness is set very high, at 171. There are many areas of gray in the selection, especially in the canopy of the tree. These gray areas are partially selected pixels.

3. This selection has too wide of a range to be effective. After accepting the selection by pressing OK, use the Delete key to erase the selected pixels. The selection creates a ghosted image of a tree after the selected pixels are erased. The gray pixels in the canopy of the tree are partially erased along with the rest of the sky.

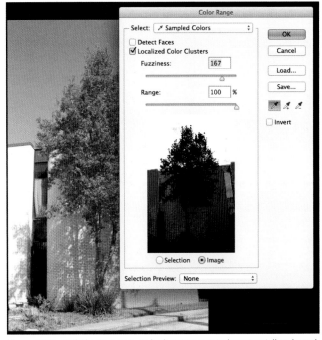

Figure 7.19. With the Fuzziness set high, too many pixels are partially selected. This selection is too broad to be used.

4. To make this selection more accurate, while preserving all of the pixels in the tree, use a low value for the Fuzziness and select multiple sample colors. Select multiple sample colors by using the Plus Eyedropper on the Color Range dialog box. Using the Color Range selection, the Fuzziness will be set to a value in the 20s. This value will depend on the image used, but will usually be lower than 40 to be effective. This is what the selection looks like at this Fuzziness level after the first sample color is selected from the sky.

5. The white/light gray areas are the selected pixels. Very little of the sky is selected because the Fuzziness value is set low, making it more precise. The concept for this technique is to keep the Fuzziness precise, but add to the number of colors from which the Color Range tool picks. This is almost like doing multiple Color Range selections on top of each other. To select multiple color samples, choose the Plus Eyedropper from the bottom right of the dialog box. Click in a different area of the sky. Notice that the selection increases, making more of the sky white.

6. With the Plus Eyedropper still selected, continue to pick multiple other points in the sky. Without changing the Fuzziness, more of the sky is added to the selection. However, the pixels in the tree canopy remain completely masked, or deselected. Continue to click on other areas of the blue sky until most of the sky is selected, but the tree is still black.

Figure 7.20. If the Fuzziness is set too high, pixels in the canopy of the tree will be partially selected. The resulting image is a poor representation of the tree.

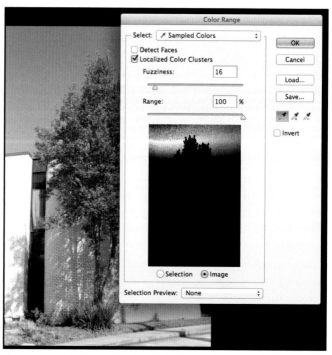

Figure 7.21. To select the sky using a Color Range selection, set the Fuzziness low and select one area of blue.

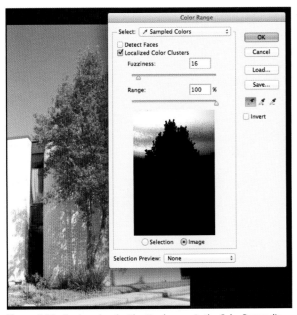

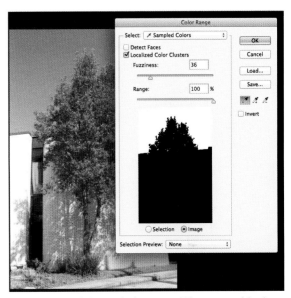

Figure 7.22. By choosing the Plus Eyedropper in the Color Range dialog box, multiple sample colors can be added to the selection.

Figure 7.23. By clicking multiple times on different areas of the sky, the entire sky will be selected, yet the tree remains completely masked.

7. Click OK to accept the Color Range selection. Use the Delete key to remove the blue pixels from the image. Notice that the selection of the tree canopy is fuller and the edges are less ragged than when the Fuzziness was set too high.

8. This selection looks good on first observation; however, along the edge of the canopy, blue pixels are forming a halo around the tree. This halo effect is more apparent with a dark background behind the tree. To create this dark background, go to **Layer > New Fill Layer > Solid Color** and choose a dark color for the fill. Place this layer below the layer with the tree.

9. At this point, there are two ways to proceed. The first and best method is to deselect and try to make a more precise selection using more sample colors.

10. The second method is to zoom into the blue halo and use the Color Range selection to select just those blue pixels.

11. Erasing those blue pixels leaves you with an accurate, but slight choppy, selection.

Figure 7.24. This selection preserves the colors in the canopy and produces a much less ragged edge.

The By Pixel method was used to select these dispersed pixels from the solid color background. For the lower part of the tree, making the selections by hand will be easier and more accurate than using the Color Range or Magic Wand selections. The final steps to selecting away the entourage element from the background are shown here:

12. Use the Eraser tool to remove the larger parts of the background around the trunk.
13. Using the Lasso tool, select the areas around the trunk to be removed and press the Delete key.
14. The final entourage element is ready to be used in a section or perspective.

Figure 7.25. Place a dark background behind the entourage to test for a halo effect.

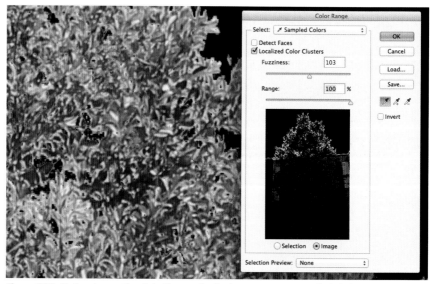

Figure 7.26. Performing another Color Range selection is one way to remove the halo from the entourage.

Figure 7.27. After the blue pixels are selected, the pixels can be deleted or the color of the pixels can be changed to match the background of the image.

Figure 7.28. Use the Eraser tool to quickly remove large parts of the background.

Figure 7.29. Using the Lasso tool, select the areas near the trunk, and erase the pixels using the Delete key.

Figure 7.30. The final image is ready for use as entourage.

Chapter 8
Managing Large Files

Figure 8.1. Each layer increases the memory the Photoshop file will need.

Architectural sheet sizes are typically very large; a 36 inch × 48 inch rendering at 120 ppi can easily become a 1.5GB (gigabyte) file, as layers and symbols are created throughout the illustration. Understanding how to work with these large files in order to keep Photoshop running smoothly is important. The goal is to always maintain the highest quality image with maximum editability, while not slowing down the computer. The problem is that these goals completely counteract each other, making it a constant struggle to keep down file size.

A file consumes computer memory through either RAM or hard drive space. Hard drive space is typically cheap, and RAM is typically expensive; therefore, most computers have much less RAM (4 to 8 gigabytes) than hard drive space (100 to 1,000 gigabytes). When a Photoshop file is open, two file size numbers appear at the bottom left of the screen. The first number shows what size the file would be if the image were flattened to a single layer. The second number shows the actual size of the unflattened file. If a single, digital photo is opened with no layers, the two file sizes will be exactly the same. As layers, symbols, smart objects, and effects are added to the file, the size on the right will continue to increase.

Flattening Layers

In most cases, layers are what quickly increase the file size. Imagine each layer as another file stacked on the original file. If there are more variations and more pixels, the larger the file will become. To cut down on the file size, it is possible to flatten the layer stack and combine layers.

1. Click on Layers in the menu bar. At the bottom of the Layer menu, there are three options for flattening layers: Merge Layers, Merge Visible, and Flatten Image.
2. Merge Layers (Ctrl+E) will merge the currently active layer with the layer below it. This is a quick way to combine two layers. Merge Layers will also merge multiple layers if they are all selected. To select several layers, hold down the Ctrl key and click on them, or click on one layer and hold down the Shift key to select a range of layers. With all the layers selected, merge the layers to create one layer from all of them.

3. Merge Visible (Shift+Ctrl+E) will take all of the currently visible layers and create one new layer. This is a good way to flatten everything except for a few specific layers, such as text layers.

4. Flatten Image will flatten the entire image and discard any hidden layers. This is a quick way to get rid of everything and make one composite image.

It is important to remember that any time a layer is merged or artwork is flattened, the ability to isolate that information on its own layer is lost. This will make the image much smaller but will take away much of the flexibility that is necessary to make edits. Any flattening of the image should be taken with some reservation because it is not reversible.

Figure 8.2. It is possible to merge one layer or several layers at once.

Saving Layer Groups for Flattening

In the quest for smaller file sizes, it is possible to export portions of the document to other files to maintain editable portions of the document in case edits are needed. This is possible by grouping layers into layer groups and then duplicating the layers to new files.

1. Create a new layer group and name it something that describes the layers that are going to be flattened.

2. Move all of the layers into this group by dragging and dropping them. This can be done one layer at a time or several layers at a time.

3. Right-click on the layer and select Duplicate Group. A dialog box will appear. In the Destination section for the document, choose New. The name of the group should be the same as the name that was given earlier. This creates a new document with the layer group in it. Save this document for later use.

4. Go back to the rendering and select the layer group. Merge the group (Ctrl+E). This will make a new layer from the layer group.

5. If the layers that were flattened in the group need to be edited later, simply open the document with the layers and reverse the duplication process. Select the group, right-click, and choose Duplicate in the Layer palette. The destination should be the rendering instead of a new image. All the layers will be fully editable.

Figure 8.3. Layer groups can be used to organize many layers that will be duplicated to a new file.

Figure 8.4. Right-clicking on a layer group and selecting Duplicate Group will bring up the Duplicate Group dialog box. The group can be duplicated to another file or to a new file.

Figure 8.5. The layer group can be merged to create a new single layer.

Printing Issues

Another issue that occurs with large files is failure to print: the printer runs out of memory while printing or otherwise crashes. Prints should be made from flattened versions in most cases. There is no benefit in printing from a 1.5GB Photoshop file with all of its layers intact. If the image is to be printed on a typical inkjet plotter, the image can be converted to a JPEG file (.jpg) to further reduce the file size. Some color quality may be reduced, but overall most renderings won't have any significant loss in color quality and, most importantly, the image will be printed. Most architectural renderings have a limited color palette and, therefore, suffer less when the image is compressed to a format such as JPEG.

Chapter 9
Automation

Certain tasks in digital media are repetitive. Often, the same sequences of steps are executed several times over with little or no change. Simple tasks of resizing and renaming a file become daunting when extrapolated over hundreds of files. Automating these types of tasks, however, can play an important role in both efficiency and consistency. The ability of contemporary software to repeat a user-defined sequence can save tremendous amounts of time in a digital workflow.

Automation is built into software like Photoshop, primarily through the use of Photoshop Actions. Actions record user-generated commands that are then stored within the program. Once recorded, the action can be automated on any document to execute the exact same sequence of commands. Any process that is consistently repeated in a standard, non-site-specific way should be recorded through Actions. If, for example, a design office has a standard layering system for all Photoshop plan renderings, an action can be recorded that creates, names, and modifies the blending mode for those base layers. When played on a newly imported CAD file, the standard layers will be generated and quickly prepare the document for rendering purposes. The aggregate time saved by incorporating these types of actions can be significant and is the primary benefit of incorporating automation.

Actions can also be used to record a very specific rendering process. When creating texture on a base color, like a grass texture, the user might apply certain blending modes, filters, or other techniques that create a particular rendered look. If that process is recorded, the specific settings used to modify the base color are stored in the Action. When played back on a separate grass layer, the steps are repeated precisely. This can be an important tool when attempting to produce a larger cohesive set of images. Automating the process ensures consistency, and, if needed, allows for editing of the final result.

The examples presented here will explore the use of Photoshop Actions and Batch Processing in both Adobe Photoshop and Adobe Bridge. They will walk through the creation of new Actions, and their applications in both Photoshop and Bridge. The final portion of the chapter will look at file organization and the use of Batch Renaming in Bridge.

Recording Actions in Photoshop

Photoshop Actions can be used to automate a series of tasks to be played back on one or multiple files. The process begins with recording the original sequence of tasks on a file and storing those steps in an Action. When recording, the Action stores the all steps applied to the file currently open. This includes, but is not limited to, changes to resolution, image adjustments, new layers, and applied filters. As long as the Action is recording, these steps and settings are being sequentially stored in the Action. Selecting the square "Stop" symbol on the Actions palette will suspend the recording.

The following example will create a Photoshop Action to record image size, saturation, and histogram adjustments made to a single site photograph. The intention is to shrink the file size and modify the image to reveal textures in site photographs. Subsequent examples in the chapter will utilize this Action to automate the photograph adjustments on other images from the same series of photographs.

1. Begin by opening a photograph that will serve as the test subject for the recorded Action.
2. To open the Actions menu, go to **Window > Actions**. By default, the Actions menu contains a folder (referred to as a "Set") of predefined actions called "Default Actions." New actions can be added to the "Default Actions" Set. For this example though, a new Set will be created. To do this, click the Folder icon at the bottom of the menu (highlighted in red). Name this new set "Custom Actions."

Figure 9.1. The Actions palette is preloaded with Default Actions. To create a new folder, known as an Action Set, click on the Folder icon that is highlighted in red. To create a new Action, click on the New Action icon that is highlighted in blue.

3. To create an Action, click the New Action icon at the bottom of the Actions menu. Name the Action "Resize to 800" and select "Custom Actions" as the Set. Leave the remaining dialogs as the defaults and click Record. Notice the red Record button at the bottom of the Actions menu. With the Record activated, any adjustments will be recorded and stored in this Action.
4. The initial step in this particular sequence is to resize the image to 800 pixels wide. To execute this step, select **Image > Image Size**. Under Pixel Dimensions in the dialog box, change the width to "800" and verify that the unit type is "Pixels." Click OK to close the dialog. Notice that "Image Size" has appeared under the newly created Action.
5. The next two adjustments will attempt to accentuate the textures in the photographs. At the bottom of the Layers Panel, click the Adjustment Layer icon and select Hue/Saturation. In the Hue/Saturation menu, move the saturation slider to −70 to desaturate the image.
6. Create another adjustment layer by clicking on the Adjustment Layer icon and selecting Levels. In the Levels menu, move the black point slider (shadows) to up to 60 and the white point slider (highlights) down to 185. By removing color saturation and amplifying the contrast, the image emphasizes texture over color. These particular settings work well for this particular photograph based on the site and weather conditions but may need to be tweaked based on conditions unique to a different series of photographs.

Figure 9.2. For this example, a new Action Set is created containing a new Action name "Resize to 800." The red Record button indicates that any adjustments performed will be recorded as a part of this Action.

Figure 9.3. The list underneath the new action indicates the five steps that were applied to the photograph and recorded as part of the Action. The adjustments can be seen in both the photograph and in the Layers panel.

Figure 9.4. The final Action includes the image resizing, image adjustments, flattening, saving, and closing of the file.

7. Notice that four new steps have been generated in the Action that is currently recording. One for the creation of each new adjustment layer and one for the adjustments to each of the settings.

8. Before finalizing the Action, it can be helpful to record the flattening and saving of a file. By recording this sequence in addition to the adjustments, the Action will perform the adjustments, save, and close the file as part of playing the Action. With the Record button still activated, select **Layer > Flatten Image, File > Save,** and **File > Close**.

9. Click the Stop button on the bottom left portion of the Actions menu. The Action is no longer recording steps and can be automated across other site photographs.

Expand the details of any step in the Action by using the arrows adjacent to the name of the particular step. Individual steps or the entire Action can be deleted by clicking and dragging the Action layer to the trashcan on the bottom right of the Actions menu. New steps can be recorded by enabling the Record button and performing additional commands.

Playing Actions in Photoshop

Once an Action is recorded, the process for playing the Action is straightforward. Simply highlighting the Action and clicking the Play icon on the Actions menu will execute each step of the Action on the open file. Regardless of the amount of time it took to record, Photoshop will perform the sequence of steps within the Action as rapidly as possible. To skip any part of an Action, simply uncheck the box on the far left of the menu that corresponds with the command to skip. To prompt a pause and adjust settings on any step, click the box next to the check mark of that command.

Actions will automatically be saved in the Photoshop presets and available for use at any point in the future. Action Sets can also be saved and shared on other computers. This is a common practice, especially in photography, as users will generate and share custom Actions made to alter photographs. Actions can be saved by selecting the Action Set, clicking on the menu icon in the top right corner of the Actions Menu, and selecting "Save Actions." Similarly, Actions can be imported by clicking the same menu icon in the top right and selecting "Load Actions" and then navigating to the Action Set file (known as an .ATN files).

For this example, the previously created Action will be applied to a different photograph from the same set of site photographs.

1. Begin by opening a new image from the same group of site photographs. The site and weather conditions are similar to the original photograph on which the Action was recorded.

2. With the Action Menu open, select the "Resize to 800" Action that was created. The Action will appear highlighted in the Actions panel.

3. Click the Play icon on the bottom of the Actions menu. Photoshop will begin automatically performing the sequence of steps associated with the Action.

4. The final steps of the Action will save and close the image file. Use a browser to navigate to the image to see the end result from the Action. Bear in mind that in this example the original file is replaced with the smaller, desaturated, and high-contrast image. If it is important to keep the unedited images, consider making copies of the image prior to playing the Action or recording a "Save as" as part of the last step of the action.

Figure 9.5. A new site photograph from the same series is shown in Photoshop. Within the Actions menu, the recorded Action is selected and can be applied to the currently open file.

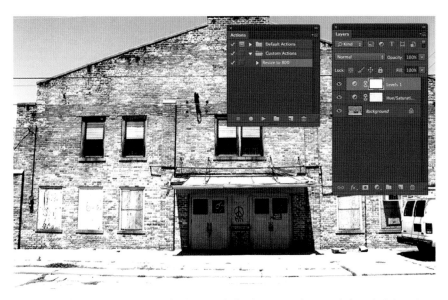

Figure 9.6. The "Resize to 800" Action has been applied to the current photograph through clicking the Play button in the Actions menu. This particular image captures the results prior to the Action completing the Layer Flatten command, Save command, and Close command.

Batch Processing in Adobe Bridge

Opening individual files in Photoshop and playing a custom Action is certainly faster than the manual alternative. Batch processing, however, can automate a single Action over multiple images. Adobe Bridge works seamlessly with Photoshop Actions to achieve this task. Bridge is typically used to sort, filter, manage, and process various file-types utilized in Adobe platforms. The following two sections of this chapter will explore the use of Adobe Bridge as a tool for working with large sets of files.

This first example will utilize the custom Action made in the first example of the chapter and apply the same Action sequence to the remaining photographs from the site visit.

1. With Adobe Bridge open, there are several workspace options available, each with a unique organization designed for specific tasks. This example will operate using the Essentials interface. To enable this interface, click **Windows > Workspace > Essentials**.
2. Using the navigation bar or Content panel, navigate to the files that will be processed using a Photoshop Action. In the Content panel, select all the photos to process. Note that all photos selected appear tiled within the preview panel.
3. Once the files are highlighted, select **Tools > Photoshop > Batch** to open the Batch dialog in Photoshop.
4. The first section in the Batch dialog denotes the type of Action that will be played across the files selected from Bridge. The Set should be "Custom Actions" and the Action should be "Resize to 800," the Action previously created for the texture study. When initiated from Adobe Bridge, the source will default to "Bridge" which will be appropriate for this example. The remaining sections will remain as the default setup. Click OK.

Figure 9.7. Select the images for Batch Processing in the Content panel of Adobe Bridge and then select **Tools > Photoshop > Batch….**

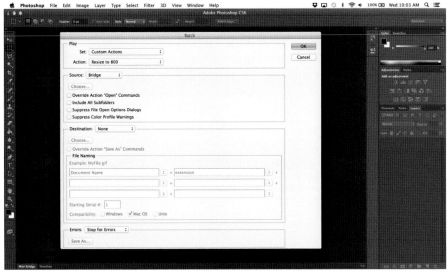

Figure 9.8. In the Batch dialog, choose "Custom Actions" as the Set and "Resize to 800" as the Action.

5. Based on the recorded steps in the selected Action, each file from Bridge will open, run the recorded steps, including saving and closing every file after the adjustments are made. Depending on the number of files and complexity of the Action, Photoshop will operate on its own to automate the Action across all the select images.

Batch Rename in Bridge

Digital photographs downloaded from cameras are often named with a seemingly cryptic numerical sequence. The file names have no relation to the site or project, though the metadata may contain date, time, and even a geo-tag. File management software like Adobe Bridge can batch rename files in a similar manner to the batch processing conducted in the previous example. This example will utilize the software to rename the site photographs to reflect the name of the project site and date the photos were taken.

1. Using the same Essential workspace in Adobe Bridge, select all the photographs from the site photography session in the Content panel.
2. With the files selected, click **Tools > Batch Rename** to open the Batch Rename dialog.
3. Within Batch Rename, the files can be saved in the current or another folder. The renaming capabilities are vast and can include any combination of the current name, new text, date/time derived from metadata, sequence numbers or letters, among other options. The preset pull-down menu at the top can be used to rename files with a default preset or to save custom configurations for future use.
4. For this example, the destination folder is the same folder and the new filename is comprised of the site name, date/time, and a number sequence. Use the preview at the bottom of the dialog to compare the current filename with the new filename based on the input settings.

101

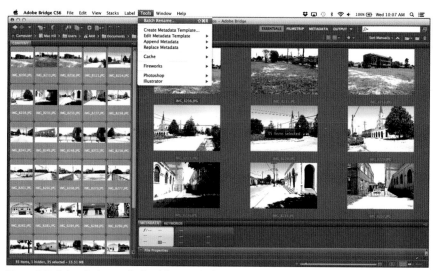

Figure 9.9. Select the images for Batch Rename in the Content panel of Adobe Bridge and then select **Tools > Batch Rename**.

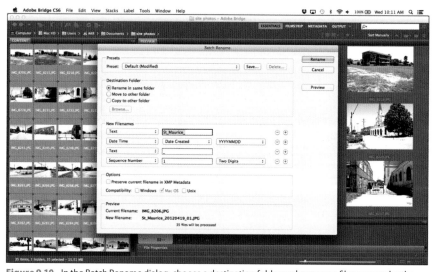

Figure 9.10. In the Batch Rename dialog, choose a destination folder and prepare a filename under the New Filenames portion of the dialog. This example will save the files in the same folder and with a filename that includes the site, date/time, and a two-digit sequence number.

5. Consider saving the preset for future use and then click Rename to execute the Batch Rename. The changes are often immediately reflected in both the Bridge interface and in the finder window itself.

As design offices and personal libraries become increasingly more digitized, the importance of proper file organization increases as well. Developing a system of organization is paramount for efficiency and consistency. Understanding the benefits of automation can assist in establishing organization, and more importantly, maintaining that organization.

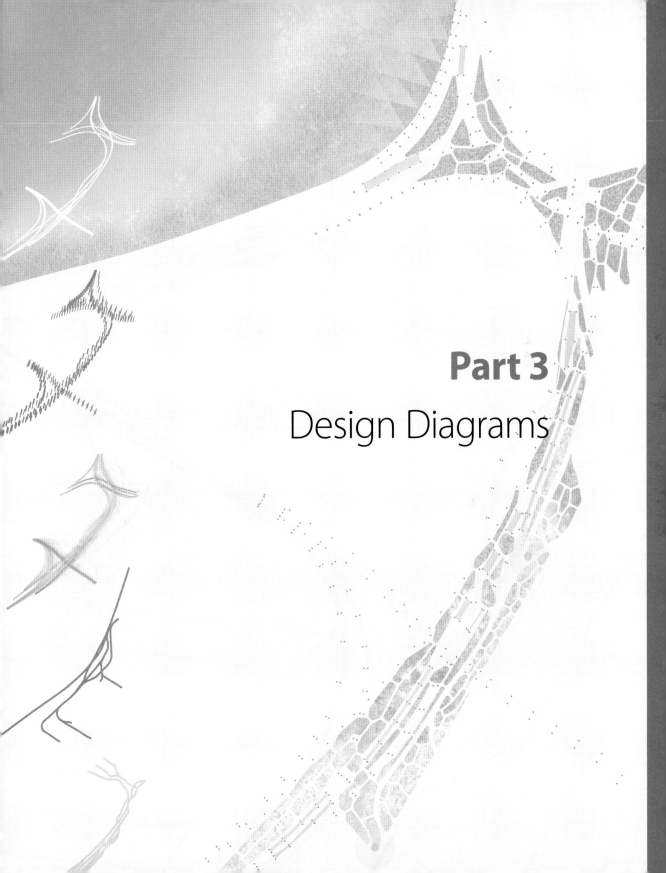

Part 3

Design Diagrams

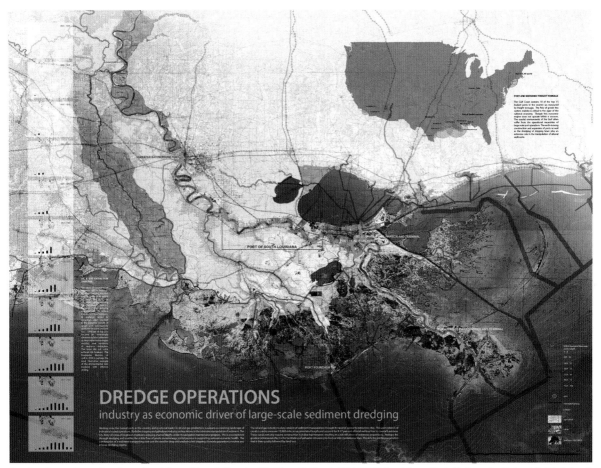

Dredge Operations. Southeast Louisiana (Matt Seibert).   **Matthew Seibert, MLA 2013, Louisiana State University Robert Reich School of Landscape Architecture**

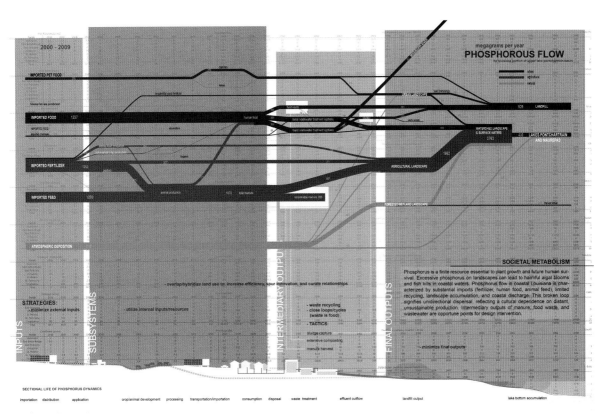

Phosphorous Flow Diagram.   Matthew Seibert, MLA 2013, Louisiana State University Robert Reich School of Landscape Architecture

Design Diagrams

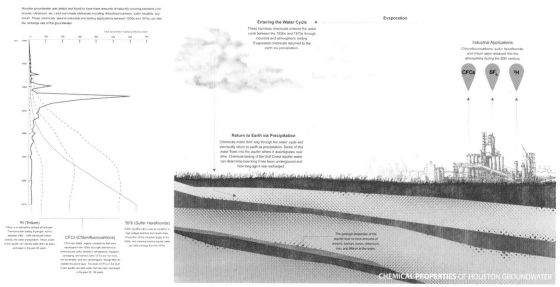

Chemical Properties of Groundwater Visualization. Houston, TX. Anna Shaw, MLA 2014, Louisiana State University Robert Reich School of Landscape Architecture

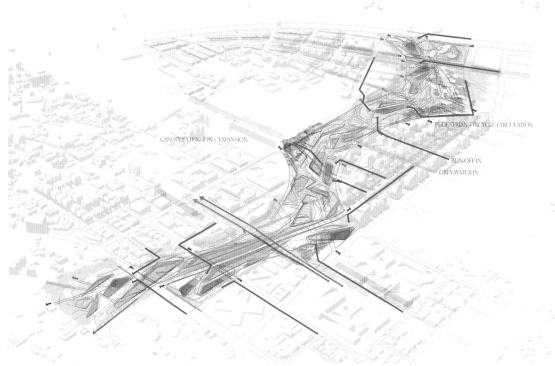

Analysis Diagrams. Stoss Landscape Urbanism

FUTURE ECOLOGICAL NETWORKS
- Carbon Forest
- Industrial Buffer
- Blue Infrastructure
- Innovation Productive
- Innovation Ecological
- Greenway
- Dispersed Green Landscapes
- Dispersed Blue Infrastructure
- Large Parks
- Network

Ecological Networks Diagram. **Stoss Landscape Urbanism**

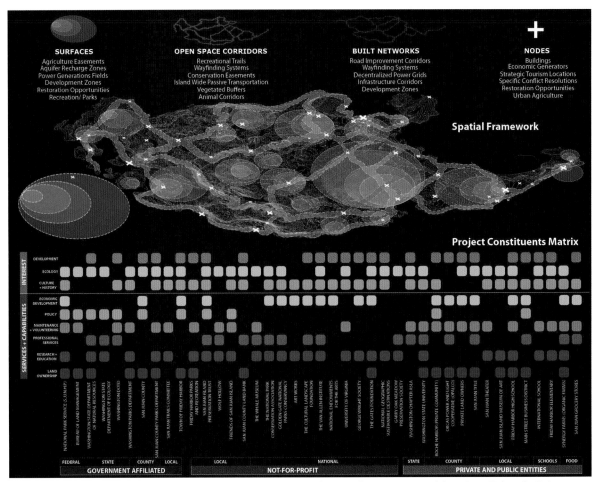

Spatial Framework for San Juan Islands, Puerto Rico. (Josh Brooks).   Joshua Brooks, BLA 2012, Louisiana State University Robert Reich School of Landscape Architecture

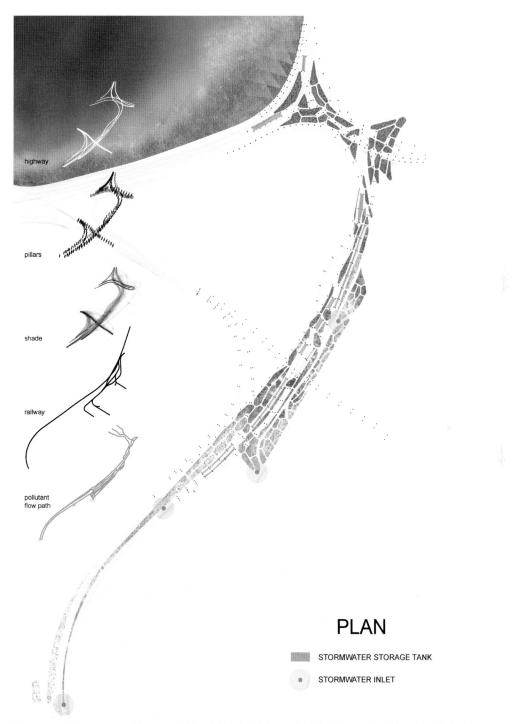

highway

pillars

shade

railway

pollutant
flow path

PLAN

STORMWATER STORAGE TANK

STORMWATER INLET

Stormwater Infrastructure Diagram. Oakland, CA.   Erin Dibos and Ju Liu, MLA 2014, Louisiana State University
Robert Reich School of Landscape Architecture

Design Diagrams

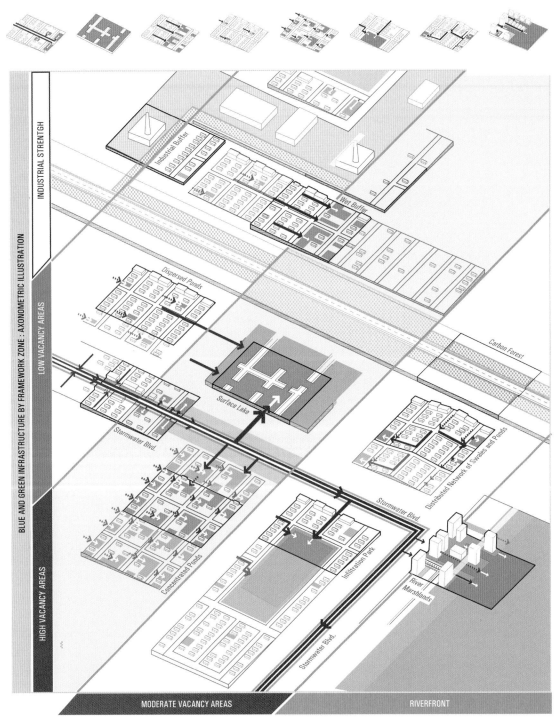

Industrial Buffer

Wet Buffer

Dispersed Ponds

Carbon Forest

Surface Lake

Stormwater Blvd.

Distributed Network of Swales and Ponds

Stormwater Blvd.

Concentrated Ponds

Infiltration Park

River Marshlands

Stormwater Blvd.

BLUE AND GREEN INFRASTRUCTURE BY FRAMEWORK ZONE : AXONOMETRIC ILLUSTRATION

INDUSTRIAL STRENTGH

LOW VACANCY AREAS

HIGH VACANCY AREAS

MODERATE VACANCY AREAS

RIVERFRONT

Blue and Green Infrastructure. Axonometric Diagram. Stoss Landscape Urbanism

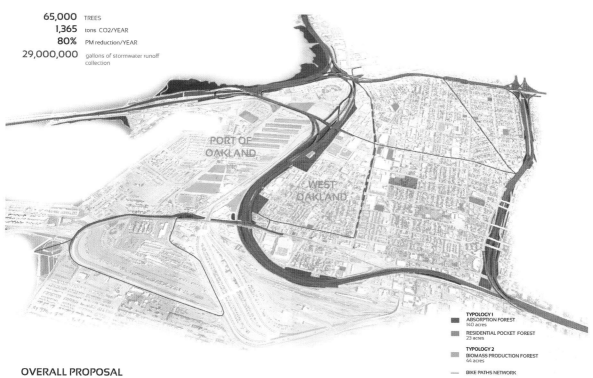

65,000 TREES
1,365 tons CO2/YEAR
80% PM reduction/YEAR
29,000,000 gallons of stormwater runoff collection

PORT OF
OAKLAND

WEST
OAKLAND

TYPOLOGY I
ABSORPTION FOREST
140 acres
RESIDENTIAL POCKET FOREST
23 acres
TYPOLOGY 2
BIOMASS PRODUCTION FOREST
44 acres
— BIKE PATHS NETWORK

OVERALL PROPOSAL
Urban Forest Network. Oakland, CA. Prentiss Darden and Silvia Cox, MLA 2014, Louisiana State University Robert Reich School of Landscape Architecture

Design Diagrams

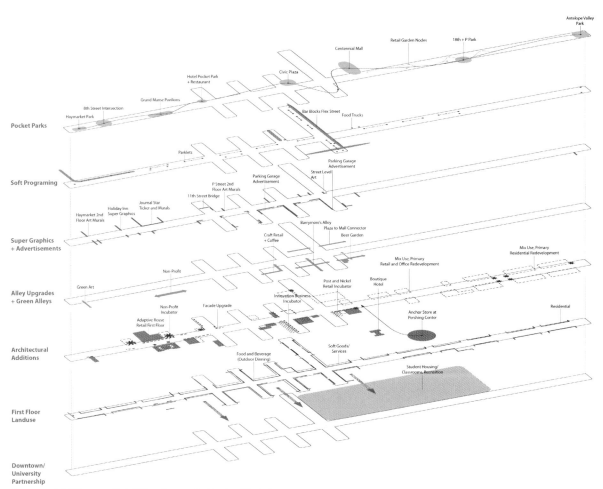

Pocket Parks

Soft Programing

Super Graphics + Advertisements

Alley Upgrades + Green Alleys

Architectural Additions

First Floor Landuse

Downtown/ University Partnership

Antelope Valley Park

Retail Garden Nodes

18th + P Park

Centennial Mall

Civic Plaza

Hotel Pocket Park + Restaurant

Grand Manse Pavilions

Bar Blocks Flex Street

Food Trucks

8th Street Intersection

Haymarket Park

Parklets

Parking Garage Advertisement

Street Level Art

P Street 2nd Floor Art Murals

Parking Garage Advertisement

11th Street Bridge

Journal Star Ticker and Murals

Holiday Inn Super Graphics

Haymarket 2nd Floor Art Murals

Barrymore's Alley

Plaza to Mall Connector

Beer Garden

Craft Retail + Coffee

Mix Use, Primary Residential Redevelopment

Non-Profit

Green Art

Post and Nickel Retail Incubator

Boutique Hotel

Mix Use, Primary Retail and Office Redevelopment

Non-Profit Incubator

Facade Upgrade

Innovation Business Incubator

Residential

Adaptive Reuse Retail First Floor

Anchor Store at Pershing Center

Food and Beverage (Outdoor Dinning)

Soft Goods/ Services

Student Housing/ Classrooms, Recreation

Axonometric Diagram. Retail Development.   Design Workshop

Chapter 10
Setting up an Illustrator Drawing

The artboard in Adobe Illustrator is the canvas where an illustration or layout will begin. Understanding the basic parameters and how they affect the rest of the process before embarking on a new project is important, and it will save headaches. Depending on how Illustrator will be utilized, the artboard can be thought of as a sheet of paper or a workspace used to create a diagram or illustration.

Document Size/Color Mode

Setting the document size correctly at the beginning of a project is not as critical in Illustrator as it is in Photoshop or other raster-based programs. This is because vector-based drawings can be rescaled with no loss of image quality. The exception is when a raster image is inserted. Once a raster image is inserted into the vector-based program, all of the same size limitations that traditionally apply to raster images apply. Raster images are typically inserted as base material for a diagram, such as an aerial photograph, or during the layout of a presentation board with multiple raster files such as plans and sections. With Illustrator, if the final size of the image is not known at the beginning of a project, the document can be set to a standard size, such as 11 inches × 17 inches, and adjusted later. RGB mode is the recommended mode in which to work. See Chapter 3 for an explanation of color modes.

The Raster Effects setting will affect how certain effects such as Drop Shadows, Inner Glow, and Outer Glow will appear on an image. There may also be situations where you want to rasterize part of the vector data; in those cases, the resolution of the rasterization will be determined by the Raster Effects setting.

Based Programs for Design Diagrams

Vector-based programs are good for creating diagrams because of the ease with which the lineweights, the placement of the lines, and colors of lines can be edited. There are many vector-based programs used in design offices, with AutoCAD, Illustrator, and Vectorworks being among the most widely used. For the techniques discussed in this section, Illustrator will be used as the primary vector-based program, although there are many other programs that have similar capabilities.

Illustrator is a robust program with a powerful set of drawing and editing tools. Illustrator has an entire set of tools that are geared toward the creation of websites, animations, and graphic design applications. Many of the advanced tools and techniques used in Illustrator are beyond the scope of this book and are rarely used in a typical architectural workflow. One of the strengths of Illustrator is the relatively easy learning curve and the short amount of time required to become proficient with the program. There are several basic techniques that must be mastered to effectively use Illustrator, including how to use the Pen tool, how to use layers, and how to adjust the Stroke, Fill, and Weight of the linework. These beginning techniques are explained briefly in the following section, but more in-depth coverage of these techniques can be found in numerous free tutorials online.

Importing an Aerial Photo into Illustrator

Techniques for constructing base images, such as aerial photographs, were discussed in Chapter 6. One powerful and simple technique for setting up a diagram is to import the raster-base image into Illustrator and then draw a diagram over it. When a Photoshop or other raster file is being importing into Illustrator, the first consideration is whether to link the image or embed it.

Link versus Embed

There are advantages to either linking an image or embedding an image into an Illustrator document. However, it is easy to change the status of an image from linked to embedded and back again. A *linked file* is similar to an external reference in AutoCAD. The file itself is saved separately from the Illustrator document. If the linked file is changed and resaved, the image in the Illustrator file will reflect those changes. An *embedded image* places the entire file into the Illustrator document. If the original file changes, these changes will not be reflected in the Illustrator document. If the embedded file is a Photoshop image, or any other layered raster image, the Embed command will flatten the image before inserting it. This reduces the ability to edit the image once it has been embedded. With a linked file, all the layers remain intact in the original file.

The advantage of linking files is the ability to update a file without having to reinsert it into Illustrator. For example, consider a plan that has been inserted into a final presentation board with text, leaders, and other images on the board. In this situation, it is typical for the plan drawing to have been placed precisely on the board, with the text and leaders corresponding to certain parts of the drawing. If the plan is updated to reflect new site conditions, it is much easier to have the plan automatically reflect the changes in Illustrator than to attempt to import a new plan into the board and place it in the exact location as the previous plan.

However, there are times when it is advantageous to embed the files—for example, when a single Photoshop file has several different layers, with each layer representing a different phase of the project. On a single Illustrator board, there may be the need to show several phases at once. It is easier to turn on the layers that show Phase 1 and embed the file into Illustrator. After that file is embedded, the layers that show Phase 2 will be turned on and the file will be embedded into Illustrator again. Now the board has two views of the same Photoshop document.

Other times when embedding files is advantageous include at the end of a project and when the file is going to be sent to another person. It can be confusing to have several different linked files in several different folders. The linked files often become lost or the link does not work after the folder structure changes. In these cases, it is easier to just embed the images into a single file. Of course, the files can be relinked at a later time if needed.

The following demonstration will show how to place, link, embed, and relink an aerial image in Illustrator:

1. After setting the Document Size to the correct value, choose **File > Place** to place the aerial image into the Illustrator document. To link the image, check the option for Link. If this box is not checked, the file will be embedded.

2. To see a list of all linked or embedded images in the document, go to **Window > Links**.

Figure 10.1. The Links palette shows the linked file. All linked and embedded files placed in the Illustrator document will appear in this palette.

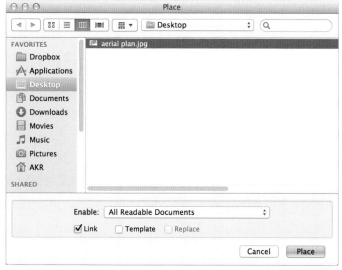

Figure 10.2. Check the Link box in the Place dialog box to link the file.

3. To understand how links work, leave Illustrator running in the background, return to the original image in Photoshop, and change the Saturation of the image to –100, making the image appear as a grayscale image. Save the image in Photoshop. The file will automatically update in Illustrator.

4. The menu option on the Links palette shows several options for altering the linked file. To embed the image, select the linked image from the list in the Links palette and choose Embed under the menu options.

5. Once an image is embedded, it can be relinked from the same menu by choosing Relink.

Figure 10.3. After the file is altered in Photoshop and saved over the original image, the file is updated in Illustrator. A dialog box will appear asking if the image should be updated. Click Yes to accept the changes.

Figure 10.4. The image was changed to grayscale in Photoshop and saved. The updated image reflects the changes to the Photoshop file.

Figure 10.5. Several options including Embed Image are found under the Links Palette menu.

Chapter 11
Linework in Illustrator

Illustrator excels at manipulating and modifying vertices and lines, as well as improving their appearance. When a designer is working with linework, maintaining clean consistent lines that develop a clear hierarchy throughout the drawing is important. Typically, linework is created using lineweights that appropriately represent an object's weight in the landscape or hierarchy in the design proposal. There are many conventions for how lineweights can be assigned within a drawing; in most cases, the designer will be able to experiment with these conventions as long as the illustration is consistent.

The following sections assume some familiarity with Illustrator. Techniques for navigating the workspace, creating new layers, moving objects between layers, selecting multiple objects, and other basic skills are beyond the scope of this book. Many free resources that provide tutorials on basic Illustrator skills are available online and in the Illustrator Help files. Illustrator is a powerful program. It has so many tools that the program's simplicity and ease of use is often obscured. However, for most office design work, only a handful of those tools are needed to complete most tasks. The tools most frequently used to demonstrate the Illustrator techniques in this book are the Selection tool, the Direct Selection tool, the Pen tool, the Type tool, and the Shape tools (such as the Rectangle tool and the Circle tool).

Shape Tools

Drawing shapes in Illustrator is easy. Several predefined Shape tools can be used to draw predefined geometries such as rectangles, circles, and polygons. With a little care, you can also draw these shapes with the Pen tool,

Figure 11.1. Most Illustrator techniques can be performed using only a handful of tools.

but the Shape tools make it much easier. Consider the following example of how to draw predefined geometries in Illustrator:

1. To draw a rectangle, choose the Rectangle tool. Click, drag, and release.
2. When the Shift key is held down, the proportions of the geometry is constrained. For rectangles, holding down the Shift key creates a square.
3. To create other shapes, click and hold the Rectangle tool to reveal other Shape tools.
4. For ellipses, holding down the Shift key will create a circle.
5. To draw a shape to a predefined set of dimensions, select the tool (for this example, the Rectangle tool is used). Click on the drawing. A dialog box will appear, allowing the dimensions of the shape to be entered.

Figure 11.2. When the Shift key is held down, the Rectangle tool and the Ellipse tool are constrained to create squares and circles, respectively.

Pen Tool

The Pen tool is the primary tool used to draw complex shapes in Illustrator. Although the Shape tools make drawing predefined geometries easier, anything that can be drawn in Illustrator can be drawn with the Pen tool. Learning how to use the Pen tool can be difficult at first. However, learning to effectively use this tool will open some powerful features in many Adobe programs. Versions of the Pen tool can be found in almost all Adobe software used in design offices, from Photoshop to Flash.

To draw straight lines with the Pen tool, consider the following example:

Figure 11.3. When the Rectangle tool is selected and the workspace is clicked, a dialog box will appear. The dimensions of the rectangle can be entered in it.

1. Select the Pen tool and click on the workspace.
2. Click on another area of the workspace and then another. Press Enter to end the line.
3. To draw horizontal or vertical lines, click on the workspace.

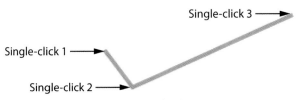

Single-click 3

Single-click 1

Single-click 2

Figure 11.4. Click with the Pen tool to draw lines.

Figure 11.5. To create horizontal and vertical lines, click the Pen tool with the Shift key held down.

4. While holding down the Shift key, click to the right of the first point. The line will be constrained to a horizontal line.
5. The default constraints for the Pen tool are horizontal, vertical, and 45-degree angles. These constraints can be changed to angles other than 90 degrees and 45 degrees. To change the constraint angle, select **Preferences > General**. A dialog box will appear that allows any constraint angle to be entered. This technique can be used to draw a series of parallel and perpendicular lines in a drawing at an angle other than 90 or 45 degrees.

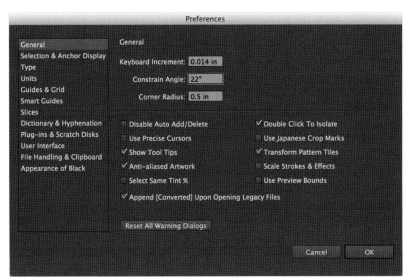

Figure 11.6. The angle of constraint can be changed in the Preferences dialog box.

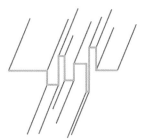

Figure 11.7. The constrained angles of the lines can be used to create a series of parallel and perpendicular lines at any base angle. In this figure, the blue lines are constrained to a 22-degree angle and drawn with the Pen tool.

The Pen tool can be used to draw more than straight lines. It can also be used to draw complex curves or multiple segment lines that are a combination of lines and curves. The curves that the Pen tool draws are called Bézier curves because of the mathematics used to draw the curve. The Bézier curve is named after a French engineer who originally used these types of curves to design automobile bodies in the 1970s. Bézier curves are now widely used in a variety of digital representation packages.

Instead of using an arc that has a beginning, middle, and end, the Pen tool uses a unique mathematical formula to draw the curves. A simple Bézier curve has two *endpoints* (or anchor points) and two *direction lines*, as Adobe refers to them (or *handles,* as referred to in this book). The handles control the direction and tangency of the arc. These handles represent the tangent line of the curve. By moving the handles closer or farther away from the anchor point, you can control the shape of the curve.

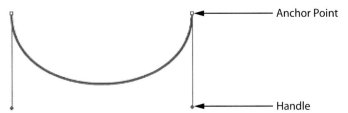

Figure 11.8. A simple Bézier curve consists of two anchor points and two handles.

To draw a simple Bézier curve, do the following:

1. Select the Pen tool. Click and drag the mouse on the workspace.
2. Click and drag a second point.

Figure 11.9. The blue rectangle on the top left is altered with the black arrow to get the blue shape below. Although the shape has different dimensions, it is still a rectangle with four parallel sides. The orange rectangle on the top right is altered to get the orange shape below. This object is no longer a rectangle with four parallel sides. The white arrow can alter the fundamental shape of an object.

3. By clicking and dragging a third point, you lengthen the curve.
4. A single click will create a straight segment in the line.

Editing Tools

Two main editing tools are used to alter lines and shapes in Illustrator: the Selection tool (the black arrow) and the Direct Selection tool (the white arrow). To understand how the black arrow edits objects, consider the following example:

1. When an object is selected with the black arrow, a *bounding box* with small grips attached to it appears.
2. To move an object, click on the object and drag it to another location.
3. To make a copy of this object, hold down the Alt key while dragging the object. A second arrow will appear to indicate that the object is being copied.
4. To copy an object horizontally or vertically, hold down the Shift key while the object is being moved.

To change the size of an object, or rotate an object, do the following:

1. Change the size of the object by clicking on a corner and dragging the corner to another point.
2. By holding down the Shift key while dragging the object, you can constrain the proportions of the object.
3. When you hold the cursor near one of the grips, a small rotation arrow will pop up.
4. Click and drag the grip to rotate the object. Holding down the Shift key will again restrict the angle of rotation.

To draw accurately with the Pen tool, you need to edit the lines after they have been drawn. It is impossible to draw every shape with the Pen tool on the first pass. Although you can do some editing with the black arrow, you will need to use the white arrow for most fine-tuning of a shape. The black arrow selects the entire object and changes its dimensions. The white arrow selects the control points of an object, rather than the entire object. This allows the shape of an object to be changed.

The white arrow is used to select and manipulate the anchor points of an object. To understand how anchor points are selected and used to alter the shape of an object, consider the following example:

Figure 11.10. The upper-left anchor point is selected. The other three anchor points are unselected. The anchor point in the middle is not used very often, but selecting it will select all anchor points in the object.

1. To select an anchor point, use the white arrow. Either click directly on the point, or click and drag a box around the point. It is important to be precise when you select anchor points. The white arrow must be exactly on top of the anchor point for it to be selected. Clicking slightly to one side or the other of the point will prevent the anchor point from being selected. Most problems with using the white arrow can be traced back to an imprecise selection of the anchor point. A small box with a white center will appear next to the cursor when it is directly over the anchor point. Watch for this box to appear before clicking on the anchor point.

2. Once an anchor point is selected, it will be filled in and no longer have an open or white middle. This indicates that it is selected. Unselected anchor points will have a white area in the middle of the anchor point. Again, it is important to look closely at the anchor points to ensure that only the intended anchor point is selected.

3. To manipulate an anchor point, use the white arrow to click and drag the selected anchor point to another location.

4. Two anchor points can be selected at the same time by holding the Shift key and selecting multiple points with the white arrow, or by dragging a box around multiple anchor points with the white arrow.

5. If more than one anchor point is selected, the anchor points will move together.

6. You can use the white arrow to drag and move points.

The white arrow is also used to adjust curves to different shapes. When you are adjusting curves, selecting and moving the anchor points is similar to the techniques shown in the following example. However, a second element in curves must also

Figure 11.11. Multiple anchor points can be selected on different objects. In this figure, the upper-right anchor point of the blue rectangle is selected and the upper-left anchor point of the orange rectangle is selected.

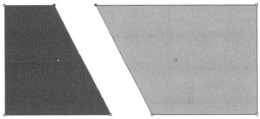

Figure 11.12. When one of the anchor points is clicked and dragged with the white arrow, both anchor points move at the same time.

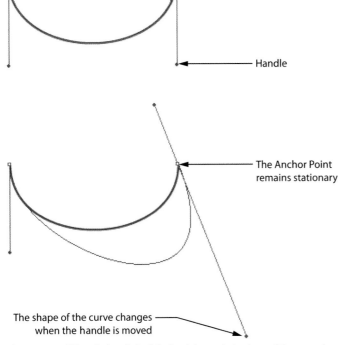

Anchor Point

Handle

The Anchor Point remains stationary

The shape of the curve changes when the handle is moved

Figure 11.13. When the handle is clicked and dragged, the shape of the curve changes.

be adjusted: the handles. The handles are not selected like the anchor points. The handles appear on the curve when the anchor point is selected. To move the handles, use the white arrow to click on the end of the handle and drag the handle to a new position.

Mastering the use of curves in Illustrator takes practice. Following are some techniques that can be used to increase proficiency with the Bézier Pen tool:

Figure 11.14. Select the Convert Anchor Point tool and click a curved anchor point to convert it to a straight point, or Click+drag a straight point to convert it to a curve. Select the Add Anchor Point tool and click on the line to add an anchor point. Select the Delete Anchor Point tool and click on the anchor point to be deleted.

- The majority of curves drawn with the Pen tool will need to be edited to achieve the final shape. Try to approximate the shape on the first pass quickly, and then fine-tune the shape later with the white arrow.

- Use fewer anchor points when possible. The Add Anchor Point tool can be used to increase the number of anchor points if needed later. Using too many anchor points can create "wobbly" curves and make them difficult to edit. Adding or subtracting anchor points can be accomplished by clicking and holding the cursor on the Pen Tool icon. A second set of tools will appear, including the Add Anchor Point tool, the Delete Anchor Point tool, and the Convert Anchor Point tool.

- When drawing a curve from scratch, do not drag the handles very far. For most curves, two handles should not cross one another. Handles normally do not cross the same line.

- To cut a line into separate segments, use the Scissors tool (located below the Eraser tool). Choose the Scissors tool and click at the point where the line is to be split.

- To join two separate lines, use the white arrow to select the two endpoints of the two lines. The endpoints do not need to be touching for this command to work. Select the **Object** > **Path** > **Join** command from the menu. Illustrator will draw a line between the two points.

Appearance of Lines and Shapes

One significant advantage of drawing in Illustrator compared to AutoCAD is the ability to see the final product on the screen as it is being drawn. Seeing the interplay of colors, transparencies, and lineweights onscreen allows more experimentation with the drawing technique and gives immediate feedback about how different techniques affect the image. While there are always differences between a printed version of a drawing and an image on the screen, there is less guessing in Illustrator about lineweights and colors than in AutoCAD. There is no need to create a preview to see how an image will look. The image on the screen is very close to what the image will look like when printed properly.

Illustrator colors its objects using *fills* and *strokes*. Every object, except for a straight line, can have both a fill and a stroke. Each object can also have only a fill or only a stroke. The fill and the stroke each have their own independent color, and they can have independent transparencies and other effects as well.

The following is an example of how to change the fill and stroke of an object:

1. Select the object using the black arrow.
2. To change the color of the fill, click on the Fill box in the Tools palette. If the Fill icon is behind the Stroke icon, the Fill icon will come to the front.

Figure 11.15. The rectangle in this figure has an orange fill and a blue stroke. Notice the Fill and Stroke colors in the Tools palette.

Figure 11.16. When the None swatch is selected, the fill is removed from the object.

3. Select a color for the fill from the Swatches palette by selecting **Window > Swatches** and clicking a color.
4. To change the stroke color, click on the Stroke icon to bring it to the front and select another swatch.
5. To remove a fill or a stroke, select the icon with the red stripe going through the swatch. This sets the value of the color to None, or invisible.

It is usually better to use the Swatches palette in Illustrator rather than the Color Picker. There are a few reasons for this. The first is that Illustrator comes with many predefined color palettes that provide sets of colors that work well together. Many other color combinations, such as the ones in Kuler, are also available from outside Illustrator.

Figure 11.17. Many predefined sets of swatches are available in Illustrator. These swatches can be found through the pull-down menu in the Swatches palette.

It is useful to use these predefined palettes when several documents are being worked on, or when a group of people are working on a project. Custom swatches can be saved into new palettes and used to create a set of standard colors for an office.

Another reason it is a good idea to use swatches is that the Eyedropper tool works slightly differently in Illustrator than in Photoshop. In Photoshop, it is less important to use predefined colors because the Eyedropper tool can copy a color from one area to another. However, in Illustrator, the Eyedropper not only copies the color, but it copies the other properties of an object as well, including any effects or transparencies. This can cause problems when all that is needed is to copy the color of one object to another. It is much easier to just choose the color from the Swatches palette than use the Eyedropper tool.

A final reason for using swatches is the ability in Illustrator to select all objects that are the same color. For instance, using the **Select > Same > Fill Color** operation from the menu bar, all objects in the drawing with a red fill can be selected at once. If the colors are slightly off due to the use of the Color Picker, this option is difficult to use.

Stroke Weight and Dashed Lines

The *stroke weight* is how thick or thin the stroke is in an object. You can change the stroke weight by selecting the object and choosing a new stroke weight from the Strokes palette. The Strokes palette can be found under **Windows > Strokes**.

Dashes lines are simple to use in Illustrator and offer a great advantage over Photoshop when it comes to creating diagrams. Creating dashed lines in Photoshop is cumbersome and the lines are not easily edited. To understand how to create a dashed line in Illustrator, consider the following example:

1. Select a line using the black arrow. Open the Strokes palette and expand the palette to reveal the Dash Lines option.
2. Check the Dashed Line box.
3. The dash size of the line can be altered by entering values in the Dash/Gap sections of the palette.
4. The dashed line can be changed back to a solid line by selecting the line and deselecting the Dashed Line box.

Figure 11.18. The Strokes palette can be found under **Windows > Strokes**.

Figure 11.19. Double-click on the word Stroke to reveal the expanded options.

Figure 11.20. Select a line and check the Dashed Line box to create a dashed line.

Figure 11.21. The dashes and gaps in the line can be altered. Selecting the Round Cap option creates the rounded edges of the dash.

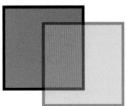

Transparency

The transparency of objects is changed through the Transparency palette. Transparencies are extremely useful for creating diagrams. Illustrator makes using transparencies easy.

1. Open the Transparency palette from **Windows > Transparency**.
2. To make an object transparent, select the object and enter the value in the Opacity box. This affects the overall transparency of the object, so both the fill and the stroke are the same opacity.
3. It is possible to make just the fill transparent or just the stroke transparent by using the Appearance palette.

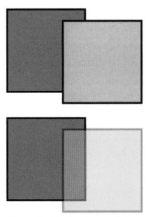

Figure 11.22. When using the Transparency palette, the entire object, including fill and stroke, is rendered with the same opacity.

Appearance Palette

The appearance of the objects in an Illustrator drawing is a combination of underlying vector linework and a series of effects that create what is seen on the screen. For example, when the stroke weight of a line is changed from 2-point to 7-point, the underlying vector geometry does not get larger, only the appearance of the line increases. Stroke weight and color are effects that are rendered on the screen in real time. Switching to Outline mode will display the underlying geometry of a drawing without the effects applied. The figures displayed here show how switching between Preview mode and Outline mode changes the way the drawing is presented on the screen. To switch between Preview mode and Outline mode, select **View > Outline** from the menu.

The Appearance palette shows the effects that rendered onto the underlying geometry of the object. From the Appearance palette it is possible to alter all of the parameters that contribute to the appearance of the object. To understand how the Appearance palette affects a drawing, consider the example shown here:

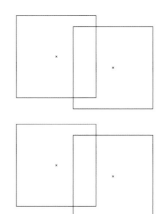

Figure 11.23. Preview mode is the standard view for working in Illustrator.

Figure 11.24. Outline mode shows only the underlying geometry without any effects such as stroke weight or fill color. This is similar to a Wireframe view in 3D modeling software.

1. Select an object in the drawing. The Appearance palette can be found in the menu under **Window > Appearances**.

2. All of the components that make up the object's appearance are listed in the Appearance palette. For a simple object, the only components listed are the Stroke, the Fill, and the Transparency.

3. As shown in the previous example, changing the transparency of an object using the Transparency palette alters the Default Transparency setting.

4. Change the Default Transparency setting back to 100%. To change the transparency of only the fill, click on the Fill box in the Appearance palette.

5. A change to the transparency using the Transparency palette now produces a transparent fill, while the stroke remains opaque.

6. Any item that affects the appearance of an object will appear in this list. For example, when a dash is added to the stroke, the description of the stroke changes in the list.

7. If an effect, such as a Drop Shadow, is added from the Effects menu the effect will also appear in the list. The effect can be altered later by double-clicking on the effect. It can be removed from the object by deleting the effect from the Appearance palette.

Figure 11.25. The Appearance palette lists all the components that make up an object's appearance. Only the stroke, fill, and transparency components are shown when a simple object is selected. To change the Stroke or Fill settings, double-click on the item in the list.

Figure 11.26. Changing the transparency of an object using the Transparency palette changes the Default Transparency setting for the entire object. Both the Fill and Stroke settings are changed to 42% opaque in this figure.

Figure 11.27. The fill is transparent, while the stroke remains opaque. The Default Transparency has returned to 100% opaque. The Appearance list has expanded to show the transparency of the fill.

Figure 11.28. When an object changes its appearance, the change shows up in the Appearance palette. The addition of a dash to the stroke is shown in the list.

Figure 11.29. Effects will show up in the Appearance palette. To alter an effect, double-click on the effect in the list.

Chapter 12
Custom Linework

Beyond using the Pen tool and other standard drawing tools to create diagrams, Illustrator offers techniques for creating custom linework through the use of brushes. Brushes in Illustrator are different from the brushes used in Photoshop. Brushes in Illustrator can be thought of as "effects" placed on the vector linework. There are several ways to build custom lines for use in diagrams. The lines can include symbols, words, custom dashes, or shapes. The custom lines that are developed can be saved in libraries and used on different projects.

Creating a Pattern Brush from Shapes

Figure 12.1. For text to be used in a custom line, it must first be converted to geometry. The text cannot be edited once it has been converted to outlines.

Custom linework is created from shapes drawn in Illustrator using the drawing tools. The custom lines can have different start points, middle segments, and endpoints. Custom corner shapes that keep the linework consistent can also be created. Custom linework is created using the Pattern brush in Illustrator. For each segment of the line, a custom shape is drawn. To understand the anatomy of a Pattern brush, consider the following example:

1. Create three different shapes to use as the start, middle, and finish of the line. This example uses text to help explain the makeup of the line. However, if text is used, the text must first be converted to geometry, rather than editable text. For more information on text and how to use the Type tool, Chapter 15: Text, Leaders, and Page Layout.
2. To convert the text to geometry, select the text with the black arrow and select **Type > Create Outlines**. This changes the editable text into simple line drawings. The text can no longer be changed using the Type tool.

start middle end

Figure 12.2. The text has been converted to geometry. This text behaves the same as any other line or object in Illustrator.

3. To create the Pattern brush, bring the Brushes palette to the workspace from **Windows > Brushes**. To create a new brush, click and drag the middle segment into the center of the Brushes palette and release.
4. A dialog box will appear. Choose Pattern Brush as the type of brush to create.

start middle end

Figure 12.3. To create a new Pattern brush, drag the object into the Brushes palette and release. Notice that the entire border around the Brushes palette is bold. This signifies that a new brush is being created. An existing brush will be edited later in this section.

5. Once the new Pattern brush has been created, the Pattern Brush dialog box appears. This dialog box contains all the elements of the brush. The "middle" geometry will appear in the corresponding area at the top of the dialog box. Not all of the segments

need to be defined for the brush to work. In practice, it is often enough to simply define the middle segment.

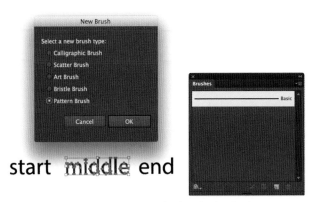

Figure 12.4. Choose New Pattern Brush. The other brushes have interesting effects and work in a similar way to the Pattern brush. However, they are not often used in a design office and are beyond the scope of this book.

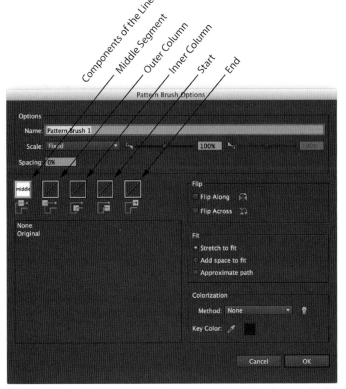

Figure 12.5. All of the elements that make up a Pattern brush are shown in this dialog box. Not all elements need to be defined, however. It is often enough to simply define the middle segment.

6. To apply this brush to a line, select OK to close the dialog box. Draw a line with the Pen tool or any other drawing tool. Select the line with the black arrow. In the Brushes palette, select the brush to apply.

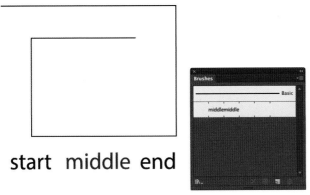

Figure 12.6. To use a Pattern brush, first draw a line using the Pen tool.

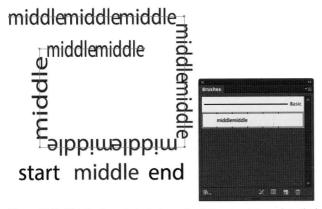

Figure 12.7. With the line selected, choose the Pattern brush to apply to the line.

7. To add a start and end segment, select the "Start" geometry and drag it over the brush while holding the Alt key. The small box will be highlighted to indicate that the line is being changed and a new line is not being created. This will place the start and end geometry at the beginning and end of the line, respectively.

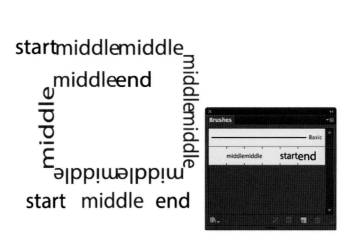

Figure 12.8. Hold the Alt key while dragging the start and end geometry over the definition of the Pattern brush in the Brushes dialog box.

To see how the Pattern brush is used in diagrams, consider the following example:

1. The diagram shown in this figure uses only standard linework at varying weights. The arrowheads are applied using the Stroke dialog box.
2. To create an arrowhead for a custom line, draw a line with the Line Segment tool (or the Pen Tool) in the shape of an arrowhead.

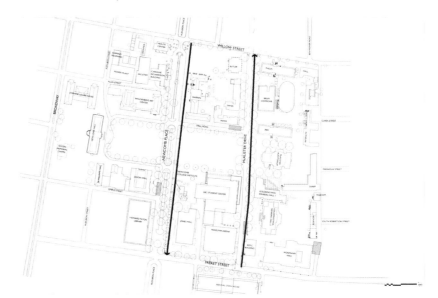

Figure 12.9. The linework in this diagram was created using the Pen tool and applying varying stroke weights. The arrowheads were created using the Stroke Palette.

3. To create a new Pattern brush, drag the arrowhead into the Brushes dialog box.

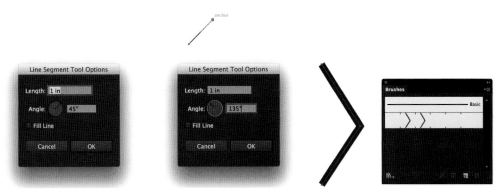

Figure 12.10. Create an arrowhead for the Pattern Brush by using the Line Segment or Pen Tool to draw an arrowhead.

Figure 12.11. Drag the newly drawn arrowhead into the Pattern Brush dialog box.

4. Select the line and choose the new Arrowhead Pattern brush from the Brushes palette.

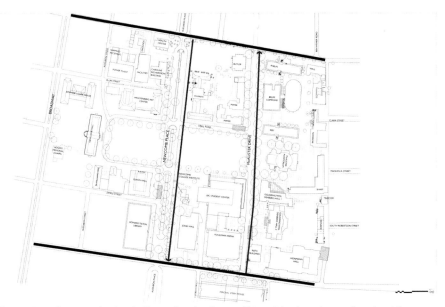

Figure 12.12. Draw a path using the Pen tool on the diagram. This path is where the new Arrowhead Pattern brush will be drawn.

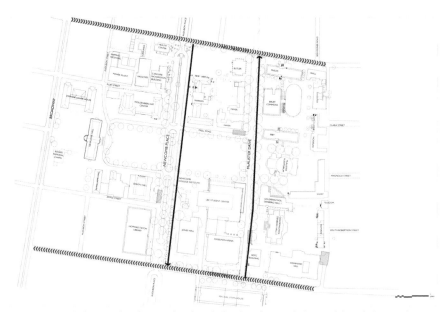

Figure 12.13. Apply the Arrowhead Pattern brush to the line by selecting the line and then clicking on the Arrowhead pattern in the Brushes palette.

Altering the Pattern Brush

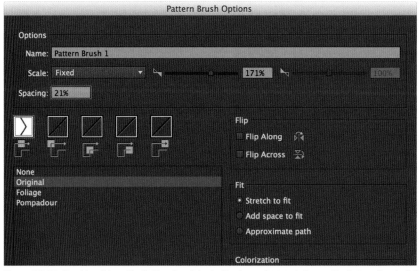

Figure 12.14. Double-click on the Pattern brush in the Brushes palette to bring up the Pattern Brush dialog box. Alter the spacing and scale of the brush in this dialog.

The spacing of the elements, as well as the scale of the brush, can be altered once it has been created. By altering the spacing and scale of the brush, the custom linework can be made to work with other elements on the diagram. To see how to alter the spacing and scale, consider the following example:

1. Double-click on the brush that will be altered in the Brushes palette. A dialog box will appear with several options for altering the appearance of the brush. Change the scale and spacing of the brush to see the effects.
2. One thing to consider is that once the Pattern brush has been altered, all of the lines in the drawing that use that pattern will be affected.

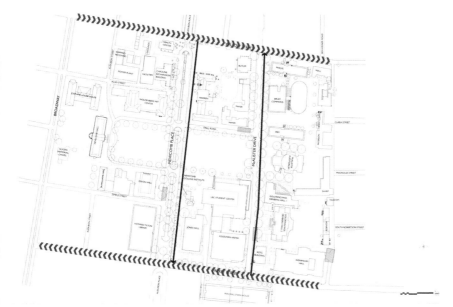

Figure 12.15. The spacing and size of the Pattern brush is applied to lines in the drawing that use that pattern.

Updating the Pattern Brush with New Shapes

Replacing the original geometry with new shapes can change the look of the brush completely. Any single element (such as middle, start, or end) can be replaced individually, or all of the elements can be replaced to create an entirely new brush. To understand how to replace the geometry of a brush, consider the following example:

1. Create a new set of shapes to use in the brush. In this example, the words "SHUTTLE ROUTE" are going to be added to the line. Use the Type tool to create the text. Go to **Type > Create Outlines** to change the text into geometry. More than one element can be used to create a line. Add a line on either side of the text to create the rest of

the brush pattern. Select all three objects that will create the Pattern brush and drag them over the original geometry of the brush with the Alt key held down.

Figure 12.16. More than one piece of geometry can be used to create a brush. Drag the text and two lines over the arrowhead while holding down the Alt key. This will replace the arrowhead geometry with the text and lines. The Pattern brush will be redefined.

2. The line will be updated with the new geometry.

Figure 12.17. Once the geometry has been redefined, the linework will be updated.

3. To remove a Pattern brush from a line and return the line to a simple stroke, select the line and choose the Remove Brush button (the icon in the Brushes palette that shows a paint brush with a cross through it).

Chapter 13
Additional Diagramming Tools

Diagramming enables us to visually express complex concepts. Adobe Illustrator contains several powerful tools that allow us control over vector information.

Blend Tool

The blend tool essentially takes two or more shapes and morphs the first shape into the second and so forth. Double-click the Blend Tool to bring up the blend options dialog box and select one of three blend methods—Specified Steps, Smooth Color, or Specified Distance.

Specified Steps is a good method for creating conceptual diagrams with dynamic line work. In addition to the number of steps, you can also alter the thickness and color of each path or shape to create varied effects. It is even possible to blend objects that have a custom brush or pattern applied. After the objects have been blended, they can further be manipulated by using **Object > Expand**.

In this example, a simple section is made from three paths. The Blend Options are set to 30 Specified Steps. Click the first path, and then the second path to connect, and finally click to connect the third path for a total of 60 steps.

Figure 13.1. Select one of three blend methods.

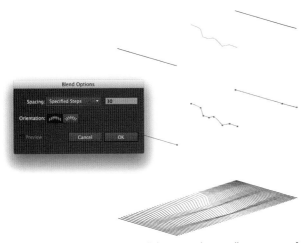

Figure 13.2. The number of steps will determine the overall appearance of the blended paths.

Figure 13.3. Live Paint is located under the Shape Builder option in the Tool palette.

Live Paint

Live Paint gives you the ability to apply color in a manner similar to the Paint Bucket tool in Photoshop. This tool is particularly useful when applying color to a composite area consisting of many shapes. It can be found under the Shape Builder tool.

When creating a complex live paint group it may be difficult to ensure all lines create closed shapes. Use **Object > Live Paint > Gap Options** to close any areas that may not be entirely connected.

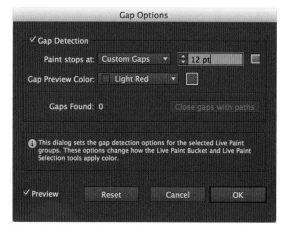

Figure 13.4. Gap options can close disconnected paths of a certain tolerance using a straight line.

Live Paint groups have the advantage of remaining completely editable with both the Select and Direct Selection tool. These qualities are ideally applied as an editable section. Consider the following example:

1. Select all objects, points, and paths you would like to be included and choose the Live Paint tool (K).

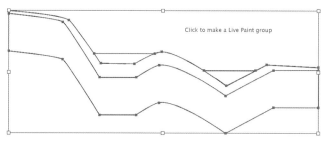

Figure 13.5. All objects to be converted into a live paint group will be outlined in red.

2. Click the canvas when prompted to make a live paint group.

3. Hover over each area of the live paint group and notice the red border that lines the entirety of the shape to be painted with the color or pattern of the foreground color.

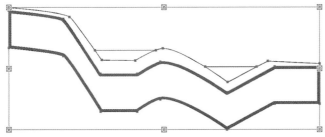

Figure 13.6. The red border shows you which shape to color or pattern to apply.

4. Once the desired colors and patterns have been applied you now have the ability to move the anchor points while the fill automatically adjusts to the new position.

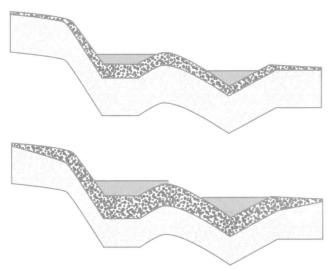

Figure 13.7. The changes made to the section intuitively adjust as seen in the before and after images.

When you are satisfied with the result of the Live Paint Object it can then be converted into ordinary vector paths rendered into separate objects by choosing **Object > Live Paint > Expand**. The objects will be black stroke paths and filled objects with the designated color or pattern, but keep in mind you will lose any specified opacity or brush stroke.

If you are dissatisfied with the result of the Live Paint Group it can always be undone and converted to its original state prior to painting by choosing **Object > Live Paint > Release**.

Transform Each

Transform allows you precise control of exactly how the selected objects are transformed. Right-click and hover over Transform to bring up additional options.

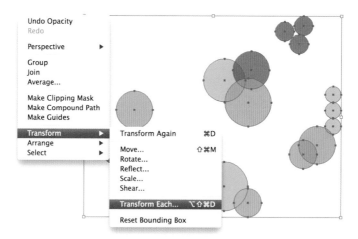

Figure 13.8. With the objects selected, right-click. Under Transform choose Transform Each.

Unlike the free transform, Transform Each will be applied to the objects according to their respective origin, similar to a pivot point. Transform Each gives you the option to affect the object, pattern, stroke, and effects. There are also options to reflect and apply a random effect. In this example the green canopy of the trees is being transformed to vary their size, shape, and orientation.

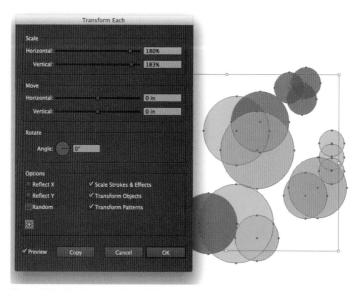

Figure 13.9. The Transform Each dialog box.

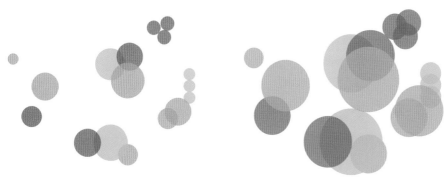

Figure 13.10. The resulting transformation is applied to each object according to its origin.

Image Trace

This powerful tool has the ability to convert raster images into vector data and is unique to Illustrator. Converting to vector data gives you the ability to infinitely resize the object without losing detail. With your raster image selected, choose Windows > Image Trace to bring up the Image Trace dialog box.

The Preset option contains 11 different methods to trace the raster image. View determines how the preview will appear and Mode relates to the color mode. Palette specifies where the resulting colors are sampled from. Take a look at the varying tracing results of this raster image.

Figure 13.11. The Image Trace dialog box contains several specific settings to achieve the desired result.

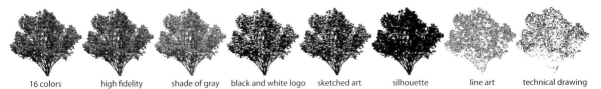

| 16 colors | high fidelity | shade of gray | black and white logo | sketched art | silhouette | line art | technical drawing |

Figure 13.12. Comparison of Image Trace Presets.

Images that have been made into vector paths by Live Trace are ideal for creating icons or any other component of graphic information. Consider the example shown here for creating a bike icon.

1. Begin with a simple raster image with a clean white background.
2. Test different tracing methods and click Preview so you can observe the results.

Figure 13.13. A raster image of a bicycle with a white background is chosen as the source imagery.

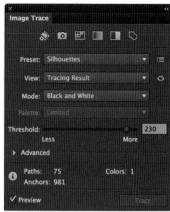

Figure 13.14. For this image the Silhouettes Preset is most effective and the threshold has been adjusted to maximize clarity.

3. You may add a path to define the shape of the icon and group them to complete the graphic.

Figure 13.15. The bicycle icon can be used to designate bike paths on several graphics throughout a project.

Chapter 14
Symbols

Symbols can be powerful tools for working with Illustrator diagrams. They allow you to place a graphic in a drawing and update it later as necessary. A *symbol* is similar to a block in AutoCAD. A symbol has only one definition, a *master symbol,* and any number of copies in the drawing. A symbol is much more than a copy; it can be thought of as a *container* for content. The content (lines, fills, images, etc.) always represents the current information in the symbol library. If the contents of the container are altered, the information is updated throughout every instance of the symbol in an illustration. This makes it easy to update geometry across the drawing at the same time, increasing consistency and saving time.

When copies of a symbol are made throughout a drawing, the contents of each symbol are linked back to the master in the symbol library; however, the container for each symbol's content is a unique object. This means that it is possible to transform each symbol independently by moving, rotating, scaling, tinting, or using any number of other effects. Each symbol will maintain its original content but may be rotated slightly, may be scaled up or down, and may even have a slight tint applied. Transformations can be applied with the normal transformation tools or with a series of tools available in the Symbol Sprayer rollout.

For example, during the early stages of an illustration, it is possible to define a tree symbol simply with a circle. The symbols can be placed throughout the drawing and scaled with slight variations. As the project progresses, the symbol can be replaced with a highly detailed symbol in order to more fully represent the tree species by updating the master symbol in the library. The symbols will be updated, but the position and scaling of each symbol will remain the same. It is possible to test alternatives or to use a simple symbol while working in order to keep the file size down and then replace the symbol before printing or exporting.

Creating Symbols from Custom Artwork

Creating symbols is similar to creating the Pattern brush. Each symbol begins as geometry and is converted to a symbol using the Symbols palette. To create a symbol, first draw the graphic in Illustrator. You can also import lines from other vector applications, such as

AutoCAD, to use as a symbol or import a raster graphic, such as a JPEG or Photoshop file. Consider the example shown here:

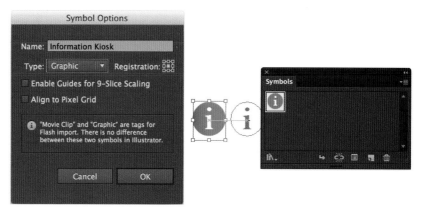

Figure 14.1. To create a symbol, drag the artwork that will serve as the symbol into the Symbols palette.

1. To create the symbol, draw or import the artwork for the symbol. In this example, a symbol for information kiosks will be used. Drag the artwork into the Symbols palette. When the dialog box appears, choose Graphic. A movie clip symbol is used for symbols that will be used in Adobe Flash, and using it is not recommended for work in Illustrator.
2. After dropping the graphic into the Symbols palette, the source object automatically becomes a symbol. Using the Move tool, you can copy this symbol to other areas of the drawing, or you can drag the symbol from the Symbols palette to the drawing.

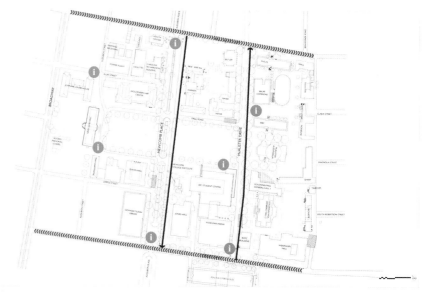

Figure 14.2. Once a symbol is created, drag it from the Symbols palette onto the drawing. The symbol can then be copied around the drawing to place the symbol instances.

If the symbol instance is scaled or rotated, that transformation will not affect the master symbol. Additionally, if an instance has been scaled or rotated and the definition of the symbol is changed, the rotation on the instance will not be affected.

Updating/Replacing Symbols

The advantage of using Symbols instead of simply copying objects throughout a drawing is that a symbol can be replaced throughout the entire drawing. There are two ways to approach this. Redefining the symbol will update all of the symbols in the drawing automatically. This is a good approach if the existing symbol is no longer needed for the drawing. However, if there is the possibility that the symbol will be needed later, a second symbol can be created and all of the existing symbols can be replaced with the new symbol. The advantage of this method is that you can return to the previous symbol if desired. To understand how this might work, consider the example shown here.

Figure 14.3. To redefine a symbol, start by creating a new symbol instance.

1. To redefine an existing symbol, it is usually easiest to break the link to an instance of the symbol, which will make the symbol into standard geometry again. To do this, drag the symbol from the Symbols palette onto the workspace.
2. To break the symbol instance and return the symbol to standard geometry, right-click on the symbol and choose Break Link to Symbol.
3. Once the symbol link is broken, the symbol graphic can be updated. In this example, the color of the symbol will be changed. However, the symbol can be edited in any way, even with additional new geometry. The symbol may need to be *ungrouped* in order to edit certain parts of the geometry. To do this, right-click the geometry and choose Ungroup.
4. To redefine the current symbol, drag the new geometry over the current symbol in the Symbols palette while holding the Alt key.
5. The symbols in the drawing will automatically update to reflect the redefined symbol.

Figure 14.4. Right-click the symbol and choose Break Link to Symbol. After the link has been broken, the geometry can be altered.

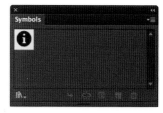

Figure 14.5. To redefine the symbol, hold the Alt key and drag the new geometry over the existing symbol in the Symbols palette.

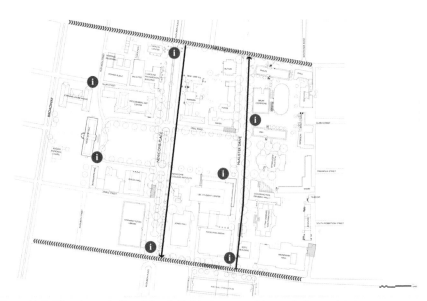

Figure 14.6. When the symbol is redefined, all of the instances of that symbol are updated.

An alternative method for replacing symbols throughout a drawing is to create a second symbol. The alternative symbol can be swapped for all of the instances of the original symbol. To understand how this technique works, consider the following example.

1. Create an entirely new symbol or, as in the previous example, place an instance of the existing symbol and break the link. In this example, a completely new symbol will be created.

2. To replace all of the instances of one symbol in the drawing with another, select all of the symbol instances that will be replaced. This is easily accomplished via the menu in the Symbols palette. Select the symbol and in the Symbols menu, choose Select All Instances. This will select every instance of that symbol in the drawing.

Figure 14.7. An alternative method to redefining the symbol is to create a completely new symbol and replace that symbol with the new symbol. To do this, a new symbol must first be created.

3. After all of the instances of the original symbol are selected, click the new symbol in the Symbols palette. Go to the menu on the Symbols palette and choose Replace Symbol.

4. The symbols will be replaced throughout the drawing.

New Symbol...
Redefine Symbol
Duplicate Symbol
Delete Symbol
Edit Symbol

Place Symbol Instance
Replace Symbol
Break Link to Symbol
Reset Transformation

Select All Unused
Select All Instances

Sort by Name

✓ Thumbnail View
Small List View
Large List View

Symbol Options...

Open Symbol Library ▶
Save Symbol Library...

Figure 14.8. To select all of the instances of a symbol in the drawing, go to the Symbols menu. Click the symbol that is to be selected and choose Select All Instances.

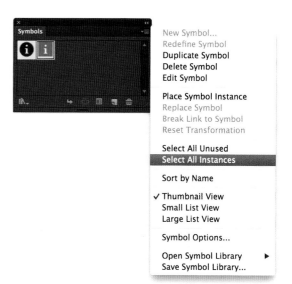

New Symbol...
Redefine Symbol
Duplicate Symbol
Delete Symbol
Edit Symbol

Place Symbol Instance
Replace Symbol
Break Link to Symbol
Reset Transformation

Select All Unused
Select All Instances

Sort by Name

✓ Thumbnail View
Small List View
Large List View

Symbol Options...

Open Symbol Library ▶
Save Symbol Library...

Figure 14.9. After all symbol instances are selected, choose the alternative symbol in the Symbols palette by clicking it. From the Symbols menu choose Replace Symbol.

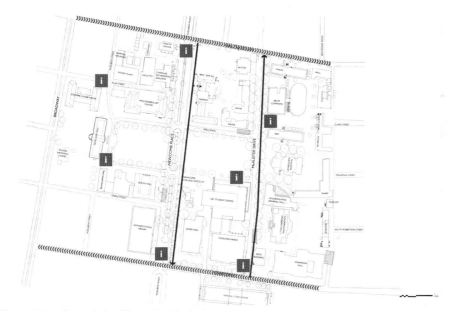

Figure 14.10. The symbols will be replaced in the drawing.

Figure 14.11. Symbol libraries can be saved to use on future projects or to share with others working on the project.

Managing Symbols

After several symbols have been created, they can be saved to a symbol library for future use or to share with other people working on the project. This is an easy way to create a standard set of symbols for an office. To save the symbols, click the drop-down menu on the Symbols palette and select Save Symbol Library.

Creating Clipping Masks for Image Symbols

Using images as symbols can be an effective technique to display graphical information in a diagram. To use an image as a symbol, it is often necessary to crop the image to a certain shape, as shown here.

A *clipping mask* hides a portion of the image to which it is attached. Each clipping mask is connected to a single object. To understand how clipping masks work, consider the following example:

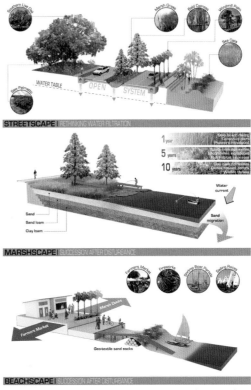

Figure 14.12. The circular images were cropped using a clipping mask in Illustrator. The smaller icons were created in Photoshop and cropped to their circular shape in Illustrator.

Figure 14.13. This image will be used to create a symbol.

1. Place an image into Illustrator using **File** > **Place**.
2. Create a shape to be used as the clipping mask.
3. Select both the image below and the Clipping Mask shape. Go to **Object** > **Clipping Mask** > **Make**.
4. The image now has a clipping mask attached to it. The clipping mask and the image can be disconnected from each other by choosing **Object** > **Clipping Mask** > **Release**.
5. The image with the clipping mask can be used as a symbol, or it can be used in the diagram as is.

Figure 14.14. Create the object that will serve as the clipping mask and place it over the image. Both the Clipping Mask and the image below must be selected.

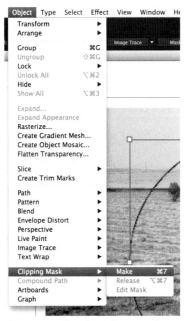

Figure 14.15. Turn the circle on top of the image into a clipping mask by going to **Object > Clipping Mask > Make**.

Figure 14.16. The clipping mask and the image are attached.

Figure 14.17. To create a symbol from the final image, drag the image with its clipping mask into the Symbols palette.

Chapter 15
Text, Leaders, and Page Layout

The text for labels and layouts should be created using a vector-editing application. The tools available in Illustrator work better than raster-based applications such as Photoshop. Raster illustrations can be linked into an Illustrator layout in order to apply titles, leaders, notes, and labels in order to take advantage of the tools that are available in Illustrator. It is also possible to create text directly in Photoshop, and both sets of tools are very similar. Illustrator has a larger set of options, particularly for text windows and text-box linking. Illustrator also has the ability to convert text to vector paths in order to transform characters individually if necessary.

Text Tools

Illustrator has two basic Text tools and several other advanced text options. The Type tool is used to create the two most basic forms of text: point text and paragraph text.

Point Text

The first method of creating text uses *point text*. To insert this type of text into your drawing, select the Type tool and click on the drawing. As you enter text, the line expands. If you press Enter, a new line will form below. The text box will keep expanding as long as type is added.

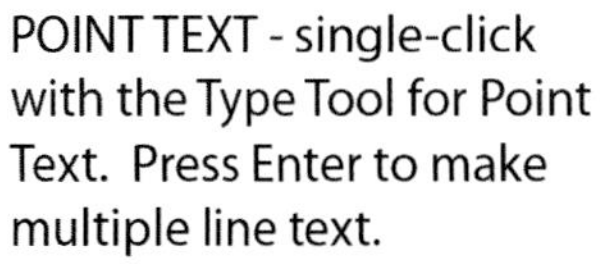

POINT TEXT - single-click with the Type Tool for Point Text. Press Enter to make multiple line text.

Figure 15.1. Insert point text into the drawing by choosing the Type tool and clicking on the drawing.

Paragraph Text

A second way to insert text uses *paragraph text*. Insert paragraph text by clicking and dragging to form a text box. The size of the text box will determine the boundaries of the text.

The text box will continue to expand as long as *point text* is being typed. *Paragraph text* will disappear from the screen once the limits of the text box are reached. The text still exists; it is simply outside the parameters of the text box. Once the limits of the box are reached, a small, red plus mark (+) will pop up at the bottom-right of the text box. This indicates that

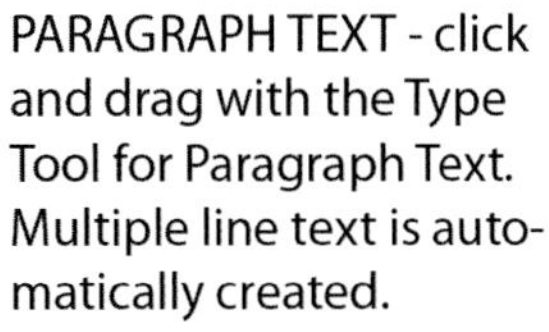

PARAGRAPH TEXT - click and drag with the Type Tool for Paragraph Text. Multiple line text is automatically created.

Figure 15.2. Insert paragraph text into the drawing by choosing the Type tool and clicking and dragging a text box.

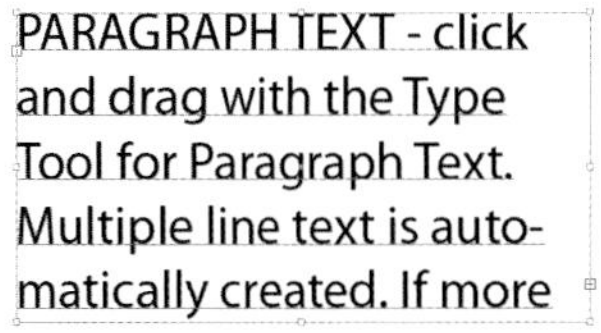

PARAGRAPH TEXT - click and drag with the Type Tool for Paragraph Text. Multiple line text is automatically created. If more

Figure 15.3. A small, red plus sign (+) indicates that there is more text than the text box can hold.

there is text outside the limits of the box. The text is still there; it can be seen by dragging a corner of the box with the black arrow to make the text box larger.

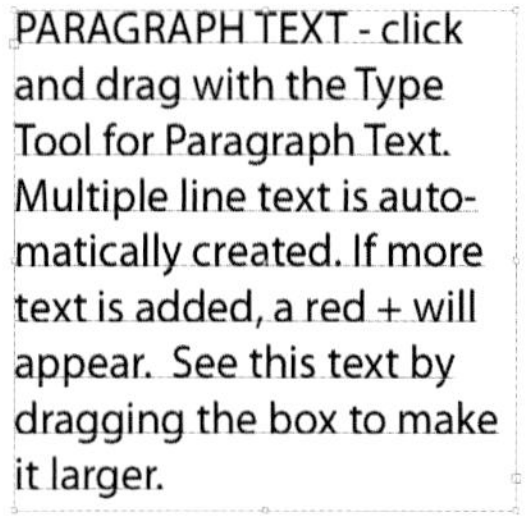

Differences between Point Text and Paragraph Text

The main difference between point text and paragraph text is how the text is affected when the size of the text box is changed after the text has been entered. With point text, the size and shape of the text changes when the size of the text box is changed. With paragraph text, the font stays the same size and adjusts to the dimensions of the new text box.

Another difference can be seen when the text boxes are rotated. The Point Text box rotates the text, where the Paragraph Text box maintains its orientation and adjusts to the parameters of the box.

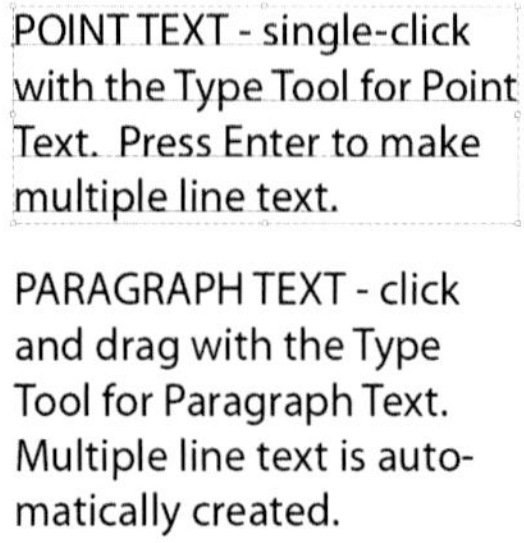

PARAGRAPH TEXT - click and drag with the Type Tool for Paragraph Text. Multiple line text is automatically created. If more text is added, a red + will appear. See this text by dragging the box to make it larger.

Figure 15.4. To see the text, click and drag one of the corners of the text box to make it larger.

POINT TEXT - single-click with the Type Tool for Point Text. Press Enter to make multiple line text.

PARAGRAPH TEXT - click and drag with the Type Tool for Paragraph Text. Multiple line text is automatically created.

Figure 15.5. Point text and paragraph text differ in the way the text appears when the text box is altered.

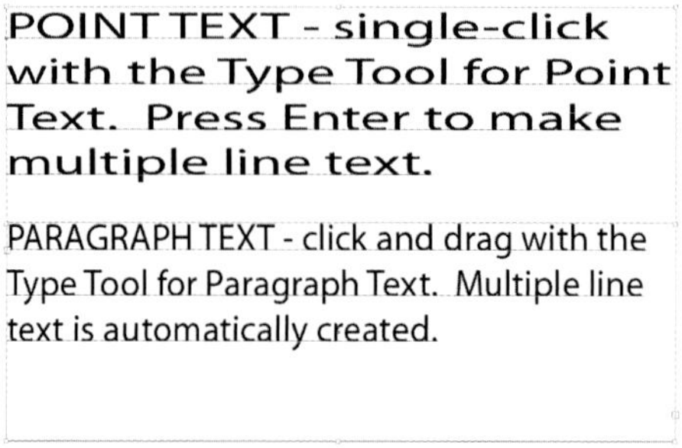

POINT TEXT - single-click with the Type Tool for Point Text. Press Enter to make multiple line text.

PARAGRAPH TEXT - click and drag with the Type Tool for Paragraph Text. Multiple line text is automatically created.

Figure 15.6. When a Point Text box is expanded, the text changes size and shape. When a Paragraph Text box is expanded, the text's font size stays the same but readjusts to fill the dimensions of the new box.

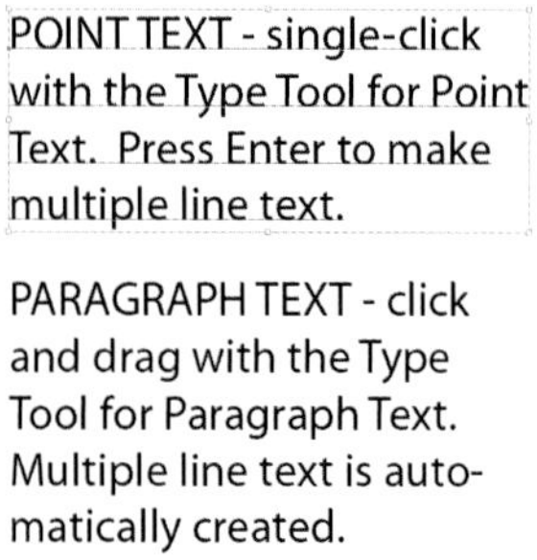

POINT TEXT - single-click with the Type Tool for Point Text. Press Enter to make multiple line text.

PARAGRAPH TEXT - click and drag with the Type Tool for Paragraph Text. Multiple line text is automatically created.

Figure 15.7. Point text and paragraph text also differ in how a rotation affects the text box.

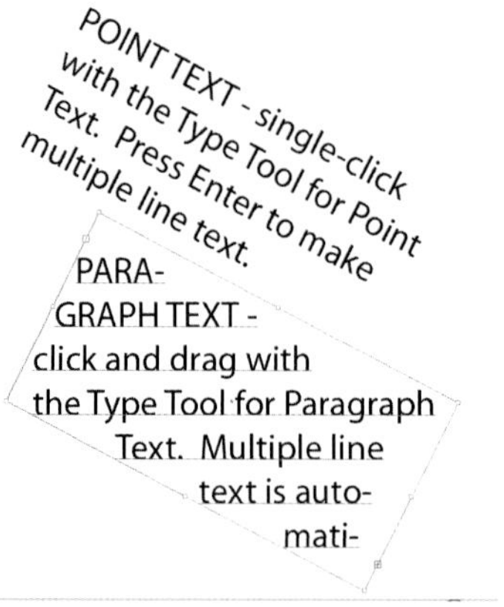

POINT TEXT - single-click with the Type Tool for Point Text. Press Enter to make multiple line text.

PARA-GRAPH TEXT - click and drag with the Type Tool for Paragraph Text. Multiple line text is auto-mati-

Figure 15.8. The Point Text box rotates the text, while the Paragraph Text box maintains its orientation when the text box is rotated.

Point text is most often used to create labels or other short text items, such as titles, and the like. Paragraph text is better used to create longer descriptions. Another feature of paragraph text is that the text can be linked to flow between two separate text boxes. To better understand the technique, consider the following example.

1. Make two Paragraph Text boxes and enter text into the first Paragraph Text box. Enter more text than the first text box will hold. The red plus sign (+) should appear at the bottom-right corner of the text box.
2. Click the red plus sign (+) on the first text box and then click in the next text box. The text from the first box will flow into the second box.
3. You can set up multiple text boxes, and copy and paste text from Microsoft Word or any other word processor into your Illustrator file.

PARAGRAPH TEXT - click and drag with the Type Tool for Paragraph Text. Multiple line text is auto-

Figure 15.9. Create two Paragraph Text boxes. The text in the first box extends beyond the dimensions of the text box. The red plus sign (+) in the corner of the box indicates that more text is contained in the text box than can be displayed.

PARAGRAPH TEXT - click and drag with the Type Tool for Paragraph Text. Multiple line text is auto-

matically created. To link one Text Box to another click on the red + and then click on the second Text Box.

Figure 15.10. Click on the red plus sign (+) and then click in the second text box to link the text boxes. The text from the first text box will flow into the second text box.

Formatting Text

To format text in the text boxes, use one of the Type palettes. This Type palette has several subpalettes. The two most important are the Character palette and the Paragraph palette. The Character palette can be found under the menu item **Window > Type > Character**. The basic feature of the Character palette is the ability to change the font and font size.

The other useful features of the Character palette are leading and tracking. *Leading* changes the spacing between lines of text. *Tracking* changes the spacing between the characters of the text. To understand how leading and tracking affect text, consider the following example:

1. To use any of the features of the Character palette, the text box must be selected. The leading will change the spacing between lines of text. In this example, the leading has been changed from Automatic, which is 25.2 point, to 21 point. This has the effect of decreasing the spacing between the lines of text.

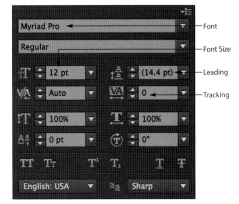

Figure 15.11. The Character palette offers tools for changing the font, font size, leading, and tracking.

LEADING set to Automatic, or in this example 25.2 pt.

LEADING set to 21 pt. This has the effect of decreasing the spacing between lines.

Figure 15.12. The leading is changed from 25.2 point to 21 point. This makes the spacing between the lines closer. Changing the leading to a value greater than 25.2 would increase the spacing between the lines.

TRACKING SET TO -50
TRACKING SET TO ZERO
TRACKING SET TO 200

Figure 15.13. The tracking is set to three different values. The tracking changes the spacing between the characters.

153

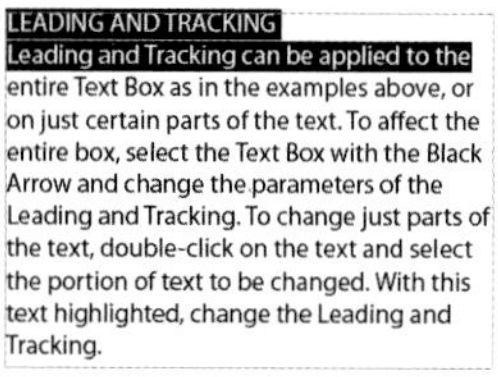

LEADING AND TRACKING
Leading and Tracking can be applied to the
entire Text Box as in the examples above, or
on just certain parts of the text. To affect the
entire box, select the Text Box with the Black
Arrow and change the parameters of the
Leading and Tracking. To change just parts of
the text, double-click on the text and select
the portion of text to be changed. With this
text highlighted, change the Leading and
Tracking.

Figure 15.14. To select individual portions of text, double-
click on the text box with the
black arrow. Selecting the first
two lines of the text and changing the leading will customize
the spacing between the title
and the paragraph text.

LEADING AND TRACKING
Leading and Tracking can be applied to the
entire Text Box as in the examples above, or
on just certain parts of the text. To affect the
entire box, select the Text Box with the Black
Arrow and change the parameters of the
Leading and Tracking. To change just parts of
the text, double-click on the text and select
the portion of text to be changed. With this
text highlighted, change the Leading and

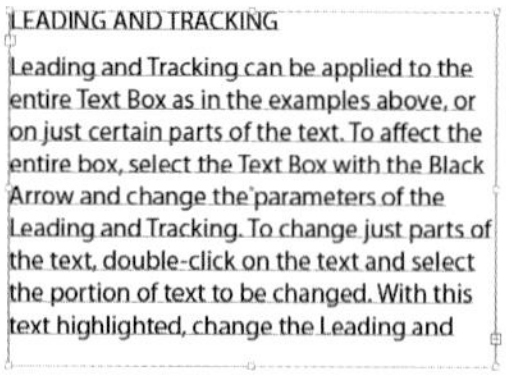

Figure 15.15. When the first
two lines are selected, a change
in the leading affects only the
spacing between these two
lines. The spacing between the
title and the paragraph text can
be customized using this technique. If the spacing is not customized, the spacing between
the title and the paragraph is
set by pressing Return between
the title and the paragraph.

2. Tracking changes the spacing between the individual characters. In this example, the same text is copied three times and the tracking is set to three different values.
3. Leading and tracking can be applied to the entire text box, as in the previous exam-ples, or on just certain parts of the text. To affect the entire box, select the text box with the black arrow and change the Leading and Tracking parameters. To change just parts of the text, double-click on the text and select the portion of text to be changed. With this text highlighted, change the leading and tracking.
4. To change the leading between a title and the text that follows it, select the first two lines of text.
5. With these two lines selected, change the leading to a larger value. This will provide a space between the title and the paragraph text that follows it.
6. To change the tracking of just the title, select the title using the Type tool.
7. Changing the font to Bold and adjusting the tracking will set off the title from the rest of the paragraph. In this example, the font was changed to Bold Italic and the track-ing was increased to 75.

The Paragraph palette offers ways to control the *justification* of the text, as well as hyphenation and indentations. The Paragraph palette is found under **Windows > Type> Paragraph**. To change the justification of the text, select one of the options at the top of the palette. The boxes below the justification types will adjust the indentation of the text box. To control the hyphenation of the text within the box, adjust it in the drop-down box from the Paragraph palette.

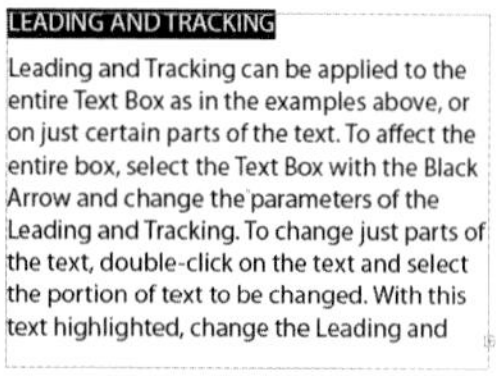

LEADING AND TRACKING
Leading and Tracking can be applied to the
entire Text Box as in the examples above, or
on just certain parts of the text. To affect the
entire box, select the Text Box with the Black
Arrow and change the parameters of the
Leading and Tracking. To change just parts of
the text, double-click on the text and select
the portion of text to be changed. With this
text highlighted, change the Leading and

Figure 15.16. The font and
other attributes, such as tracking, are changed only on the
text that is selected.

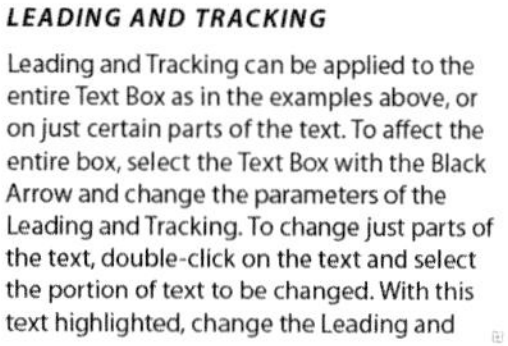

LEADING AND TRACKING
Leading and Tracking can be applied to the
entire Text Box as in the examples above, or
on just certain parts of the text. To affect the
entire box, select the Text Box with the Black
Arrow and change the parameters of the
Leading and Tracking. To change just parts of
the text, double-click on the text and select
the portion of text to be changed. With this
text highlighted, change the Leading and

Figure 15.17. In this example,
the title was changed to Bold
Italic and the tracking was
increased to 75. The font size
could be changed if desired.

Figure 15.18. The Paragraph palette controls the justification and
hyphenation of the text in a text box.

Custom Type Tools

There are several Type tools that provide unique ways to place text into a drawing. These tools offer different techniques for creating vertical text, having text follow a path, and creating text within a custom shape.

The following examples show how these different techniques create custom text:

1. Vertical text can be created by choosing the Vertical Type tool and either clicking (for point text) or clicking and dragging (for paragraph text) in the workspace. The text entered into the text box will be oriented vertically.

2. Text can be set to follow a path created in Illustrator or imported from another vector-based program, such as AutoCAD. First, draw the path for the text to follow.

3. Choose the Type on a Path tool. Select the path and type the text to appear on the path.

4. The text can be altered and transformed like other objects in Illustrator. To change the color, select the text and choose a new swatch.

5. Text can be created within a custom shape as well. Any shape created with the Pen tool or the Shape tools can be used. Start by creating the custom shape.

6. Select the Area Type tool and click on the custom shape. The text entered into this shape will follow the dimensions of the shape, similar to a regular text box.

Figure 15.19. Several custom Type tools provide techniques for creating vertical text, creating text that follows a path, and creating text within a custom shape.

Figure 15.20. When the Vertical Type tool is chosen and placed in the workspace, the text maintains a vertical orientation. Point text and paragraph text can be created using this tool.

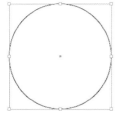

Figure 15.21. To create text that follows a path, first create the path.

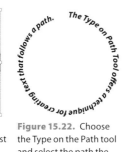

Figure 15.22. Choose the Type on the Path tool and select the path the text will follow. The original path will disappear after the text is added.

Figure 15.23. The text and the path can be copied and manipulated like other geometry.

Figure 15.24. To use the Area Type tool, first create a custom shape using either the Pen tool or the Shape tools.

Figure 15.25. Select the Area Type tool and click on the shape. The text entered into the shape will follow the shape, similar to a regular text box.

Creating Text with a Clipping Mask

A useful technique for creating text in combination with an image is to use a clipping mask with the text. Clipping masks are discussed in Chapter 14: Symbols. To see how text can be created using a clipping mask, consider the following example.

Figure 15.26. Place the image and place the text to be used over the image.

1. Place an image into Illustrator. Create the text to be used over the image.
2. Transform the text into geometry by selecting the text and choosing **Type > Create Outlines**.
3. Ungroup the text. When text is converted to outlines, it is grouped together to allow the text to be moved easily. However, for this technique, the text needs to be ungrouped.

Figure 15.27. Select the text and choose **Type > Create Outlines**.

Figure 15.28. The text will be placed into a Group. Right-click the text geometry and choose Ungroup.

4. The text must be turned into a *compound path*. When the text is ungrouped, each individual letter is turned into an individual object. To make a clipping mask, all of the letters need to be a single path. To change the text into a compound path, select all of the letters and choose **Object > Compound Path > Make**.
5. Select the image and the text, which is now a single compound path, and choose **Object > Clipping Mask > Make**.

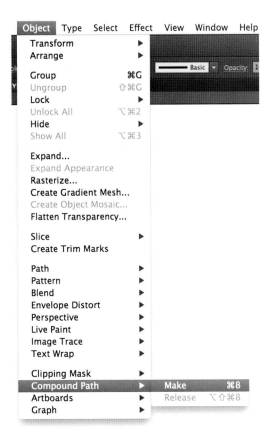

Figure 15.29. All of the letters need to be turned into a single path to make the clipping mask. Select all of the letters and choose **Object > Compound Path > Make**.

Figure 15.30. Select both the image and the compound path of text and choose **Object > Clipping Mask > Make**.

Figure 15.31. The text does not have a stroke applied.

6. To add an outline to the text, select the text. Notice that the Stroke is empty in the color swatch. Choose a color and weight for the Stroke in the color swatch to make an outline of the letters.

Figure 15.32. To create outlines of the letters choose a Stroke color and weight.

7. The final text is not editable because it was turned into outlines.

Figure 15.33. The final text has the image behind it, and a stroke is applied to the edges.

Leaders

Creating *leaders* in Illustrator is much simpler and more flexible than creating them in Photoshop. Leaders can be created from a combination of a text box and a line with the Arrowhead effect on it. The leaders in Illustrator are easy to move once they are created on the page. The techniques for creating leaders in Illustrator are demonstrated in the following example.

1. To draw a leader, first create a text box and add text. Draw a line from the text to the part of the drawing the label references.
2. Under the Stroke palette there is a drop-down box for Arrowheads.
3. To move the text only, use the white arrow. This technique moves the text and the end of the leader together, while keeping the reference arrow in place.

Entrance Pathway

Figure 15.34. Draw a line from the text box to the reference area on the drawing.

Figure 15.35. There are several arrowhead options from which to choose. The size of the arrowhead is related to the stroke weight of the line. The arrowhead size can be adjusted using the Scale option.

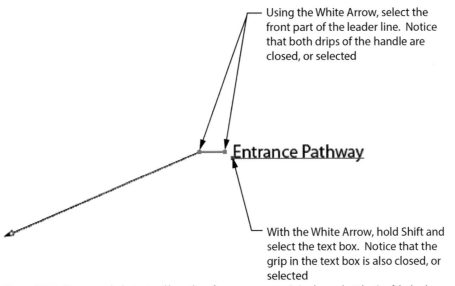

Using the White Arrow, select the front part of the leader line. Notice that both drips of the handle are closed, or selected

Entrance Pathway

With the White Arrow, hold Shift and select the text box. Notice that the grip in the text box is also closed, or selected

Figure 15.36. To move only the text and have the reference arrow remain in place, select the tip of the leader line and the text box together.

4. First, select the tip of the leader line and the text box. Then, while holding the Shift key, select the text box.

5. Use the white arrow to move the text. When the text is moved, the arrowhead stays in the same place, but the text and the rest of the leader will move. This makes it easy to reposition text dynamically on a drawing as you add more leaders.

Figure 15.37. Using the white arrow, move the text. The leader will reposition itself with the new placement of the text while the reference arrow will remain in its original position. The gray text/leader in the figure is the original position of the text/leader before being moved.

Figure 15.38. Hold the Alt key while the leader is in the process of being moved. If the Alt key is held down before then, the technique will not work.

6. To create two leaders, use the white arrow to select the leader line. Click on the end-point of the leader and begin to drag it to another part of the drawing. While the line is being moved, hold the Alt key. If the Alt key is pressed before the line is moved, the technique will not work.

Layout

Illustrator offers some useful techniques for laying out graphics and images on a board. These tools can be used to diagram or to lay out a presentation board with plan, section, and perspective images.

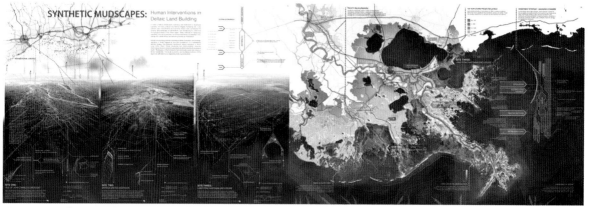

Figure 15.39. Illustrator offers some useful techniques for laying out graphics on a board. This figure has images created in Photoshop and Illustrator, as well as site images arranged in Illustrator. Text and leaders can be added in Illustrator once the layout has been set.

One technique that is worth mentioning is linking Photoshop files into Illustrator. See Chapter 10: Setting up an Illustrator Drawing for more information on how to link Photoshop files into Illustrator. When files are linked, the layout board can be arranged before the Photoshop files are completed. This offers the opportunity to see how individual drawings will look at the size they will be displayed at on the board earlier in the process. As the Photoshop files evolve, they will be updated in the Illustrator layout.

The most useful tool for layout is the Align palette. This set of tools will line up and space images in a number of ways. The following examples show how the Align palette is used.

1. Place the images to be used in the layout into Illustrator.

Figure 15.40. Place the images that will be in the layout on the workspace in Illustrator.

2. Open the Align palette from **Windows > Align**. The Align options work in a similar way to text justification in word-processing programs. Vertically, the objects can be aligned to the left, to the center, or to the right. Horizontally, the objects can be aligned to the top, to the center, or to the bottom. When clicked, the Distribute Objects icons will space the objects equally between the two outer objects.

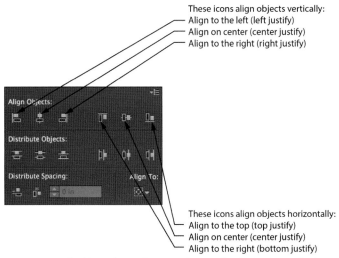

These icons align objects vertically:
— Align to the left (left justify)
— Align on center (center justify)
— Align to the right (right justify)

These icons align objects horizontally:
— Align to the top (top justify)
— Align on center (center justify)
— Align to the right (bottom justify)

Figure 15.41. The Align palette offers several options for aligning images both horizontally and vertically. It also has Distribute Objects icons, which can be used to evenly space the images.

3. To align the images for layout, select all the images and choose to align horizontally along the center.

4. The objects will be aligned along the center axis. When Center Justify is chosen, the objects align along an axis that is the center of all the objects in the group.

Figure 15.42. Center-justify the images from the Align palette.

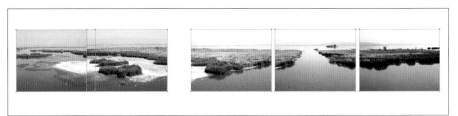

Figure 15.43. The objects are aligned along the central axis.

5. To space the objects evenly, click the Distribute Objects icon. This will space the objects evenly between the outer two objects.

Figure 15.44. Click the Distribute Objects icon to space the objects evenly between the two outer objects.

Figure 15.45. The objects are spaced evenly.

Chapter 16
Exploded Axonometric Diagrams

The distillation or culling of information can often lead to diagrams that are void of contextual references. It is possible to represent the context throughout each diagram in order to provide a reference, tying together the unique information from each diagram. It is also possible to create exploded *axonometric diagrams,* which are useful to show multiple layers of information and how they relate to one another spatially. An exploded axonometric drawing pulls the information apart vertically in order to maintain a reference between each component of a site. This provides a space for each layer of information, while maintaining a clear spatial relationship among individual parts. Lines may be drawn in order to link upper and lower layers, linking edges or points that are critical between each layer.

Creating an Exploded Axonometric Diagram

Several methods are used to create drawings similar to exploded axonometric diagrams. The most common method is to create the diagram from a layered plan drawing. The basic elements of the exploded axonometric diagram are placed on separate layers of the drawing, and each layer is stacked on top of the layer underneath. The following example shows a technique for creating these diagrams.

1. Start with a plan view of the project. Collect all of the elements that will be in the diagram into a single file. Each layer in the diagram should reside on an individual layer in Illustrator.
2. Select the entire drawing by pressing Ctrl+A. Make sure that all layers are unlocked. Rotate the drawing to approximate the final orientation of the diagram.
3. The blue line is the *bounding box*. The bounding box is the master editing box that contains all of the selected objects. It appears only when the black arrow is being used to move or transform objects. It allows the user to transform multiple objects simultaneously. Depending on the settings, the bounding box may not "reset" to an orthogonal position after items are rotated. If the bounding box does not reset, with all of the objects selected, go to **Transform > Reset Bounding Box**.

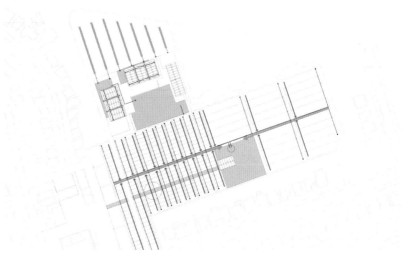

Figure 16.1. Collect all of the elements that will be in the diagram into a single plan drawing. Place each layer in the drawing on a unique layer in Illustrator.

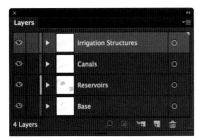

Figure 16.2. The four elements that will create the diagram are on separate layers.

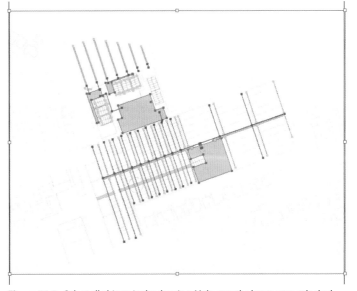

Figure 16.3. Select all objects in the drawing. Make sure the layers are not locked.

4. Using the black arrow, click and drag the top-center grip to flatten the plan view.

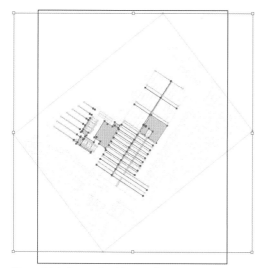

Figure 16.4. Rotate the objects to the proper orientation.

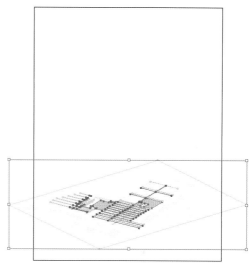

Figure 16.5. To flatten the drawing, click on the top-center grip and drag it downward.

5. To move them to the top of the layer stack, select the objects on the top layer of the diagram and use the Move tool while holding the Shift key. To select all of the objects on a single layer, click in the far right area of the layer box.

6. Repeat the process for the other layers in the drawing.

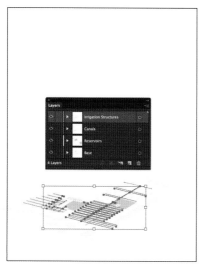

Figure 16.6. To select all of the objects on a layer, click in the far right portion of the layer list. The blue box will indicate where to click.

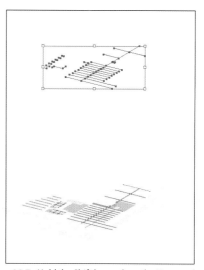

Figure 16.7. Hold the Shift key and use the Move tool to position the layer in the drawing.

7. Adding vertical lines often helps ground the layers above the base.

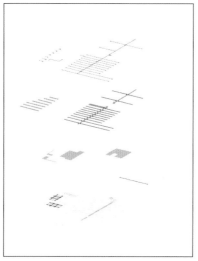

Figure 16.8. Repeat the same process for the other layers in the drawing.

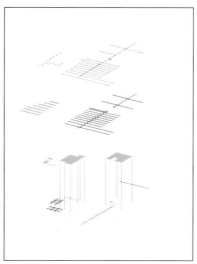

Figure 16.9. Adding vertical lines helps ground the floating layers to the base.

Chapter 17
Time-Based Imagery

Time is a critical component of landscape representation and digital tools provide methods for working with time-based sequences and overlays. These forms of representation can be used to examine phasing, site evolution, traffic (human or vehicular), or more ephemeral phenomena such as erosion or light patterning. It is also possible to visualize or explain complex information through basic animations within the design process with colleagues or with clients. With basic time-based tools integrated directly into Adobe Photoshop it is possible to use layers and effects within the timeline and to repurpose current diagrams and illustrations.

Adobe Photoshop has two methods for manipulating time, the timeline that allows for the keyframing and tweening of layers and image stacks.

Loading an Image Sequence

The timeline can be useful with existing video content such as image sequences that may be rendered from modeling software or a time lapse taken with your camera. It is possible to open this content in Photoshop, make edits, and then export the video as a movie file.

1. To open an image sequence in Photoshop, **File > Open** and browse for the first file in the image sequence. The files should be in a single folder and must be numbered sequentially, for example, filename_0000.tif, filename_0001.tif, and so on. Select the first file in the image sequence and then check the box at the bottom of the file dialog stating that this is an image sequence.

2. After clicking open a dialog will appear asking for the frame rate of the image sequence. This is dependent on the use of the sequence but for most video applications you would use 30 frames per second.

3. The image sequence will then open showing the first frame and the length of the sequence in the timeline at the bottom of the screen. You will also notice that the image sequence is loaded as a video group layer in the Layers palette.

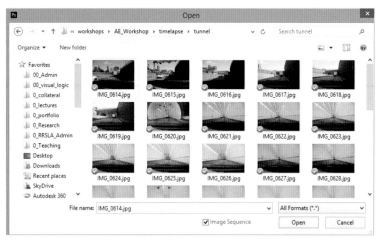

Figure 17.1. Opening an image sequence, file dialog.

Figure 17.2. The timeline showing the length of the image sequence.

4. It is possible to play the image sequence using the video controls within the timeline. When playing the sequence for the first time it will render a preview and playback will be slower than the actual speed of the video. After the initial preview, rendering the video playback will be in real time, the preview will need to be re-rendered if there are any edits.

5. Because the image sequence is loaded as a layer it is possible to create new layers with additional content such as text, annotations, or adjustments. These new layers will appear in the video timeline and within the timeline properties for each layer. They can be animated using keyframes. To create a keyframe for any layer property simply click the Stopwatch icon next to the property, this will set a keyframe at the current point. You will then move the timeline to another point and time and adjust the attribute; this will automatically set a new keyframe. Photoshop will then create the adjusted frames between these two keyframes to smoothly transition between each.

Figure 17.3. Image sequence within the Layers palette as a video group.

Figure 17.4. Initial playback will render a video preview; the green bar at the top of the sequence indicates the progress of the rendering.

Figure 17.5. Keyframes created to adjust the opacity of an image adjustment layer.

6. After making edits to the sequence it is possible to export the video to a format that is playable in external media players such as windows media player, VLC, and iTunes or to be used in presentation software such as PowerPoint. To export the video go to **File > Export > Render Video**.

7. The Render Video dialog has all of the options to define how a video or image sequence will be rendered from the current timeline. You will specify the location and name of the file to be exported within the top section. The middle area allows for rendering with the Adobe Media Encoder or as a Photoshop image sequence and to adjust the file types including video encoding, resolution, or image settings.

Figure 17.6. Render Video dialog options.

Using these basic editing tools it is possible to make small edits and adjustments to sequences and/or assemble sequences that can be rendered as new video or image sequences.

Tweening between Layer States

The previous method outlined ways to animate using keyframes based on layer properties. It is also possible to use layers and their current states to create animation. This works by turning layers off and on or adjusting properties, and then creating a frame of the current state. Within the timeline it is then possible to create a number of "in between" frames (tweening) to create smooth transition between states.

1. To create and tween between frames you will select the drop down in the middle of the timeline to create a frame animation; if you wanted a video timeline (similar to the image sequence) you would choose Video Timeline. It is possible to convert between each type of animation using the toggle in the lower left corner of the timeline. You will see a timeline with the current state of the animation—a single frame describing the current state of the canvas.

Figure 17.7. The frame animation timeline shows the animation with a single frame.

2. To create a new frame state, click the duplicate frame button at the bottom of timeline. Then make changes to the layers; turning layers off/on, adjusting screening, editing styles, and making adjustments. These changes will then be reflected in the new frame state. It is possible to give each of these frames a duration so that they are displayed for a specific amount of time.

3. To create the in between frames, select the first frame and then click on the Tweens Between Frames button at the bottom of the timeline. In the Tween dialog select the amount of frames to create and the parameters that should be considered when the frames are created.

4. It is possible to rearrange the frames, create or delete frames, and to change the duration each frame is displayed to edit the animation. After the animation is complete it is possible to render the video using **File > Export > Render Video**.

Figure 17.8. The Frame Animation dialog options.

Figure 17.9. The frame animation timeline shows the animation with tweened frames.

Image Stacks

Image stacks provide a way to combine a series of images to represent a compression of time within a single image. Typically this would be used to remove unwanted elements from a set of images with the same background or can be used to show motion within an image. It is possible to create a stack automatically using Photoshop's built-in scripts or manually by creating layers.

A typical use of an image stack is to take a set of pictures of a busy space and to then use the Median Stack mode to remove the unwanted elements, for example, people or vehicles. It can also produce interesting effects using other modes to trace change over time.

1. To create a layer stack load the images using **File > Scripts > Load Files** into Stack. The images will take a moment to load as a stack of layers. After loading the images, align the images using **Edit > Auto-Align Layers**. This will align the layers based on similar areas. At this stage the images are aligned and can be edited if necessary.

2. To create the image stack, select all of the aligned layers and go to **Layer > Smart Objects > Convert to Smart Object**. The layers are now loaded into the Smart Object. It is now possible to use one of the image stack modes to process the images by selecting **Layer > Smart Objects > Stack Mode** and choosing the appropriate mode.

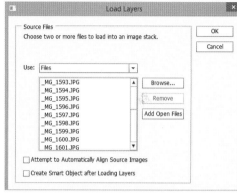

Figure 17.10. Load files into Image Stack dialog options.

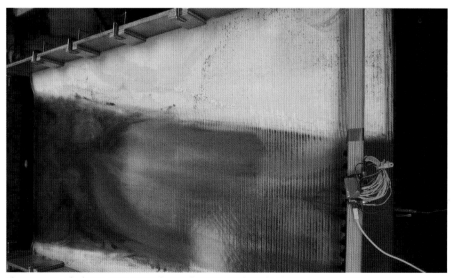

Figure 17.11. The layers are processed using the Mean Stack mode. Fluid is smoothed and surrounding movement is discarded. *Bradley Cantrell and Justine Holzman, Louisiana State University Robert Reich School of Landscape Architecture*

Part 4

Plan/Section Renderings

Plan/Section Renderings

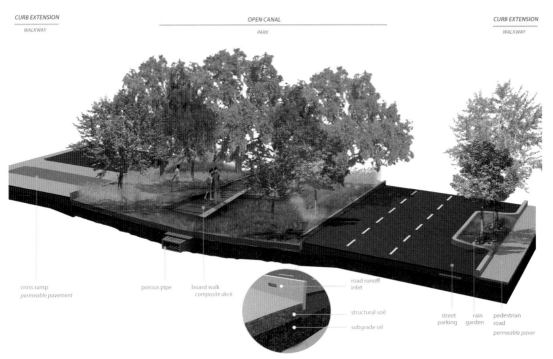

CURB EXTENSION   OPEN CANAL   CURB EXTENSION

WALKWAY   PARK   WALKWAY

cross ramp
permeable pavement

porous pipe

board walk
composite deck

road runoff
inlet

structural soil

subgrade oil

street
parking

rain
garden

pedestrian
road
permeable paver

Saint Charles Street Section Perspective. New Orleans, LA. Elizabeth Huangbo, MLA 2014, Louisiana State University Robert Reich School of Landscape Architecture

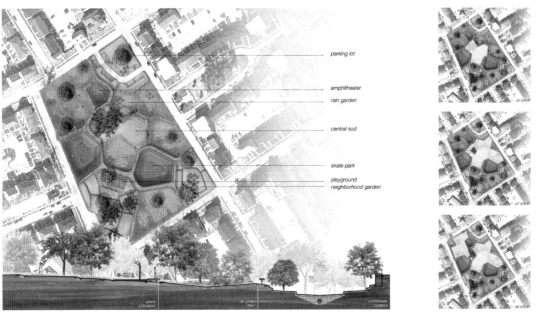

parking lot

amphitheater
rain garden

central sod

skate park
playground
neighborhood garden

30 000 ft²

57 000 ft²

80 000 ft²

89

Harmony Oaks Park Concept. New Orleans, LA. Shu Shi, MLA 2014, Louisiana State University Robert Reich School of Landscape Architecture

174

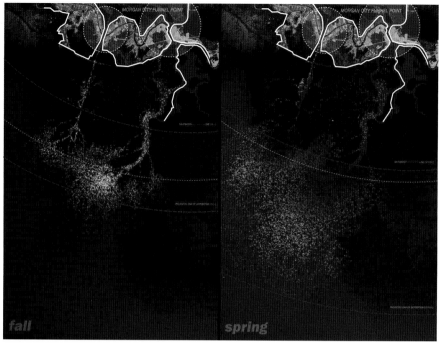

Sensing Sediment Dispersal. Morgan City, LA. **Charlie Pruitt, BLA 2012, Louisiana State University Robert Reich School of Landscape Architecture**

Section Cut Perspective. **Matthew Seibert, MLA 2013, Louisiana State University Robert Reich School of Landscape Architecture**

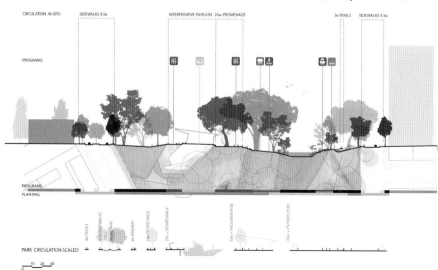

Park Circulation Diagram. Stoss Landscape Urbanism

Plan/Section Renderings

Hybrid Section Perspective. Matthew Seibert, MLA 2013, Louisiana State University Robert Reich School of Landscape Architecture

Concept Plan. San Juan, Puerto Rico. Joshua Brooks, BLA 2012, Louisiana State University Robert Reich School of Landscape Architecture

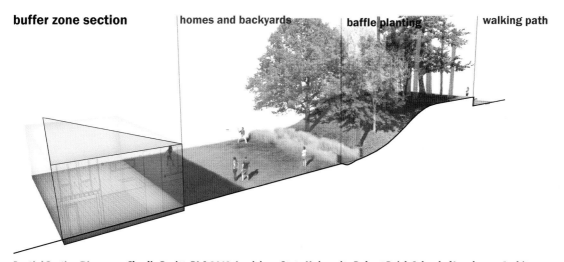

buffer zone section   homes and backyards   baffle planting   walking path

Spatial Section Diagram. **Charlie Pruitt, BLA 2012, Louisiana State University Robert Reich School of Landscape Architecture**

Concept Plan. **Lydia Gikas and Matthew Rossbach, MLA 2014, Louisiana State University Robert Reich School of Landscape Architecture**

Plan/Section Renderings

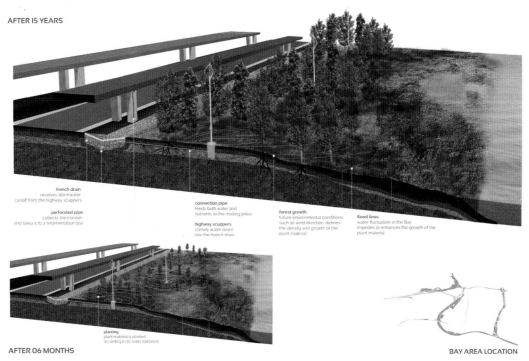

AFTER 15 YEARS

french drain
receives stormwater
runoff from the highway scuppers

perforated pipe
collects stormwater
and takes it to a sedimentation box

connection pipe
feeds both water and
nutrients to the misting poles

highway scuppers
convey water down
into the french drain

forest growth
future environmental conditions,
such as wind direction, defines
the density and growth of the
plant material

flood lines
water fluctuation in the Bay
impedes or enhances the growth of the
plant material

planting
plant material is planted
according to its water tolerance

AFTER 06 MONTHS

BAY AREA LOCATION

FOREST TYPOLOGY 1 - IMPLEMENTATION
Section Perspective. **Prentiss Darden and Silvia Cox, MLA 2014, Louisiana State University Robert Reich School of Landscape Architecture**

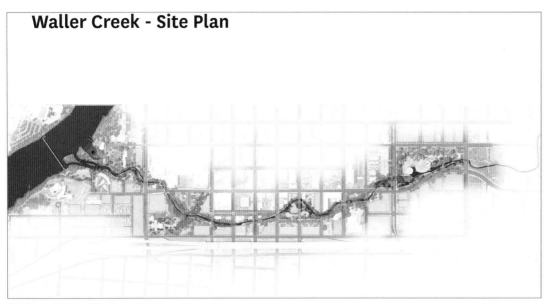

Waller Creek - Site Plan

Site Plan. **Michael Van Valkenburgh and Associates**

Tulsa - Site Plan

Site Plan. **Michael Van Valkenburgh and Associates**

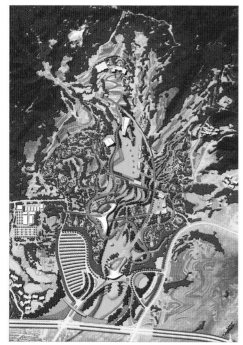

Site Plan. **SWA**

Plan/Section Renderings

Section Perspective. **SWA**

Plan. **Yitian Wang, Yi Liu, Matty Williams, MLA 2014, Louisiana State University Robert Reich School of Landscape Architecture**

Chapter 18
Importing PDF Linework

In order to develop a measured, scalable illustration, designers need to develop a method to transfer linework from a drafting (CAD) application to an illustration application such as Photoshop. Although there are plug-ins and applications that allow drawings to be illustrated directly in CAD software, the most common method is for the linework produced in AutoCAD to be rendered in Photoshop. Photoshop offers a more robust set of rendering tools than any integrated representation system, such as an AutoCAD plug-in or Vectorworks. In many workflows, CAD and illustration work is divided among staff members, departments, and even outside contractors. Because many people will use the same base linework, it is important to develop a standard approach to exporting linework from a CAD application.

The most common workflow is to print from AutoCAD to the PDF format and then to import or rasterize the PDF file into Adobe Photoshop. This method works well and is transparent for many scenarios because printing to a PDF adopts standards similar to what would be in place to print to paper, such as sheet sizes, lineweights, and scales.

Typically, linework in the CAD application will be organized to make the rendering process as easy as possible. This will include printing several PDF files, each containing separate linework that will then be layered in Photoshop. In order to increase the editability of the drawing, it is normal to print PDF files for vegetation, scoring, layout, text, topography, and utilities. This method makes choosing the areas in the drawing that will receive color much easier in Photoshop. Exporting the entire drawing as a single PDF increases the amount of time needed to color the drawing once in Photoshop.

Exporting multiple PDFs for use in Photoshop has the additional advantage of making editing easier at later stages in the project. If changes occur in the planting plan, it is then possible to simply reprint the vegetation layers and insert them into Photoshop, while leaving the rest of the drawing unchanged. This type of flexibility is one of the advantages of using digital media for representation as opposed to hand rendering.

PDF Linework

Printing a PDF file for every CAD layer is not necessary; instead, layers can be consolidated to make rendering easier in Photoshop. Each file will have a unique set of layers that can be consolidated. The key concept for grouping layers is to separate layers that have a lot of overlapping areas. For an example of how to set up a drawing in AutoCAD for exporting PDFs, consider the following:

1. The drawing in *model space* will be exported using the Paper Space tabs. The original drawing has many overlapping elements.
2. Create a Paper Space sheet layout at the correct size and scale of the final rendering. If the final rendering is to be 11 inches × 17 inches at 1 inch = 50 inches, set the Paper Space tab to these same dimensions. In this example, the page is set to 24 inches × 36 inches. Once the PDF is exported and opened in Photoshop, the size and the scale of the drawing will be the same as the Paper Space tab. Once the Paper Space tab is set up with the proper page size and scale, lock the viewport so all of the PDFs will line up in Photoshop. Locking the viewport keeps the image from moving around on the page. To lock the viewport, select the viewport and choose Lock Display from the Properties tab.
3. After creating the first Paper Space tab, copy the tab to create new Paper Space tabs. Create one Paper Space tab for each PDF that will be brought into Photoshop.

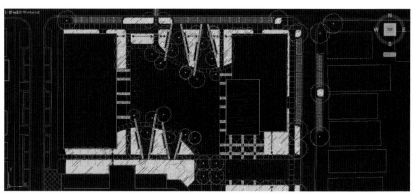

Figure 18.1. The drawing in AutoCAD, as seen in model space.

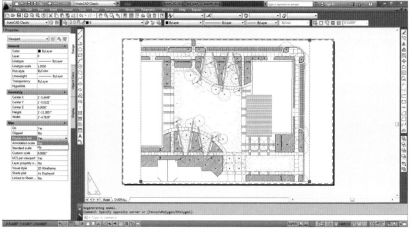

Figure 18.2. Set the Paper Space sheet layout to the dimensions and scale of the final rendering. These attributes will be the same in Photoshop once the PDFs are imported. The Properties tab has an option to Lock the Viewport.

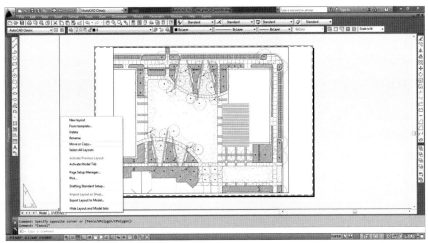

Figure 18.3. Copy the first Paper Space tab to create new sheet layouts. Each exported PDF will have a Paper Space tab.

4. To isolate the linework in each new Paper Space tab, freeze the layers in that viewport only. This will not freeze the layers throughout the drawing; it will freeze only the layers in the viewport on that Paper Space layout. To freeze only these layers in this viewport, double-click the viewport to go to Model Space, open the Layer Properties Manager, and choose VP Freeze.

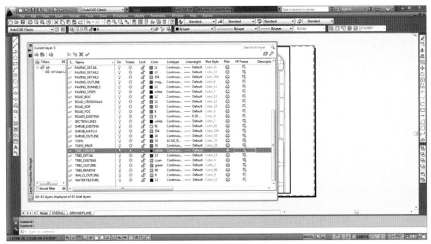

Figure 18.4. To freeze layers only in the current viewport, open the Layer Properties Manager and select VP Freeze.

5. Once the other layers are frozen, only the linework that will be exported as a PDF remains in the viewport.

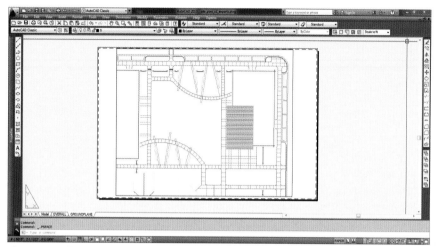

Figure 18.5. The linework remaining will be exported as a PDF and used in Photoshop.

6. Continue to create Paper Space tabs until all of the linework that needs to be isolated is on an individual Paper Space tab.

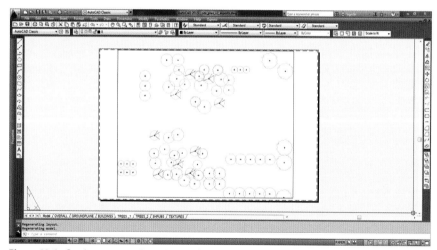

Figure 18.6. Continue to create Paper Space tabs and isolate linework.

7. To simplest way to create the PDFs from the Paper Space tabs is to print the tabs using a PDF printer. Each Paper Space tab should be printed individually. In this example, there will be seven separate PDFs. Lineweights and other attributes can be set while printing from AutoCAD.

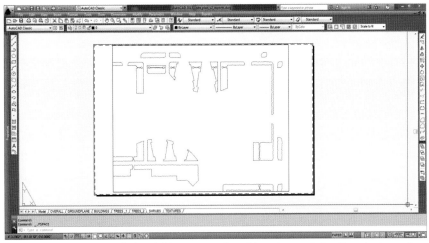

Figure 18.7. Separating small, closed objects can save lots of time when rendering. The advantages of isolating this kind of linework can be seen in Chapter 19: Applying Color to a Plan Rendering.

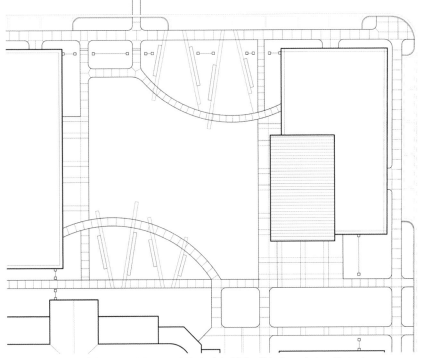

Figure 18.8. One of the seven PDFs printed. Each of the PDFs will be brought into Photoshop.

Linework printed from a CAD application to PDF is stored as vector data and requires the PDF to be rasterized when it is brought into Photoshop. *Rasterization* is the conversion of vector data into raster data; it requires that a pixel resolution be specified for the rasterized PDF file. The following example shows a technique to assemble all of the PDFs into a single Photoshop file:

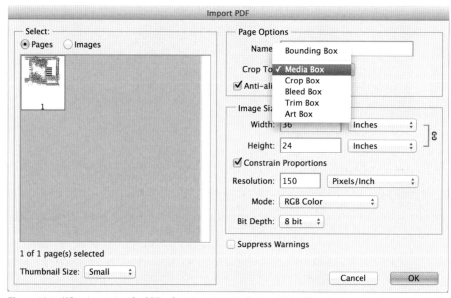

Figure 18.9. When importing the PDF, select **Crop To > Media Box**. This will retain the paper size and scale of the drawing as it was determined in AutoCAD.

1. Photoshop allows PDF files to be opened using **File > Open**. When the PDF file to be opened is selected, the Import PDF dialog box will appear. This dialog box has several options that are needed to import the PDF file successfully. The Name option sets the filename for the PDF file upon import.
2. The Crop To drop-down box has several choices. To maintain the proper scale and paper size of your drawing as it was configured in AutoCAD, choose Media Box. For example, if the Bounding Box option is chosen, any extraneous whitespace around the objects will be discarded. This will alter the page size and make registering several PDFs on top of one another difficult.
3. Make sure Anti-Aliased is selected. *Anti-aliasing* will smooth the edges of the linework upon import. If Media Box is selected, the Image Size dimensions should match the sheet size that was set up in AutoCAD. If the page size is changed here, the scale of the drawing will change.

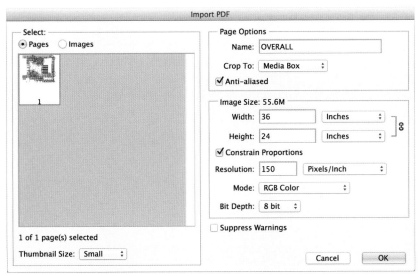

Figure 18.10. Once the Crop To selection is set to Media Box, the Image Size should reflect the image size as it was set up in AutoCAD. In this example, the image size is the same as it was in AutoCAD, 24 inches × 36 inches.

4. The Resolution should be adjusted, based on the size of the layout. It is typically set at 150 pixels per inch (ppi), unless there are extenuating circumstances such as a very large file size. (See Chapter 3: Basic Overview of Digital Concepts for more information on ppi.)

5. Once the settings have been entered into the Import PDF dialog box, click OK. The PDF will open in a new file. The PDF linework will be contained on a single layer. There are many ways to import the PDFs into a Photoshop file, but in this technique it is usually best to open the PDF with all of the linework on it first. In this example, the PDF is named Overall, as in the overall linework for the project. This linework will not typically be used in the final drawing, but it is useful when importing the other PDFs into the drawing as a method for checking the correct placement of all the layers. If a PDF is slightly off when it is imported, it will show up compared to the "overall" linework.

6. This Overall drawing will be the master file into which all of the other PDFs will be imported. When the file is first created, the background of the Photoshop file is transparent. The checkerboard boxes indicate a transparent background.

7. To provide a solid white background for the linework, go to **Layer > New Fill Layer > Solid Color** and choose White.

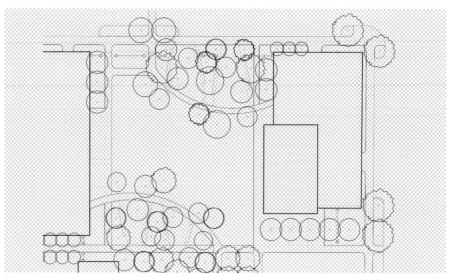

Figure 18.11. When the drawing is first created, the PDF linework will exist on a layer and the background will be transparent.

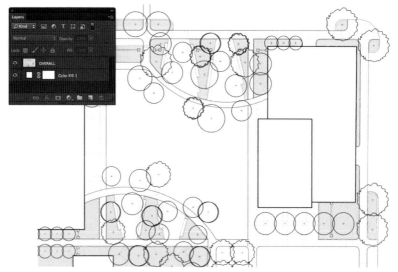

Figure 18.12. Create a fill layer to provide a white background for the linework. Remember to move the fill layer below the linework layer.

After importing the linework as PDF files, each PDF file needs to be merged into a single PSD to create the basis for your illustration. The end result will be a multilayered Photoshop file, with each PDF on its own layer. Because all of the PDF files were printed from

AutoCAD using the same Paper Space layout settings, the layers can be duplicated into your new PSD file. These layers will line up directly on top of each other, provided the same settings are used to open each PDF. The PDFs will not be imported into the master Photoshop file. Rather, each PDF will be opened individually as a new file. The linework will then be copied into the master file. To create this multilayered document, consider the following example:

1. Select the PDF file first opened—in this example, the Overall drawing—and save it as a PSD file. As indicated previously, this will become the master file. Keep this file open throughout the entire process.
2. Open a second PDF as a new file in Photoshop by choosing **File > Open**. In this example, the Groundplane PDF will be used. In the PDF Import dialog box, choose the same settings that were used for the first file. There is no need to add a Solid Color fill layer to this file, because the linework will be copied into the master file.
3. With the Groundplane file open, right-click on the linework layer in the Layers palette. Select Duplicate Layer to bring up the Duplicate Layer dialog box.

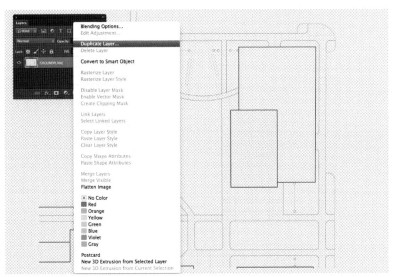

Figure 18.13. With the new PDF file open, right-click on the layer and select Duplicate Layer.

4. The Duplicate Layer dialog box has two options. The As: value determines the name of the duplicated layer. In this example, the name will be **Groundplane Linework**. The second option is to select the destination of the duplicated layer. The layer can be duplicated within the current file, to a completely new file, or to another file that is open in Photoshop. In this instance, the file will be duplicated to the master file, called Overall. Click on the drop-down box to select the file called Overall. Remember, the Overall file must be open in Photoshop to appear in this list.

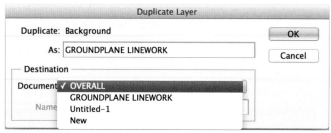

Figure 18.14. Under the Destination, choose the master file, which is called Overall in this example. The linework on this layer will be copied to that file.

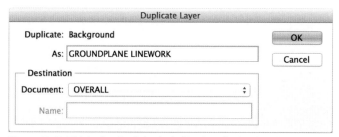

Figure 18.15. This is what the dialog looks like after all values have been entered.

5. Once the linework has been duplicated into the master file, the recently opened PDF—in this case, the Groundplane file—can be closed. It does not need to be saved.
6. The master file will now contain an additional layer with the linework from the new PDF.

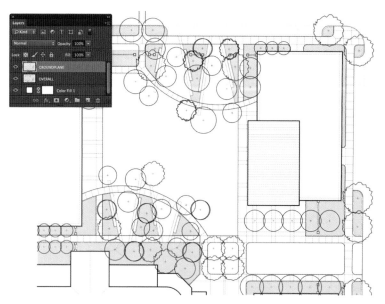

Figure 18.16. The linework shows up as a new layer in the master file.

7. Repeat Steps 1 through 6 for each of the PDF files in order to create your rendering base file. The final file will have a layer for each PDF that was exported from AutoCAD.

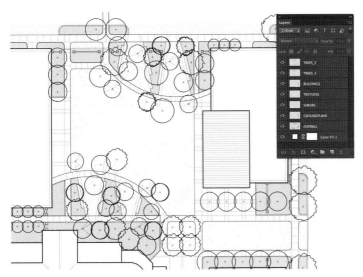

Figure 18.17. Repeat the procedure for each PDF that was exported from AutoCAD. The final Photoshop file will have a layer for each PDF.

Adjusting the Appearance of Linework

While most of the decisions about the appearance of the linework, such as the lineweight, should be made in AutoCAD during the PDF printing process, there are ways to adjust the appearance of linework once it is in Photoshop. Adjustment layers (see Chapter 19: Applying Color to a Plan Rendering) should almost always be used when editing any aspect of a Photoshop drawing, if possible. This way, the drawing can be reverted to its original state if needed. However, using adjustment layers in this case is not a high priority. If the linework is altered and the results are not desirable, and there is no way to go back in the History palette to Undo the adjustment, simply reimport the linework from the original PDF. This is one of the most powerful aspects of this technique. Furthermore, if the design changes, simply reprint a PDF from the AutoCAD file and duplicate that layer into the Photoshop drawing.

Several different techniques can be used to adjust the appearance of the linework. The following example explores some of these techniques.

1. To increase the weight of the linework, copy the layer by dragging it to the New Layer icon in the Layers palette. In this example, click and drag the Groundplane layer and release it over the New Layers icon. A new Groundplane layer will be created. This will increase the density of the linework on that layer.

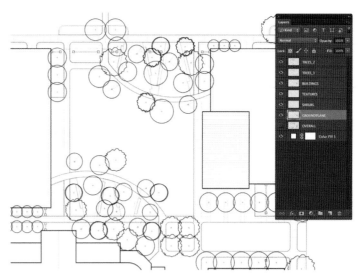

Figure 18.18. The original linework has the lineweight characteristics that were determined in AutoCAD.

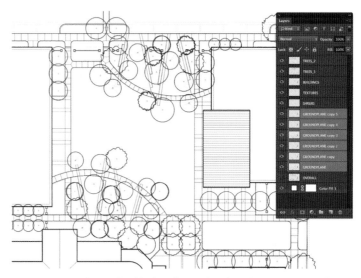

Figure 18.19. To increase the weight of the lines from within Photoshop, make a copy of the linework layer by dragging the layer into the New Layers icon at the bottom of the Layers palette. In this example, the Groundplane layer was copied several times.

2. After multiple layers are created, the layers can be merged into a single layer by selecting them all and choosing **Layer > Merge Layers** from the menu.
3. The linework can be made to appear lighter by either lowering the opacity of the layer or increasing the brightness of the linework using the Hue/Saturation dialog box.

4. The Trees and Trees 2 layers have their Opacity set to 42% to lighten the appearance of the linework.

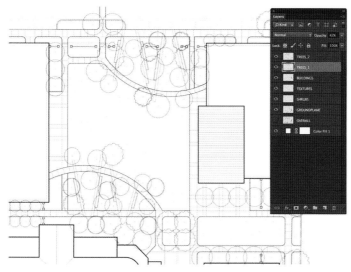

Figure 18.20. By decreasing the Opacity of the layer, the linework becomes lighter. In this example, the two Tree layers have a reduced Opacity.

5. With the Opacity reset to 100%, select the Trees and Trees 2 layers and then select **Image > Adjustments > Hue/Saturation**. The Brightness of the linework is set to +47. This lightens the linework.

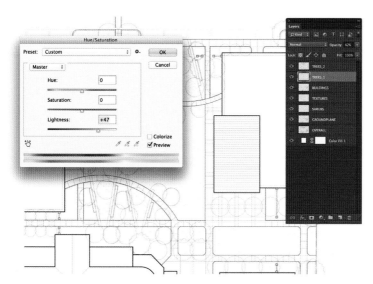

Figure 18.21. Another way to lighten linework is to adjust the Brightness using the Hue/Saturation dialog box.

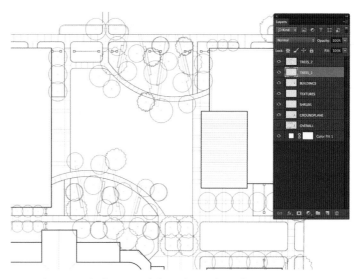

Figure 18.22. The trees in this figure were lightened using the Brightness adjustment.

Chapter 19
Applying Color to a Plan Rendering

One of the first tasks in rendering a plan is to apply a base color to all of the areas. Textures, shading, and other effects can be added later in the process. Two common techniques are used to apply color to a rendering. The most common is to use the Paint Bucket tool to simply paint areas with color. The second method uses Solid Color adjustment layers to color the plan. The techniques are similar; however, using adjustment layers adds flexibility to the drawing. Using this technique, the colors of the plan can be easily adjusted as the drawing develops. This allows all of the colors to be applied quickly, and detailed decisions about which colors to use can be made at the end of the process once all of the colors are on the rendering.

Technique 1: Applying Color with the Paint Bucket Tool

In this technique, the Paint Bucket tool is used to apply color to the rendering. The Paint Bucket tool is similar to the Magic Wand tool (see Chapter 7: Source Imagery/Entourage), except the Magic Wand tool makes a selection *and* fills the selection with a color and the Paint Bucket tool fills the canvas until it reaches adjacent pixels. Many of the Paint Bucket tool's options are similar to the Magic Wand tool's, the most critical being the Sample All Layers option and the Contiguous option. It is important to understand how these options affect the two tools. To understand how the Paint Bucket tool is used to apply color to a rendering, consider the following example.

1. Isolate a single linework layer by hiding all of the other layers. In this example, the Groundplane layer is the first isolated layer.
2. Create a new layer for the base color. It is important to apply the base color on a different layer than the linework. An explanation of how this affects the quality of the image is presented later in this section. Place the base color layer underneath the linework layer in the layer stack.

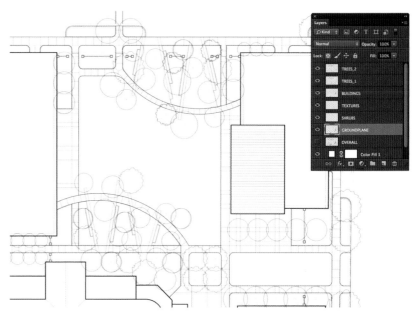

Figure 19.1. All of the layers in this drawing were imported from the PDFs created in AutoCAD. All the layers are visible, with the exception of the Overall layer, which is primarily used to double-check the alignment of PDF layers as they are imported.

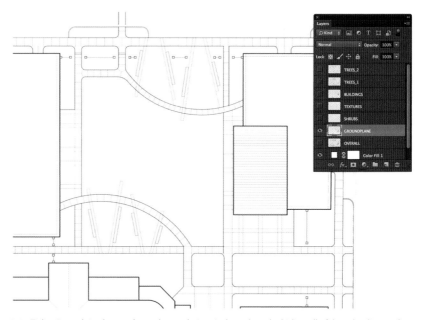

Figure 19.2. To begin applying base color to the rendering, isolate a layer by hiding all of the other linework layers.

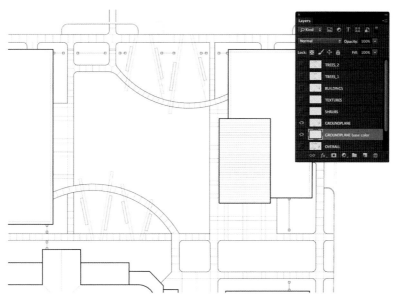

Figure 19.3. Create a new layer by clicking the New Layer icon at the bottom of the Layers palette. Place the base color layer underneath the linework layer in the layer stack.

3. Choose the Paint Bucket tool from the Tools palette. Because the base color will be applied to a different layer than the linework, it is important to have Sample All Layers selected as an option. This will use all visible layers for the boundary definition, but will put the painted pixels on the current layer: the base color layer. The linework will form the boundaries for the Paint Bucket tool. The Contiguous option needs to be selected to allow the Paint Bucket tool to perform this technique.

Figure 19.4. The Sample All Layers and Contiguous options need to be selected for the Paint Bucket tool.

4. To apply color to an area of the drawing, choose a color from the Color Picker by clicking the Foreground icon. Use the Paint Bucket tool to click an area of the drawing.
5. For the Paint Bucket tool to color a specific area of the drawing, the linework that contains it must be closed. Any small gap will allow the paint to "escape" the area. In a perfect world, the linework that comes into Photoshop from AutoCAD would have completely closed lines. This is rarely the case. For example, in this drawing, several areas in the linework are not closed.

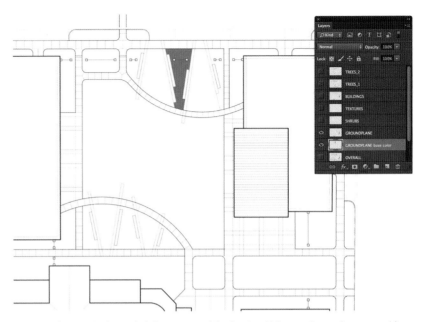

Figure 19.5. Using the Paint Bucket tool, click on an area of the drawing. Make sure the new layer created for the base color is selected. The color will be applied to this base color layer.

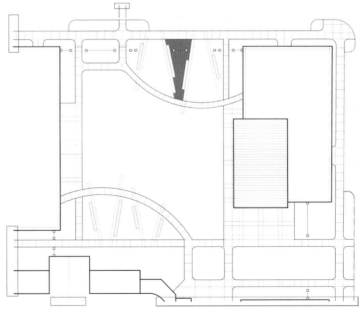

Figure 19.6. Several areas on the drawing do not have closed linework. The areas highlighted in red are open, and the Paint Bucket tool will not color these areas correctly.

6. There are two ways to close open lines. The easiest way is to use the Paint Brush tool with a small hard-edged brush and paint in the missing linework. The new lines will be painted on the linework layer, not the base color layer. However, it is sometimes difficult to get the new linework to have the same appearance as the existing linework.

7. Another technique is to create a TEMP layer that will be deleted later. Draw the lines on this layer and once the paint has filled the area, the TEMP layer can be deleted. To use this technique, start by creating a new layer named TEMP. On this layer, paint a black line to close the linework.

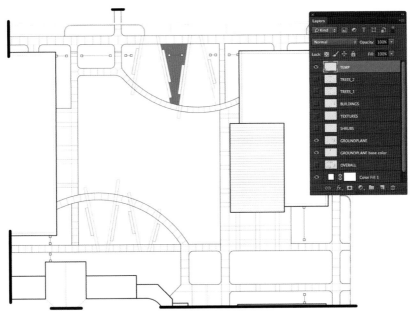

Figure 19.7. Create a new layer named TEMP. Using the Paint Brush tool, close the linework with a black line. The black lines will be removed when the TEMP layer is deleted, so they do not need to be precise.

8. Using the Paint Bucket tool, paint the recently closed areas with a color.

9. When the TEMP layer is deleted, the black lines that were used to close the lines disappear.

The process of filling areas of the rendering continues until the entire base color scheme has been applied. Typically, the fills will start at the lowest level and work their way up toward the viewer. It is important that each of the base color areas is created on a separate layer and is labeled as a "base color" layer. There are a couple of advantages to keeping the base color separate from the linework. The most important is that the quality of the linework will not be degraded if the base color is on a layer beneath the linework. If the Paint Bucket tool is used directly on the linework layer, the color of the fill will bleed into the edges of the lines. The following figures show the difference between placing the base color on the same layer as the linework and placing it on a separate layer below the linework.

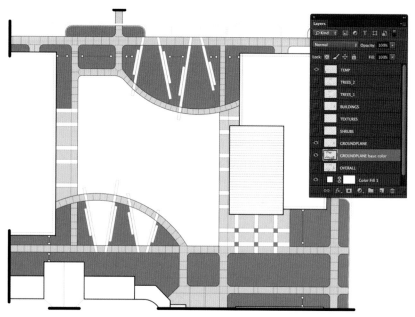

Figure 19.8. Now that the TEMP layer has been used to close the linework, the areas can be painted with the Paint Bucket tool.

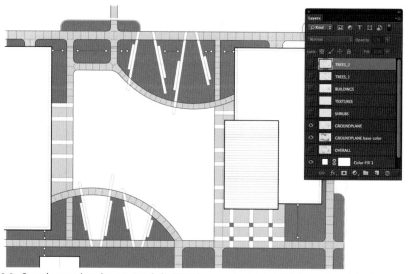

Figure 19.9. Once the areas have been painted, the TEMP layer can be deleted. This leaves the original linework intact.

Figure 19.10. When the linework is imported from AutoCAD, it is rasterized. This means that the linework is converted to a set of pixels. To replicate the smooth edges of the linework, Photoshop adds some gray pixels along the edges of the lines. From a distance, this makes the lines appear smooth. Without these gray edges, the linework would appear jagged or harsh.

Figure 19.11. When the Paint Bucket tool is used on the same layer as the linework, the pixels from the Paint Bucket tool bleed into the edges of the linework. This causes the smooth transition of the line created in the rasterization process to be degraded. On very thin linework, the lines may even appear spotty or almost disappear in places. Adjusting the Tolerance of the Paint Bucket tool can control some of the effect of line degradation, but it is almost always better to keep the linework of a separate layer.

Figure 19.12. When the base color is placed on a separate layer below the linework, the gray edges of the original linework are maintained. This keeps the crisp and smooth linework that was imported from the PDF intact.

The second reason to keep the base color on a separate layer is for selecting colors later in the drawing. One of the disadvantages of using the Paint Bucket technique is that it is more difficult to change the colors of the drawing once they are set. If the Paint Bucket technique is used, it is best to keep each different color on a separate base color layer. This will make it easier to select the colors later. To see how to change the color of a base color area using the Paint Bucket method, consider the following example.

1. The single Groundplane BASE COLOR layer from the previous example has been repainted as two separate layers. The green color is on the GRASS base color layer and the gray area is on the SIDEWALK base color layer.

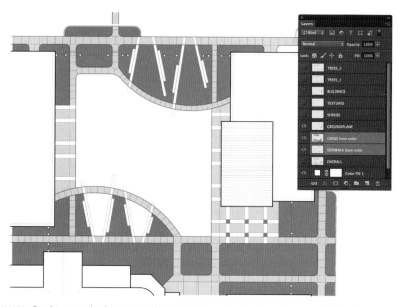

Figure 19.13. For this example, the green and gray areas of the drawing have been repainted onto separate layers.

2. Instead of being repainted, the layers could have been separated by using the Magic Wand tool, selecting each color, and using **Layer > New > Layer Via Cut**. Provided the selection is accurate, this will put the selected color on a new layer. With this method, each color would need to be selected this way and cut to a new layer individually.

3. To change the color of one of the base color layers, begin by selecting all of the pixels on that layer. This can be accomplished by Ctrl+clicking (Windows) or Cmd+clicking (Mac) on the Layer icon in the Layers palette.

4. Once the pixels on that layer are selected, choose a new color using the Color Picker. This new color will be painted into the selection using the Paint Bucket tool. Once the color is selected, click in the selection area with the Paint Bucket tool. Alt+Backspace (Windows) or Option+Delete (Mac) is another method to fill a selection with the foreground color.

5. The colors can also be changed using the Hue/Saturation adjustments instead of replacing the color with the Paint Bucket tool. Once the pixels are selected, open **Image** > **Adjustments** > **Hue/Saturation**, and adjust the color using the Hue/Saturation dialog box.

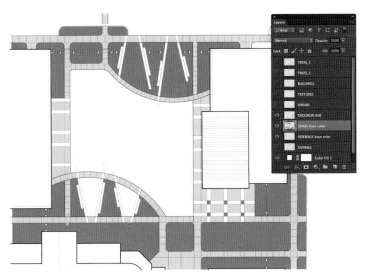

Figure 19.14. Ctrl+clicking (Windows) or Cmd+clicking (Mac) on the Layer icon will select all of the pixels on that layer.

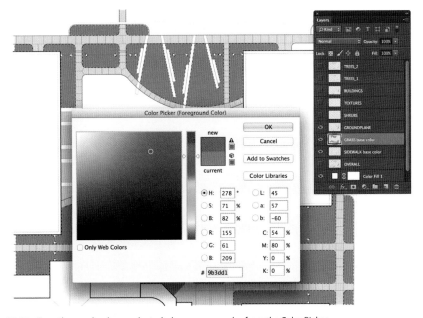

Figure 19.15. Once the area has been selected, choose a new color from the Color Picker.

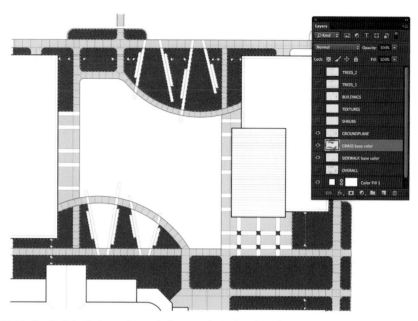

Figure 19.16. Use the Paint Bucket tool to apply the new color in the selected area. The new color will replace the old color.

Technique 2: Applying Color Using Adjustment Layers

A more effective technique is to use adjustment layers to apply the base color. Adjustment layers allow the colors to be changed easily; more importantly, the results of the color changes are displayed interactively on the screen. Changing colors using the Paint Bucket method requires choosing a color, applying it, and then examining the results. With the Adjustment Layer method, as the colors are changed they are instantly reflected in the drawing. This makes selecting colors that work well together much easier.

Using adjustment layers is similar to using the Paint Bucket tool to apply base color. However, instead of using the Paint Bucket tool to directly paint the color to the selected area, the Magic Wand tool is used to select the area first. When a Solid Color adjustment layer is applied, the selection becomes a mask for the adjustment layer. To understand how to apply base color using adjustment layers, consider the following example.

1. As in the earlier example using the Paint Bucket tool, start by isolating one of the line-work layers.
2. If a TEMP layer is needed to close areas of the drawing, create that layer and paint the areas needed to close the lines. See Steps 7 through 9 in the discussion under "Technique 1: Applying Color with the Paint Bucket Tool" for details on this operation.

3. Using the Magic Wand tool, select all areas of the drawing that will have the same base color applied.

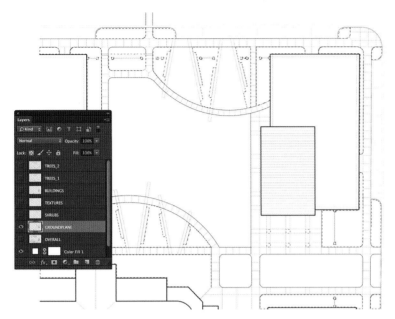

Figure 19.17. Begin the process by isolating one of the linework layers. It is usually more effective to work from the ground plane up. Select all areas of the drawing that will receive the same color. In this example, all of the areas that have groundcover have been selected. To select multiple areas with the Magic Wand tool, hold the Shift key while clicking in multiple areas.

4. From the bottom of the Layers palette, select the New Adjustment Layer icon. It is the half-white, half-black circle. A new adjustment layer can also be created by selecting **Layer > New Adjustment Layer**.
5. From the Adjustment Layers list, choose Solid Color. The Color Picker will appear. Choose a color for the area from the Color Picker. A new Color Fill layer will be created and added to the layer stack.
6. (The icons in the Layers palette were enlarged to aid this demonstration. To do this, use the Layers Palette menu and select Palette Options.) The Color Fill layer has two items: an icon that represents the color of the fill and an icon that represents the mask. The first icon represents "what" is happening on the layer (i.e., a solid green color is being applied). The second icon represents "where" the green color is being applied (i.e., to the white areas in the mask).
7. To change the color of the adjustment layer, double-click the green icon. The Color Picker will appear. Adjust the color in the Color Picker and it will be reflected on the drawing.

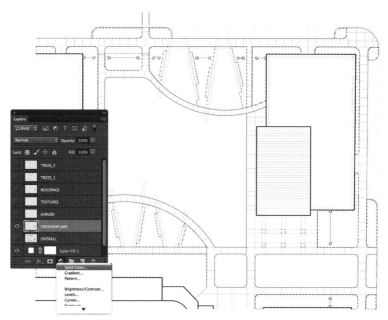

Figure 19.18. Create a new adjustment layer from the icon in the lower portion of the Layers palette. A list will pop up indicating the range of adjustments that can be made to the drawing.

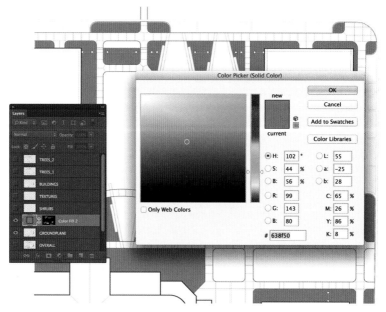

Figure 19.19. Choose a Solid Color adjustment layer from the options. This will apply a solid color to the areas of the drawing that are selected. A new Color Fill layer will appear in the Layers palette.

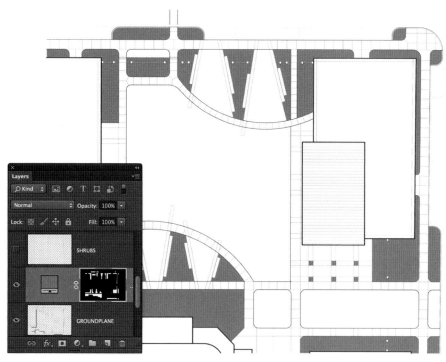

Figure 19.20. The adjustment layer has two icons. The first represents "what" is happening on the layer and the second represents "where" it is happening.

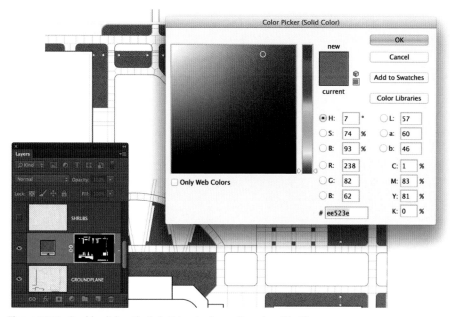

Figure 19.21. Double-click on the "what" icon to change the color of the fill.

If an area needs to be added to the adjustment layer, the mask must be altered. In this example, another area needs to be painted green. Acquiring this skill is critical if this technique is to be used to apply base color. The technique is relatively straightforward; however, attention needs to be paid to the details of this process during the first couple of attempts. The following steps cover the process in detail.

1. Click the Mask icon in the Color Fill layer. The foreground and background colors will change to black and white, or a version of gray, depending on the colors currently chosen. Remember that painting white will take away the mask and painting black will restore the mask. In other words, where white is painted, the green will show. Where black is painted, the green will go away.
2. With the Magic Wand tool, select an area of the drawing to be added to the selection.
3. Using the Paint Bucket tool or the Paint Brush tool, color the selected area white. This will "open" that area of the mask, allowing the green Solid Color adjustment to show through.
4. To remove an area of green from the layer, select an area and paint it black.

To complete the drawing, continue to create all of the base color layers for the ground plane. Each base color will be on its own layer with all of the base colors below the linework. The final colors do not need to be completely determined at this point. The advantage of this technique is that it will be easy to adjust the colors once all of the colors are on the drawing.

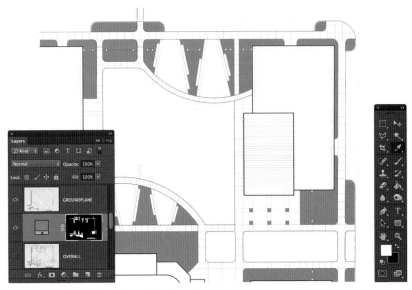

Figure 19.22. Click the Mask icon to alter the mask.

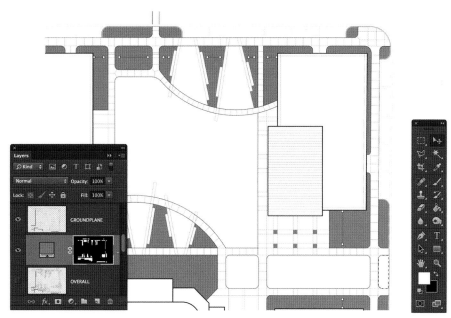

Figure 19.23. Use the Magic Wand to select the area to be "opened" in the mask.

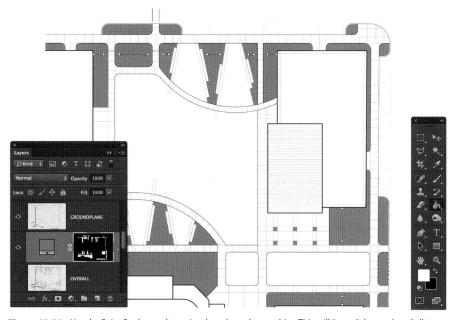

Figure 19.24. Use the Paint Bucket tool to paint the selected area white. This will "open" the mask and allow the green color to show through. The newly painted white area will be visible in the Mask icon on the Layers palette.

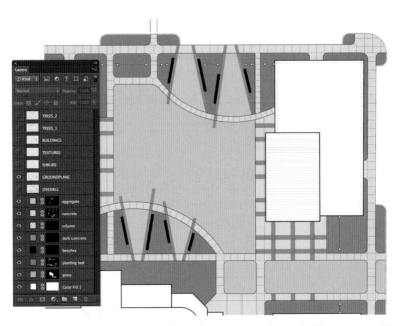

Figure 19.25. Continue to complete the base color for the ground plane. Each base color should be on a separate layer. This will make it easy to change the colors at the end of the drawing.

To complete the base color application, isolate another linework layer from the drawing and apply color to that layer. One of the advantages of separating linework onto different layers is that complex selections can often be made more easily if the linework is isolated from the rest of the drawing. Imagine how many areas would require a Magic Wand selection if all of the linework were on a single layer. Every area on the ground plane that is intersected by the trees above or by other linework in the drawing would have to either be redrawn with a Selection tool, or every area would need to be clicked.

There is another technique that allows closed objects to be selected quickly. Consider the following example.

1. Isolate the Trees linework layer.
2. Using the Magic Wand tool, click in the whitespace outside the Tree linework. Select everything except the inner area of the trees.
3. To Invert the selection, choose **Select > Inverse**. This will select the inner areas of the trees. Add a Solid Color adjustment layer to color the trees.

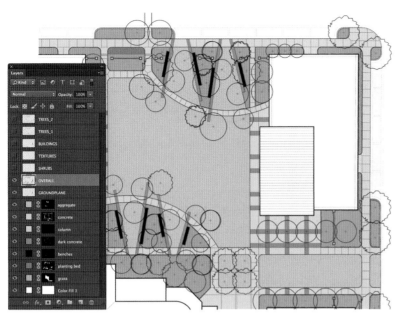

Figure 19.26. The advantages of separating the linework onto different layers become more obvious when all the linework is visible.

Figure 19.27. To begin another technique for selecting multiple items, isolate the Trees layer by making all other linework invisible.

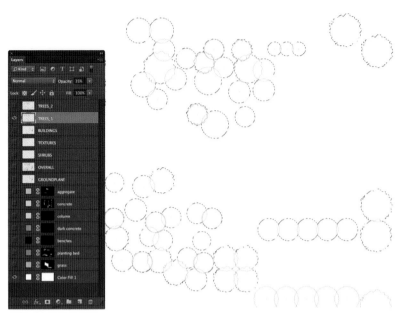

Figure 19.28. Select the whitespace outside of the trees. The "marching ants" selection box runs along the edge of the drawing.

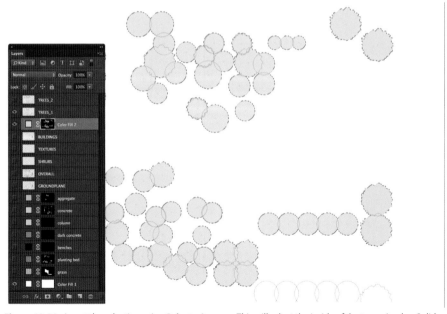

Figure 19.29. Invert the selection using **Select > Inverse**. This will select the inside of the trees. Apply a Solid Color adjustment layer to the selection.

4. The interior area of the grove of trees in the bottom portion of the drawing has the interior of the grove filled in. To remove this area from the selection, click the Mask icon in the Color Fill Trees layer. Use the Magic Wand tool to select the interior of the grove. Use the Paint Bucket tool to paint this area black.

Figure 19.30. With the Magic Wand tool, select the area to remove from the selection.

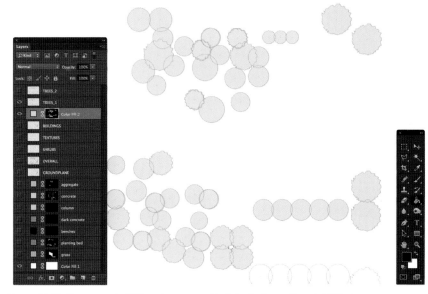

Figure 19.31. To remove the fill from the area, use the Paint Bucket tool to paint it black.

5. The same technique can be used to color the shrubs.

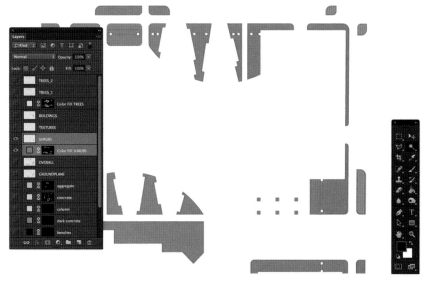

Figure 19.32. The shrubs can be colored using the same selection technique.

213

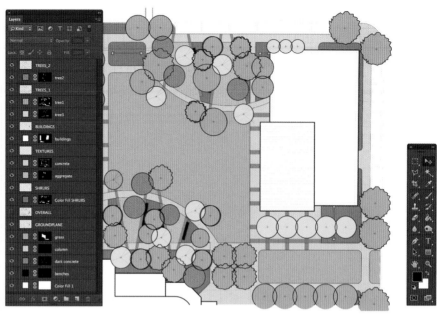

Figure 19.33. Once all of the base colors have been applied, the layer order and layer transparency need to be adjusted to make the drawing legible. At this point, double-clicking a base color adjustment layer can easily change the colors of the drawing.

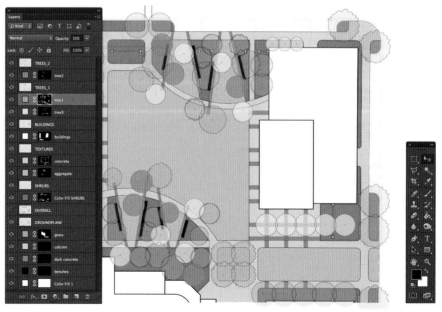

Figure 19.34. The layer order and layer transparency can be adjusted to make the drawing more legible.

The process of applying the base color to all areas of the drawing continues until all the linework has at least one base color layer. Once all of the base colors have been applied, the colors need to be adjusted, the layers need to be ordered, and the transparency needs to be adjusted to make the drawing more legible.

To adjust the transparency of the layers, select the base color layer from the layer stack. In this example, the trees are the most obvious elements that need to be more transparent. Typically, the linework layers will not be made transparent. Once the tree layers are made more transparent, the drawing will be ready to add shading, textures, and other elements that will add to the character of the rendering.

Saving Channels

If the base colors are separated onto different layers it is easy to recall the selection at any time. In essence, the layer is also saving the selection. However, it is also possible to save selections using channels. Channels provide more flexibility and more information when necessary. With channels, selections from several different layers can be saved together. A channel can translate a selection into 256 levels represented as grays from white (fully selected) to black (unselected), similar to a mask. This allows complex selections to be saved that can apply effects or procedures in a varied or gradated manner.

1. To save a channel from a selection, using one of your Selection tools (the Lasso, the Marquee), right-click within the selection and choose Save Selection. A dialog box will appear that will give you several options; the first option lets you designate the drawing in which to save the selection.
2. The selection can be saved to another drawing if necessary, or a channel can be created in the current drawing. Next, you can choose to create a new channel, create a layer mask, or add, subtract, or intersect it with an existing channel. After deciding how to create the mask, click OK and the new channel will be created. If a new channel is created, it will be added to the Channels tab; if a layer mask is created, it will appear on the specified label.

Figure 19.35. The Channel palette.

In a manner similar to the way solid fills were created, the Gradient tool can be used to create gradated fills. The Gradient tool is on the same button as the Paint Bucket tool. In order to apply a gradient, a selection must first be created so the gradient can be applied within it. The default gradient is a linear gradient and uses the foreground and background colors as the basis for the gradient. The Gradient toolbar allows you to select the type of gradient: linear, radial, angle, reflected, and diamond. Each of the gradients can be applied by clicking the center point of the gradient and dragging it to specify the length and direction along which the gradient changes.

Figure 19.36. Gradated black-and-white selection as a channel.

Chapter 20
Shading Techniques

Shading depicts a variety of conditions in landscape illustrations, particularly light and depth. In order to properly shade a drawing, it is necessary to understand the vertical height of elements, as well as the source and direction of the light. The process of shading a plan can shed light on design decisions and how elements will react with one another spatially. Shading also communicates depth and volume, as well as the material quality of a surface or element.

Shading in Photoshop is accomplished using previous or saved fills and can be done manually with brushes or automated with strokes. The following methods focus on speed while maintaining accuracy when illustrating cast shadows and highlights.

Selecting Fills

Shading is applied using fills or saved selections as masks. This provides a template that allows the shading to be applied quickly. An entire layer can be selected by holding down the Ctrl key and clicking (Ctrl+click) on the Layer thumbnail in the Layers palette. This creates a selection based on the pixels that exist on that layer. If color fills are organized on layers, it is important that the layer containing the fill is not altered during the rendering process. The fill is then used as the selection every time that area needs to be isolated. It is also possible to add or subtract from the selection using multiple layers—use Alt+Ctrl+click to add and Shift+Ctrl+click to subtract from another layer. Using Ctrl+click to select the pixels on a layer is an extremely versatile technique that preserves layer transparency, allowing extremely complex selections to be created. This method works well if a color fill already defines a space within the drawing. Because the color fill is already using memory in the drawing, it does not require another channel or work path to redefine that space.

In order to make a selection based on a layer's pixels, you can do the following:

1. Highlight the layer that contains the pixels to be selected.
2. Ctrl+click on the Layer thumbnail to select the pixels on the current layer.
3. To add to the selection, simply hold down the Shift key and press the Ctrl key (Shift+Ctrl) when clicking on the thumbnail. To subtract from the selection, hold down the Alt key and press Ctrl (Alt+Ctrl) when clicking on the thumbnail.

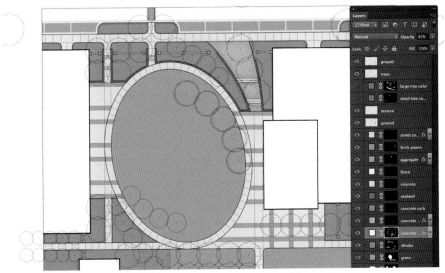

Figure 20.1. The Layer thumbnail is to the left and contains a preview of the layer's contents.

Figure 20.2. When Ctrl+Alt or Ctrl+Shift are performed, a selection box with either a minus sign or a plus sign will appear when the cursor hovers over the Layer thumbnail.

Saving Selections and Manual Shading

These selections can also be saved using two Photoshop tools: *channels* and *paths*. In order to create a new channel, first create a selection.

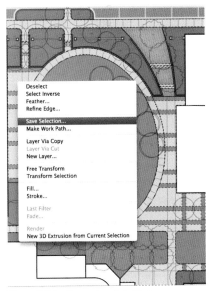

1. The selection can be made using any Photoshop method. After a selection is made, switch to one of the Selection tools in the toolbar (Lasso, Marquee, Magic Wand) and right-click in the selection on the canvas.
2. From the Context menu, select Save Selection (**Select > Save Selection**) and give the selection a descriptive name.
3. This creates a new channel that is added to the current channels on the Channel palette.
4. The channel will be added below the already existing channels in the Channel palette. Depending on the color mode for the current drawing, the channels will be displayed as either an RGB composite with individual Red, Green, and Blue channels or a CMYK composite with individual Cyan, Magenta, Yellow, and Black channels, with the saved selections as channels below.

Figure 20.3. Choose Save Selection.

Figure 20.4. The saved channel appears below the existing channels.

Figure 20.5. The Selection button at the bottom of the Channel palette.

Figure 20.6. Save the work path and access it through the Paths palette.

Figure 20.7. Reactivate the selection with the Selection button.

5. Channels work well when a color fill is not needed to define an area but a mask is necessary to define a space.

6. A channel will use less memory in an illustration because it is defined with shades of gray rather than RGB values. The selection can be recalled by Ctrl+clicking the Channel thumbnail or by selecting the channel and clicking the Selection button at the bottom of the Channel palette.

Work paths can also be used to define a selection, but they do not preserve layer transparency like layers or channels. The work path is a vector approximation of the current selection.

1. To create a work path, make a selection, switch to one of the Selection tools in the toolbar (Lasso, Marquee, Magic Wand), and right-click in the selection.

2. From the Context menu, select Save Work Path and choose a resolution to approximate the vector path. The work path will be saved in the Paths palette, and the path can be activated by selecting it in the Paths palette.

3. The selection for that path can be activated using the Selection button at the bottom of the palette.

Paths are versatile in that they are vector interpretations; this means that they can be edited using the vector-editing tools, such as the Pen, and can be used to define strokes that will be used to shade edges of spaces.

To begin shading, it is important to determine the source of light and the direction it will be casting shadows. Typically, for site renderings the light source is in the upper-left or upper-right corner and casts light to the lower-right or lower-left corner. It is also important to determine relationships between the elements and the ground plane; shadows and shading allow the viewer to determine topography and height. For example, shadows cast from objects must attach themselves to the object footprint if the object rests on the ground; otherwise, the object will float above the ground plane. Likewise, tree canopies and building awnings or overhangs must cast a detached shadow the length of which corresponds to the object's height. Shadow lengths are proportional and specific to each rendering. This means that if a building has a specific shadow length and a tree rendered next to that building is twice as tall, the shadow should also be twice as long. In some cases where shading is applied to the ground plane, the shading may not represent specific shadow lengths but instead will be used to illustrate depth; therefore, artistic license can be exercised when creating shaded surfaces.

To apply shading to an area, it is best to make a selection using one of the previously described methods. For example:

1. Ctrl+click the fill layer in the Layers palette; this creates a selection based on the pixels on the Fill layer.

2. Select the Brush tool and then adjust the size and hardness, or select a brush preset for the scale and texture of the current area to be shaded.

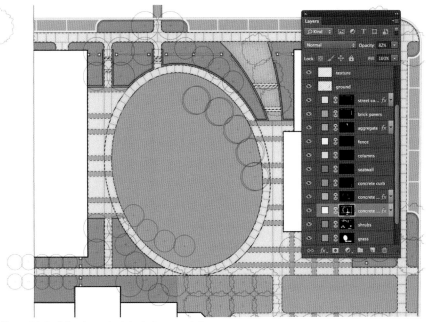

Figure 20.8. Select layer pixels in the Layers palette.

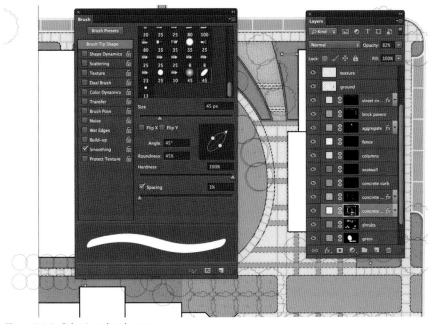

Figure 20.9. Selecting a brush preset.

3. A very fast way to begin shading an area once the Brush tool has been selected is to use the Eyedropper. Hold down the Alt key, which will change the Brush tool to the Eyedropper temporarily. Using the temporary Eyedropper, sample the fill color and then double-click the foreground color swatch to bring up the Color Picker. Select a saturation and brightness level that is much darker than the current color; the color should be darker than the desired shading effect.

4. Create a new layer and make that layer active. Using the Paint Brush tool, quickly trace the edges of the area to be shaded, applying shading to simulate light falling on the surface, most typically darkening the southeastern edge of lower areas. How the shading is applied is dependent on the surface being rendered and the style of illustration.

5. The shading will be very dark at this point and require adjustment. Because the shading was applied with a color that was darker than necessary, the opacity can be used to adjust the shading in order to get the desired effect. As the rendering progresses, the shading layers can be readjusted to make them lighter or darker. The layers can also be adjusted after printing if the shading is not dark enough or is too intense.

6. Successive layers of shading are used to further refine the shading. The first pass should lay down a field of shading, with successive passes further defining site features. The smaller brush sizes can be used to add detail and clarity.

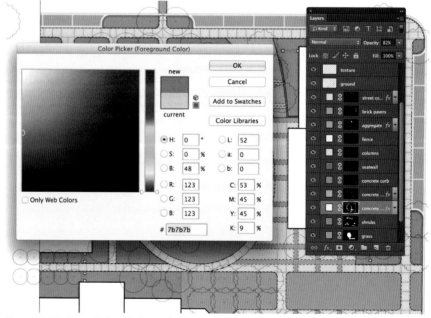

Figure 20.10. Select shade with the Eyedropper and make it darker than the intended final result.

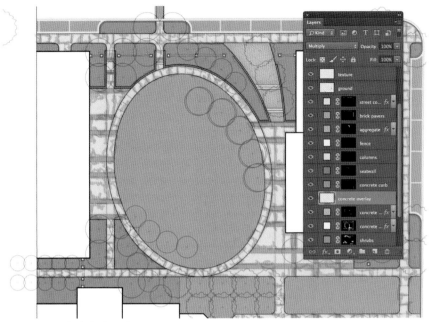

Figure 20.11. Shaded edges of area.

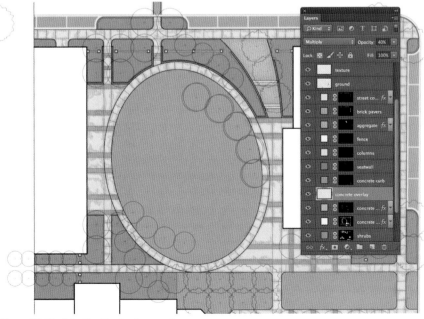

Figure 20.12. Adjusting the shading opacity.

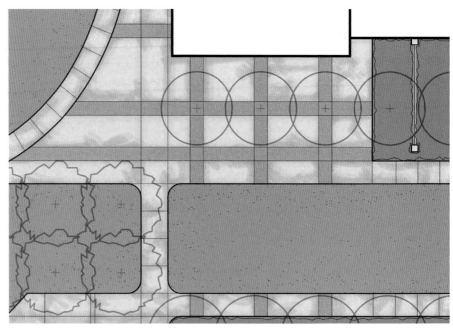

Figure 20.13. Successive shading passes.

Automating the Shading of Edges

The process of shading a plan adds richness and depth, but in some cases the edges to be shaded can be very large—for example, a master-plan with many miles of roadways and parking. Applying shading to all the edges would be extremely time-consuming. To save time and allow experimentation, a single brush stroke can be applied to an entire edge automatically.

1. Create a selection around the area to be shaded (either use a saved selection or simply Ctrl+click the Layer thumbnail to select the pixels).

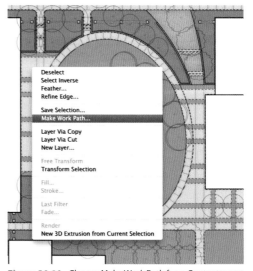

Figure 20.14. Choose Make Work Path from Context menu.

2. Make sure that one of the Selection tools is active (Lasso, Magic Wand, Marquee), right-click within the selection, and choose Make Work Path.

3. Select the Paint Brush tool, and then select a brush preset or create a new brush using the Brush palette. The purpose is to create a brush that will render a random edge rather than a perfectly aligned stroke. A random edge can be generated using the brush dynamics and irregular brush tip shapes.

4. Choose the color desired for shading the edges, create a new layer, and make it active. As explained previously, the color should be darker than the desired shading.

5. Open the Paths palette and make the previously saved path the active path. Press the Selection button at the bottom of the Paths palette. This will make a selection from the current path and keep the shading that is applied next within the desired area.

6. Switch to the Pen tool and right-click on the canvas. Select Stroke from the context menu, and then select Brush in the next dialog box to apply the current Brush settings to the stroke.

7. The edge of the work path should be shaded. Adjust the layer opacity in the Layers palette to tone down the shading effect. Deselect the current area using Ctrl+D. If the results are not quite right, delete the Shading layer, adjust the brush and color, and try again.

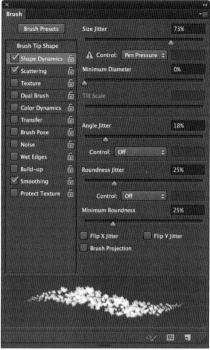

Figure 20.15. The Brush Stroke is selected to shade the edges.

Large areas can be shaded using layer effects such as Drop Shadow, Bevel, and Emboss. This is a very quick method to create a shading effect, but it lacks the richness of using a brush that utilizes the brush's ability to adjust spacing, scatter, and create patterns. See Chapter 22: Brushes for more information on creating custom brushes.

Figure 20.16. The path is selected in the Paths palette.

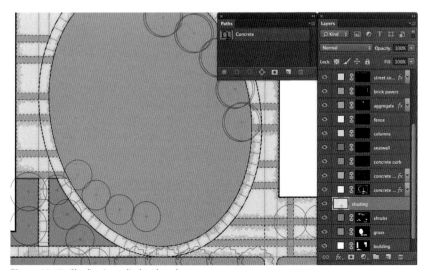

Figure 20.17. Shading is applied to the edges.

Chapter 21
Creating Textures

Landscape renderings require a range of textures to express the relationships between materials, depths, and surfaces. These relationships often have ambiguous boundaries with layered materials requiring versatile approaches to atypical conditions. Analog media has traditionally approached texturing as a layered system, applying media in order to develop mixes of color or intensity in shading. Digital media uses similar methods that also create relationships between layers with screening modes and opens the possibility to edit the texturing throughout the illustration process.

Creating a Texture from an Existing Photograph

Creating textures in Photoshop is accomplished through a variety of tools. Using images obtained from site photography or aerial imagery is an obvious method to quickly create large areas of texture. This type of texture can be abstracted in order to cover a large area of the site to convey a surface's material. When an image is used, it is important that either the scale of the texture is correct or that the image is altered enough that the material scale is not discernable. The following technique explains how this might be applied.

Figure 21.1. This mowed grass pattern in the image will be used as a texture to represent the grass within the site plan.

1. With the Photoshop rendering file open, open the file that will be used for the texture. Arrange the workspace windows so that they are next to one another, and use the Move tool to drag the image into the illustration.
2. Position the image in the area where the texture will be applied. In many cases, the image can be cut and duplicated to distribute the texture evenly across the desired area. After it has been positioned, turn off the Texture layer in the Layers palette.
3. Make a selection that represents the area where the texture will be applied. If a base color has already been applied, this can be done using any of the Selection tools or by Ctrl+clicking the Layer thumbnail.
4. At this point, turn the Texture layer back on and make it the Active layer. Create a new *layer mask* using the button at the bottom of the Layers palette. This will create a mask based on the selection that was just made. The selected area will be visible and the unselected areas will be masked. Masks are a good way to create boundaries for textures. Because they don't actually delete pixels, it is possible to readjust the texture position or to change the mask if necessary.

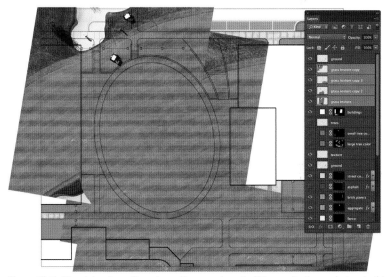

Figure 21.2. The picture is positioned over the area where it will be used in the rendering. In this scenario, the image was duplicated and cut to cover a larger area with the same pattern.

5. In order to adjust the position of the texture, it is necessary to unlink the image from the mask. This can be accomplished by clicking the Link button between the Layer thumbnail and the layer mask in the Layers palette. Select the Layer thumbnail; using the Move tool, it is now possible to move the Texture layer in order to reposition it.
6. The Texture layer can be altered using filters, adjustment layers, and blending options. The Blur filter is a useful tool in abstracting the texture of site photography when applied to a plan rendering.

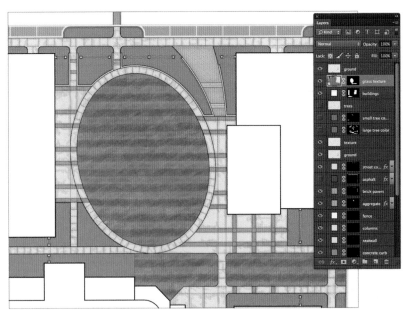

Figure 21.3. A layer mask is created to mask the image within the desired area.

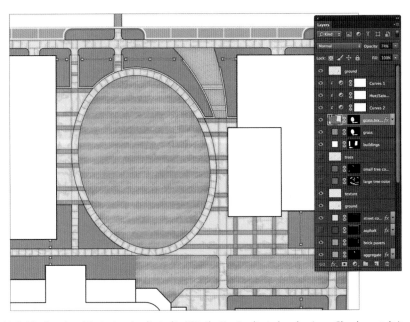

Figure 21.4. The Opacity of the texture is adjusted to 74%, the Hue is adjusted, and an Inner Glow layer style is added.

Creating a Seamless Pattern Using the Offset Filter

Patterns are helpful when creating a large field of repeating texture. Finding an image that represents the field is often difficult; however, if a small area is available, a pattern can be built. If the image is not evenly shaded, the result is a noticeable tiling effect. Because an evenly lit image is needed to create a seamless pattern, adjustments need to be made to remove any variations in lighting. This can be accomplished using the following method.

1. Open the file that will be used to create the pattern. Click **Select Image > Image Size** and determine the image's size. The image size must be divisible by 2 for the next step. The image size can be adjusted directly in the Image Size dialog box: either go up or down 1 pixel to make the number of pixels an even number. If the height and width are not the same, make note of the smallest dimension and close the Image Size dialog box by clicking OK.

Figure 21.5. The photo used to create a pattern.

Figure 21.6. When tiled, the photo displays noticeable seams.

2. Choose **Select Image > Canvas Size** and adjust the canvas size so that the longer dimension equals the short dimension. This will crop off a portion of the image, so be sure you select the side you want to crop using the dialog box and then click OK. This will create an image that is perfectly square and divisible by 2.

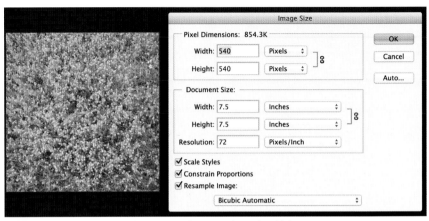

Figure 21.7. The photo is resized to a square dimension that is divisible by 2.

3. Use the Offset filter to offset the image. Choose **Select Filter > Other > Offset**. In the dialog box, enter the number of pixels to offset in the horizontal and vertical directions—this will be half the image size. Make sure that Wrap Around is selected and click OK. The image will be offset by half, which will push the image up and to the right and then wrap the pixels around to meet in the middle, effectively putting the edges into the center of the image.

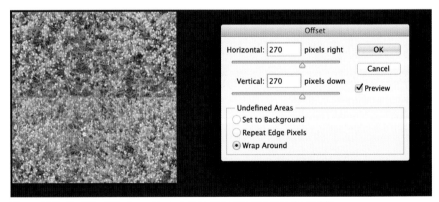

Figure 21.8. The Offset filter is used to push the edges of the image to the middle.

Figure 21.9. The Clone Stamp tool can be used to match the edges in the middle. When they are matched, use the Offset filter again to put the edges back to their original positions.

4. Use the Clone Stamp tool to even out the center edges, creating a smoothly shaded texture. When using the Clone Stamp tool, hold down Alt and click to select the area to be sampled. Release Alt and the next click will determine where the pixels will be painted. It is best to use longer strokes if possible to avoid a repeating pattern.

5. After the edges have been smoothed, reapply the same Offset filter to move the edges back to the center. If the center has been altered, the Clone Stamp tool can be used again to finish smoothing—just be careful not to alter the edges.

6. Save this texture as a new file, so that it can be used again.

Figure 21.10. The final texture tiles are smoother than in the original version.

Creating the Pattern and Applying It to the Rendering

A pattern can be created from any image with the Define Pattern command, and that pattern can be applied with the Paint Bucket, Pattern Stamp, or Pattern Overlay layer style.

1. Once the pattern is created, it cannot be edited, so it is important to scale the image for the current rendering. Drag the newly created, seamless pattern into the rendering and scale it using the Free Transform tool (Ctrl+T). If the pattern will be used as a pattern overlay, this step can be skipped and the pattern can be created directly from the source file.

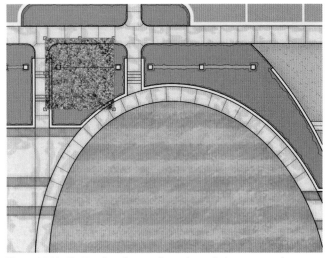

Figure 21.11. The Free Transform tool is used to scale the texture to the correct size in the image.

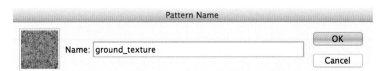

Figure 21.12. When creating the pattern, enter an appropriate name to identify the swatch.

2. Select the texture by drawing a square marquee over the texture. Make sure the Texture layer is above all the other layers. Select **Edit > Define Pattern**, and name the pattern in the dialog box that appears. The pattern will be stored in Photoshop's default Pattern Library. The Texture layer can be deleted or turned off at this point.

Three basic methods can be used to apply the pattern to the rendering: the Paint Bucket method, the Pattern Stamp method, and the Pattern Overlay method.

Paint Bucket and Pattern Stamp

The Paint Bucket and Pattern brush are two familiar tools that can also apply patterns. These tools provide all of their normal functionality, but instead of applying color will apply the selected pattern to the rendering.

Figure 21.13. Choose Pattern from the Paint Bucket pull-down list.

1. Select the Paint Bucket tool (press G or Shift+G to change from the gradient to the Paint Bucket). From the pull-down on the top toolbar next to the Paint Bucket icon, choose Pattern as the fill type.
2. Select the pattern to use for the fill by clicking on the swatch next to the pull-down. The Paint Bucket tool can now be used to fill areas with the selected pattern. Remember to make a selection before filling unless a pixel boundary is available, and remember to put the pattern on a new layer.

Figure 21.14. The texture is blended with the green base color using Layer Opacity for shading.

The Pattern Stamp works in a similar method to the Paint Bucket. The pattern type can be specified in the toolbar, and the pattern can be painted into the illustration. This method is extremely useful to touch up areas of the rendering that were not filled properly with the Paint Bucket. Because the Pattern Stamp is a brush-based tool, it is also possible to use any of the brushes or even define a new brush to apply the pattern.

Pattern Overlay

Using a Pattern Overlay layer style is an extremely versatile method for applying patterns. A layer effect is applied to a layer and affects every pixel on that layer; the pattern overlay will apply the pattern to all of the pixels on the layer. The areas need to be filled or painted with a base color before the Pattern Overlay layer style is applied.

1. Select the layer that contains the pixels for the Pattern Overlay effect. Apply a new Pattern Overlay style by clicking the *fx* button at the bottom of the Layers palette and selecting Pattern Overlay.
2. The Layer Style dialog box will appear with the pattern overlay applied. The pattern can be selected from the pattern swatches. There are settings to adjust the Blend mode and Opacity; they will affect the pattern overlay in relation to the pixels on the current layer. The texture can also be scaled at this point; it is best not to scale the texture up because pixelation can occur if the scale is increased beyond 200%. After selecting and adjusting the pattern, click OK.

Figure 21.15. Add a new Pattern Overlay style from the Layers palette.

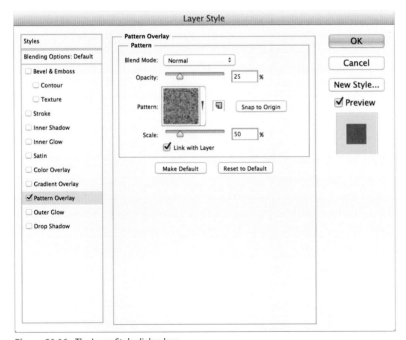

Figure 21.16. The Layer Style dialog box.

3. Layer styles are fully adjustable. To make an adjustment, double-click on the layer style in the Layers palette and the Layer Style dialog box will appear. Click on the layer style to make it Active, and make the necessary adjustments.

After the Pattern Overlay style is applied, the layer's overall opacity can be adjusted in the Layers palette. Using the Fill adjustment in the Layers palette, it is possible to adjust the application of only the layer styles; doing so will affect all of the layer styles that are currently applied to the selected layer.

Managing Patterns

Patterns can be managed using the Preset Manager (**Edit > Preset Manager**). The Preset Manager provides access to presets that are applied to a variety of tools. The Patterns preset is available in the pull-down; from this menu, it is possible to load new patterns from PAT files (.pat) or save selected patterns to a new PAT file. This is a good way to share patterns or load patterns from others.

Texturing with Filters

It is also possible to create texturing using a variety of other techniques that do not involve a source image. This typically involves using one of the filters in order to generate a texture and then manipulating the result. Filters change the appearance of the image and are applied to the current layer or selection within a layer. Filters work well because they can cover a large area with texture and do not require a pattern. Because the filters are applied based on a mathematical formula, the results are random and will not create tiling effects. In order to create a texture with a filter, consider the following example:

1. Select the layer that contains the pixels to which the filter will be applied. Duplicate the layer and make the duplicated layer Active. Select **Filter>Filter Gallery**. Within the Filter Gallery, select Grain from the Texture menu. From the Grain dialog box, change the intensity to 77, the contrast to 59, and the Grain Type to Clumped. Adjust the settings beyond the desired effect. When finished, press OK. This applies the Grain filter to a new duplicate layer.
2. The opacity of this layer can be adjusted to blend it with the original layer. By applying the Grain filter heavier than necessary, the effect can be adjusted using the Layers Opacity; this allows flexibility as the illustration progresses.
3. It is also possible to use screening modes, such as Screen or Multiply, for the layer. The normal screening mode does not interact with the layer below, but Screen and Multiply do—by either lightening or darkening pixels, respectively.

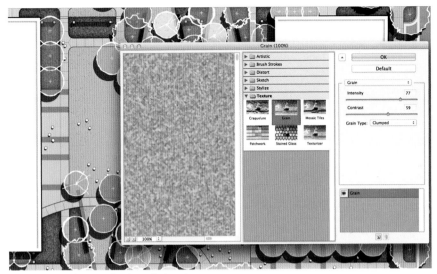

Figure 21.17. The Grain filter is applied to a layer to create a texture.

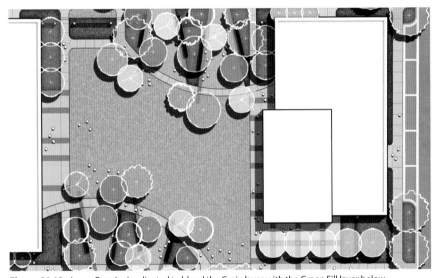

Figure 21.18. Layer Opacity is adjusted to blend the Grain layer with the Green Fill layer below.

4. It is also possible to add a mask to a layer in order to change the effect of the filter. This can make the filter heavier in some areas or remove it completely from others. To add the mask, select the layer and click Add Mask at the bottom of the Layers palette. If nothing is selected, the mask will be added as a completely white mask, meaning that everything is visible. If a selection is in place, it will create a mask for the selected area. Make the mask Active by selecting it, and paint black to mask areas or white to

unmask them. It is also possible to use shades of gray to make other areas partially transparent—this technique is similar to a feathering effect.

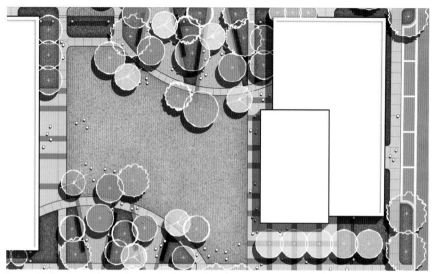

Figure 21.19. Several layers of grain, shading, and masks are used to create shaded edges.

A filter can also be altered by adding another filter—for example, pixels modified by the Noise filter can be modified by a second, third, or fourth filter. The Grain Filter and the Noise filter are related, but different. This can create interesting effects that are much more customized for specific situations.

Chapter 22
Brushes

The Brush tool is one of the most powerful tools for creating renderings in Photoshop. Brushes allow a more direct contact with the drawing and can create textures and nuances that other techniques cannot. Mastering the use of brushes opens a range of possibilities for rendering in Photoshop. A wide selection of predefined brushes come standard in Photoshop; numerous brushes can be downloaded from the Internet.

Brushes can also be created from scratch within Photoshop. Creating custom brushes offers almost limitless control over the type of brush used in a drawing. Custom brushes can also be saved and used on future projects, allowing an office to create a palette of brushes that are standardized. Using the Tool Presets options allows standard office brushes to be saved using the same colors, sizes, and other options on different drawings by several different team members who might work on the same drawing.

Standard Brushes

To use a standard brush, choose the Brush tool from the Tools palette. The options for the Brush tool include a set of predefined brushes from which to choose. Most of these brushes have two standard settings that can be altered to make the brush have different effects. The first setting is the Pixel Diameter, which is simply the size of the brush. The second is the Hardness of the brush. This option affects how crisp the edge of the brush is. To create straight segments using the Brush tool, click on an area of the drawing, hold Shift, and click on another area of the drawing.

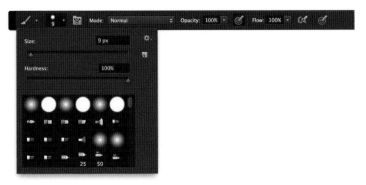

Figure 22.1. The standard options for most brushes are the Pixel Diameter and the Hardness of the brush.

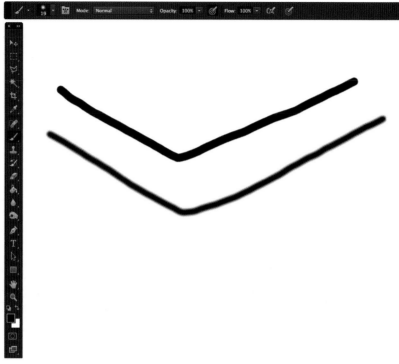

Figure 22.2. Both brushes in this figure are 19 pixels in diameter. A brush with the Hardness set to 100% was used to create the upper line. The lower line was created with a brush with the Hardness set to 0%.

Some predefined brushes, such as the Dune Grass brush, do not have an option for hardness. The settings for these brushes are controlled using the Brushes palette. The Brushes palette can be found under **Windows > Brushes**.

The Brushes palette has several options for adjusting the effects of the brush. Not all of the settings are important for general work in a design office. Only the critical and most useful settings will be covered in this section. The following example will demonstrate each section and how it affects the look of the brush.

Figure 22.3. Some predefined brushes, such as the Dune Grass brush, do not have an option for hardness.

1. The upper line painted in the example figure shows the initial, pre-defined settings of the Dune Grass brush. This is how the brush will look when it is first chosen. The upper line will remain the same throughout all of the examples as a reference point for comparing the changes.

2. The Brush Tip Shape option (the second option down on the list to the left of the Brushes palette) controls the spacing and the orientation of the brush. The spacing of the brush affects the density. The orientation affects the angle of the brush stroke.

3. The next option in the list is the Shape Dynamics. The *dynamic controls* of a brush control the randomness of the brush stroke. This creates the appearance of a random and natural pattern in the brush stroke and is useful for drawing materials. *Jitter* in this context has a similar meaning to "amount of randomness." The higher the Jitter setting, the more random the effect will appear. For example, the Size Jitter setting in the initial settings of this brush is set to 100%. That means that each "blade" of Dune Grass will have a random size, from very small to the full height of the brush as defined by the Pixel Dimensions. By setting the Size Jitter to 0%, all of the blades of the Dune Grass will be the same size.

Figure 22.4. The settings for these brushes are controlled using the Brushes palette.

Figure 22.5. The initial settings for the Dune Grass brush are shown in this figure. The upper line in all subsequent figures will have the initial settings shown for the upper line. This will allow comparisons to be made to the altered brush settings.

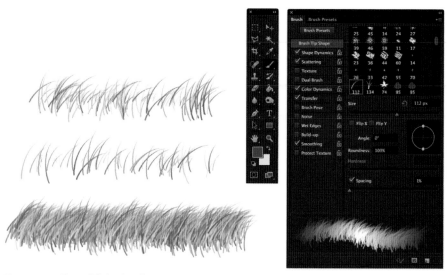

Figure 22.6. The middle line has the Spacing set to 72%; the lower line has the Spacing set to 1%.

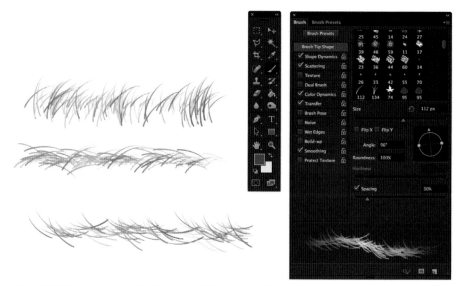

Figure 22.7. To change the angle of the brush, Click+drag the edge of the circle in the middle-right side of the Brushes palette or enter a value in the Angle box. The middle line has the angle changed to –42 degrees, and the lower line has the angle changed to 121 degrees.

4. The Angle Jitter controls the randomness of the angle at which the brush is rotated. In the Brush Tip Shape setting, the initial angle of the brush is set. In the Angle Jitter setting, the amount of random rotation is established.
5. The next option in the list is Scattering. Scattering controls how "loosely" the line is painted. A larger Scatter setting will spread out the blades of Dune Grass farther from the area where the line is painted.

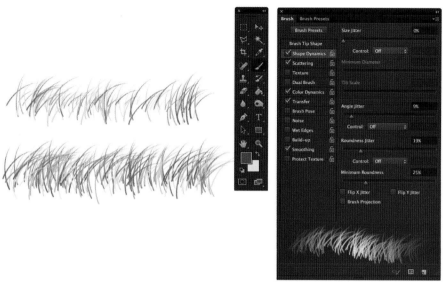

Figure 22.8. With the Size Jitter set to 0%, all of the "blades" of Dune Grass will be the same size. In the lower line, each element in the brush stroke is the same size; in the upper line, some elements are smaller than others.

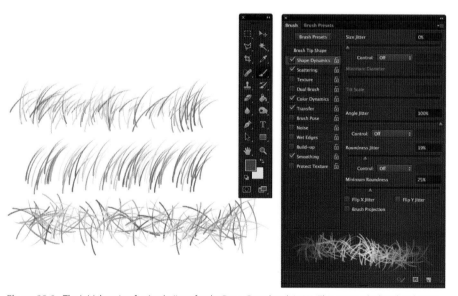

Figure 22.9. The initial setting for Angle Jitter for the Dune Grass brush is 9%. This causes the brush to be randomly rotated to within 9% of its standard angle. In the middle line, the Angle Jitter is set to 0%, preventing the brush from being randomly rotated at all. In the lower line, the Angle Jitter is set to 100%. At 100%, each blade of Dune Grass is randomly rotated between 0 and 360 degrees.

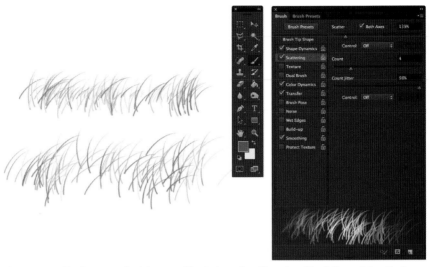

Figure 22.10. The Scatter setting is increased for the lower line. The painted line is "looser" than the line above.

6. The Count is how many blades of Dune Grass are painted each time the brush passes over an area. It is similar to setting the density of the brush with the Spacing option.
7. The Color Dynamics option controls the randomness of the brush color. The Foreground/Background Jitter determines how much the foreground color and background color are mixed. The foreground and background colors are set in the Tools palette.
8. The Hue Jitter, the Saturation Jitter, and the Brightness Jitter create random values for these three color settings.

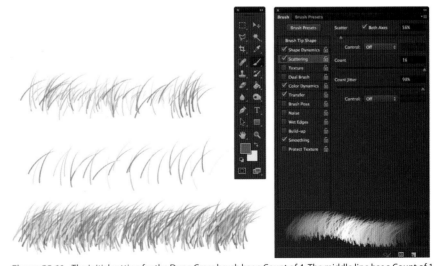

Figure 22.11. The initial setting for the Dune Grass brush has a Count of 4. The middle line has a Count of 1, which makes the brush less dense. The lower line has a Count of 16, which makes the brush denser.

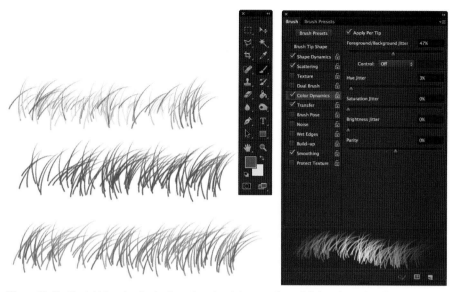

Figure 22.12. The initial setting for the Dune Grass brush is 100%. The middle line shows the effect of setting the Foreground/Background Jitter to 0%. This makes all of the blades of grass be the foreground color. The lower line has the Foreground/Background Jitter set to 47%, which mixes the foreground and background colors to a different degree.

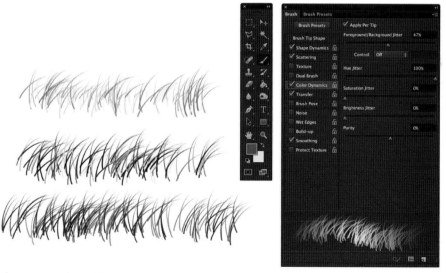

Figure 22.13. The middle line has all three color Jitters set at 100%. The lower line has the Hue Jitter set at 100%. This creates a random hue adjustment to each blade as it is drawn.

9. The Other Dynamics option offers one valuable setting: the Opacity Jitter. The Opacity Jitter randomly sets the opacity of each blade as it is being drawn.

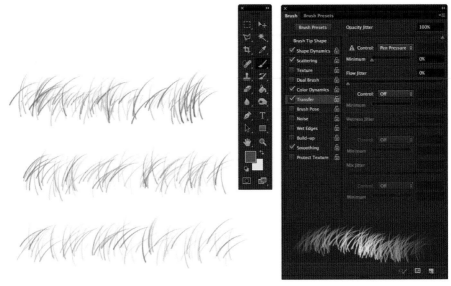

Figure 22.14. The middle line has the Opacity Jitter set to 50%. The lower line has the Opacity Jitter set to 100%. This creates a random transparency in the brush, which allows the brush to be blended with other brushes while painting.

Figure 22.15. The ground plane of this image was rendered using the Dune Grass brush.

Brushes can be used in a design drawing in a number of ways. Most often, Grass Brush or similar brush styles are used to render a ground plane. The ground plane in the following figure is rendered using the Dune Grass brush using multiple layers of brush strokes. The technique involves creating several layers of brush strokes, each with a slightly different color combination. Each layer is then set to a medium Opacity, around 50%, which allows the different layers of brush strokes to blend together.

Figure 22.16. Making several layers of brush strokes and setting the Opacity of each layer to 50% created the ground plane. This allows the different layers to blend together to create the overall effect.

Custom Brushes

Custom brushes are powerful tools that can be used to create a variety of effects. In essence, all of the predefined brushes are created in the same way that a custom brush is created. Each brush starts with a single element, or "brush tip." In the case of the Dune Grass brush, the brush tip is a single "blade" of grass. The brush tip is repeated as the brush is applied according to the settings in the Brushes palette, as shown in the previous examples within the Standard Brushes discussion. Consider the following example.

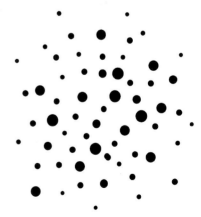

1. The Brush Tip can start out as either a single line or shape, or a combination of shapes. To create the brush, create a new file, choose a black brush, and draw the element.
2. Select the entire drawing by pressing Ctrl+A. Select Edit > Define Brush Preset from the menu. Name the brush.
3. Once the brush has been created, choose a color for the brush from the Color Picker. The brush can be used in various sizes.

Figure 22.17. Draw a pattern to create the Brush Tip. The Brush Tip must be drawn in black.

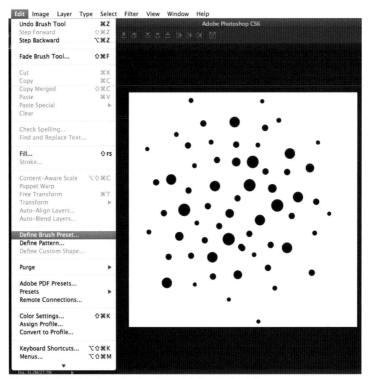

Figure 22.18. Select the entire drawing and define the Brush Preset.

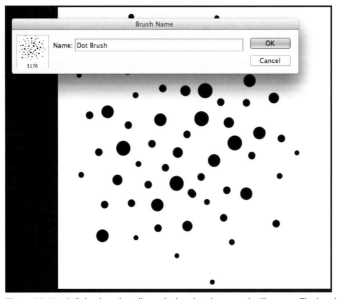

Figure 22.19. A dialog box that allows the brush to be named will appear. The brush will appear in the list of predefined brushes in the Brush Tool options. The newly created brush typically appears at the bottom of the list.

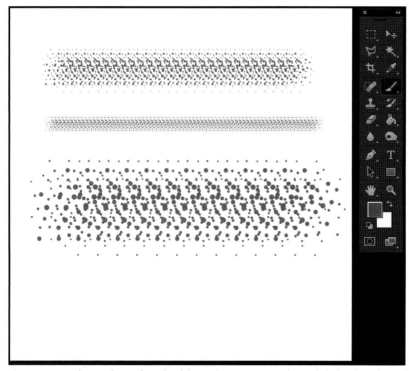

Figure 22.20. When a color is selected and the Pixel Dimensions are changed, the brush can be used as a Rendering tool.

4. Changing the settings of the brush using the Brushes palette can create many different effects for the brush.

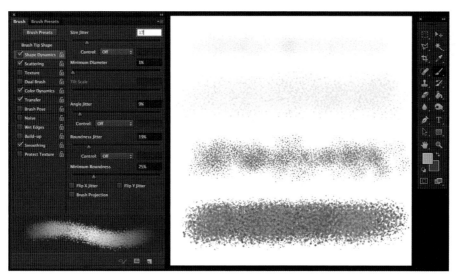

Figure 22.21. Changing the settings creates several different types of brushes from a single Brush Tip.

5. To save a particular setting for a newly created brush, create a new Tool Preset. The Tool Preset menu can be found under **Windows** > **Tool Presets**.

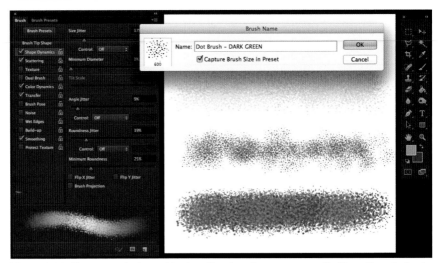

Figure 22.22. To save a particular combination of brush settings, create a new Tool Preset from the brush. The color, size, and other settings will be saved to use later in the drawing.

Chapter 23
Plan Symbols with Smart Objects

When any type of rendering is being created, many elements (typically plant symbols or images, entourage, or icons) are often repeated. These elements, which are often placed, scaled, and rotated with great precision, are copied many times within an illustration. Creating multiple copies is extremely simple; but if possible, this laborious process should not be repeated during the representation process—at least not too many times. *Smart objects* in Photoshop function in a similar manner to symbols in Illustrator or blocks in AutoCAD. They allow the user to update one instance of an object and have the changes propagate throughout the drawing. The other advantage to using smart objects is that the original object maintains the resolution that it had when it was first created. This means the smart object can be scaled down without losing pixel resolution, so that in the future it can be scaled back up again if necessary.

Creating Smart Objects

There are multiple ways to create a smart object: from layers within the current Photoshop drawing, from another Photoshop drawing, and even from Illustrator linework.

To create a smart object from layers or layer groups:

1. In Photoshop, select the layers to be used and right-click on them in the Layers palette. Select Convert to Smart Object.
2. The layers will collapse to a new Smart Object layer. The thumbnail will change to show that the layer has been converted. It is possible to convert one layer, multiple layers, or a layer group.

To create a smart object from an external raster or vector image:

1. In Photoshop, select **File > Place**. Browse to and select the file to be placed in the rendering.
2. Scale and position the artwork.
3. Press Enter or double-click on the artwork. A new Smart Object layer will be created.

Figure 23.1. Right-clicking on the layer will reveal the options. Choose Convert to Smart Object.

Figure 23.2. The layer is converted to a smart object.

To create a smart object by cutting and pasting vector artwork:

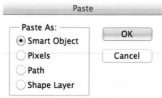

1. In Illustrator, select the vector linework to be brought into Photoshop. Copy the artwork using Ctrl+C or select **Edit** > **Copy** and then switch to Photoshop.
2. In Photoshop, press Ctrl+V or select **Edit** > **Paste** to insert the artwork into the rendering. The Paste dialog box will appear. Under Paste As, select Smart Object and click OK.
3. Scale the artwork and press Enter, or double-click the artwork to create the new smart object.

Figure 23.3. Paste the artwork as a smart object.

All of these methods create smart objects in Photoshop. Because a smart object typically can be duplicated, it is important to give the layer a name and, in many cases, place it in a layer group. The smart object is artwork that is embedded within the Photoshop file. This creates a reference file, and each copy becomes an instance of the reference or master smart object.

Duplicating and Editing Smart Objects

The Smart Object layer cannot be altered directly in Photoshop other than through transforms such as Move, Scale, and Rotate. If the embedded smart object file needs to be edited, follow these steps:

1. Select the Smart Object layer and select the Move tool. Alt+click and drag on the canvas to create a copy of the smart object. Move, scale, or rotate the smart objects on the canvas.
2. Double-click the Layer thumbnail for one of the smart objects. A dialog box will appear warning that after performing edits it requires saving the file and closing it to apply the edits. Click OK. The file will open in a new Photoshop document.
3. The document will be in the format of the original file, or if the smart object was created from layers, the file will be a PSB file (.psb). If the original document was Illustrator linework, the smart object will be opened in Illustrator rather than Photoshop.

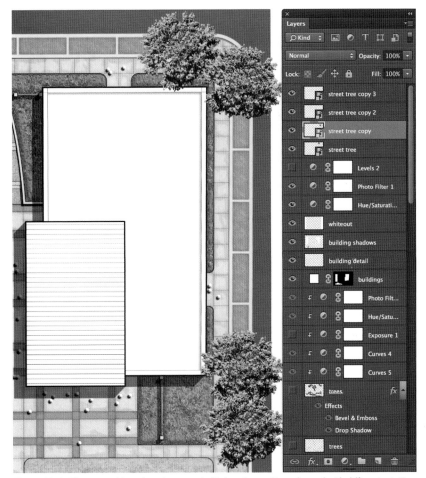

Figure 23.4. The smart objects have been copied in location and transformed with different rotations.

Figure 23.5. To edit the smart object, double-click the Layer thumbnail.

4. Editing is now possible. New layers can be added, content can be adjusted, and portions of the image can be erased. Almost any edit can be performed in this file.

5. After the edits are complete, save and close the file. All of the smart objects copied from this smart object will be updated with the edits. However, the transforms made on the smart objects (such as position, scale, and rotation) are still in place. If the adjustments were made to the sizes of all of the smart objects, the contents of the smart object file would need to be edited.

Figure 23.6. The smart object opens as a new file that can be edited. The smart object has been adjusted, and a layer mask has been added to create transparency on the edges.

Figure 23.7. The edits are propagated across all smart objects within the Photoshop file.

Managing Smart Objects

After smart objects are created, they can be stored in a library of symbols so they can be used over and over again in renderings. The smart objects are saved as external files that can be used to create new smart objects. Some options for working with smart objects include:

- Right-click on the Smart Object layer. There are several options for smart objects: the first is New Smart Object from Copy. This option will create a new smart object that is not referenced back to the other instances. This allows a smart object to create a new series of instances that when updated won't affect the instance from which it was copied. This is a good way to use an existing smart object to make something completely new.
- The layer can be rasterized by selecting Rasterize from this menu. This will turn the smart object back into a pixel layer. The smart object will be deleted.
- The Edit Contents option allows the contents of the smart object to be edited. This option is the same as double-clicking the Smart Object thumbnail.
- The Export Contents option allows the smart object to be saved as an external PSB file so it can be used in future renderings.
- The Replace Contents option will take an external file and replace the contents of the smart objects. It is possible to switch the objects completely in order to swap one symbol for another symbol. The two files, the one being replaced and the one being inserted, should be the same size in pixels. This will avoid scaling issues that might occur otherwise.

Figure 23.8. Several options for working with smart objects are available by right-clicking on the smart object in the Layer palette.

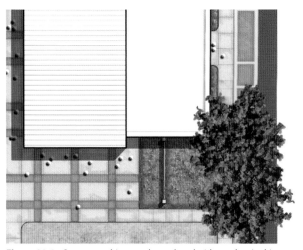

Figure 23.9. One smart object can be replaced with another. In this example, a winter tree symbol replaced the summer tree symbol.

Smart Filters

Smart filters are extensions of smart objects that are available in the latest versions of Photoshop. They provide a method for applying filters in a *nondestructive* manner, so that edits can be applied without losing information. To apply a smart filter to a layer:

1. Select the layer to which the smart filter will be applied. Select **Filter > Convert for Smart Filters**. This will essentially turn the layer into a smart object. If the layer is already a smart object, it is not necessary to use Convert for Smart Filters.
2. It is now possible to apply a filter to the layer from the Filter menu. Try **Filter > Blur > Gaussian Blur**. Adjust the settings to create an appropriate blur, and click OK.
3. Two areas are added to the Layer palette—one for the smart filter and a second for the filter that was applied. To change the settings for the filter, double-click on its space in the Layer palette. The filter's settings dialog box will open.
4. It is also possible to add multiple smart filters. Simply add the next desired filter and it will be added above the first filter. The interesting thing about this is that the order in which the filters are applied can be adjusted by moving the filters up and down in the stack. The results from adding a Blur filter *before* a Noise filter are not the same as those from adding a Blur filter *after* the Noise filter

This provides a very powerful method for applying filters to a layer. The one drawback is that if the pixels are to be edited on the layer, the editing must be done within the smart object.

Figure 23.10. A smart filter is applied to a layer. Double-click the smart filter to edit its properties.

Figure 23.11. When multiple smart filters are applied to a layer, the order can be changed and the smart filter can be edited independently.

Chapter 24
Creating a Section Elevation

Three main types of drawings are used to represent the cross-sectional space of a design: sections, elevations, and the most commonly used, a hybrid of the two called a section elevation. *Sections* are critical to the representation of a design idea. In a true section, only the information along a section line is represented. Most sectional work is used to represent spatial relationships between the landscape, buildings, and the human scale. These drawings help to relate the scale of a design alternative.

Elevations show an orthographic view of the design from one side. These drawings are similar to perspectives, except they show the information without many of the depth cues used in perspectives. *Section elevations* are a combination of the two techniques and are the most frequently used type of cross-section drawing in site design projects.

Methods

Rendering a section elevation is similar to rendering a plan. The linework for a section is drawn in AutoCAD and exported as a PDF. The PDF is brought into Photoshop, and base colors are applied in a similar fashion to plan renderings. One technique that is common in a section elevation but rarely used in a plan rendering is to use the linework to cut away portions of an image. Consider the following example of the anatomy of a section elevation drawing in Photoshop:

1. The linework from AutoCAD is exported as a PDF and brought into Photoshop.

Figure 24.1. The linework from AutoCAD is exported as a PDF and brought into Photoshop.

253

2. Place an image of background trees on a new layer in the section. Adjust the opacity of the layer to make the background images lighter. Make a selection using the existing linework of all areas that are in front of the background. Erase parts of the image where the linework is in front of the background trees.

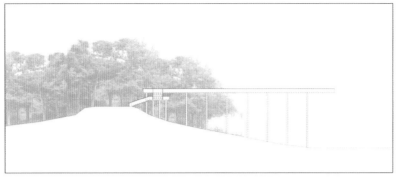

Figure 24.2. The existing linework is used to make a selection, and the background trees are erased.

3. Add entourage trees in front of the background. Each tree should be placed on a separate layer. Each tree behind the linework can be erased using the same selection used to erase the background.

Figure 24.3. Foreground trees are added. Cut away parts of the trees that are behind the linework.

4. Add the remainder of the trees in the mid-ground layer; add the grasses or groundcovers.

Figure 24.4. Continue to add trees and groundcover plants.

5. Color the linework using a Solid Color adjustment layer, similarly to how the plan rendering is colored.

Figure 24.5. Fill the linework using a Solid Color adjustment layer.

6. Add people to the image and place them in places that are key to the design. The use of people will draw attention to specific areas of the drawing.

Figure 24.6. Add people to the composition.

7. Add the front layer of trees. This creates depth in the drawing by layering the space from front to back.

Figure 24.7. The final composition. *Spackman Mossop+Michaels*

Part 5

Perspectives

Perspective Rendering. Jescelle Major, Will Reinhardt, Kelli Cunningham, MLA 2015, Louisiana State University Robert Reich School of Landscape Architecture

Aerial Perspective Rendering. **Stoss Landscape Urbanism**

Perspective Rendering. **Spackman Mossop+Michaels**

Perspectives

Hybrid Diagrammatic Perspective. LSU Coastal Sustainability Studio, Matthew Seibert, MLA 2013, Louisiana State University Robert Reich School of Landscape Architecture

Perspective Rendering. **SWA**

Aerial Perspective Rendering. **The Office of James Burnett**

Perspective Rendering. **Design Workshop**

Chapter 25
Perspective Drawings

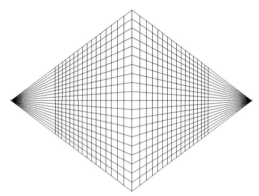

Figure 25.1. Perspective grid/chart, analog and digital.

Traditional perspective drawings have relied on the *perspective chart* or constructed perspectives to create compelling and convincing illustrations. This aid creates an underlying framework that facilitates accurate, scaled perspective drawings from measured plans. Image-editing software such as Photoshop allows for the incorporation of perspective grids using layers that contain an image of the perspective grid or an existing site photo. This allows the designer to develop an illustration using traditional drawing or collage methods within Photoshop.

Three-dimensional modeling software (such as Google SketchUp, Autodesk 3ds Max Design, Newtek Lightwave, Softimage XSI, and/or Autodesk Maya) allows designers to develop digital models of their design work. As the design model develops, virtual cameras can be used within the model to frame and compose views of a work in progress or a finished model. By combining image-editing software and three-dimensional modeling and rendering, a flexible, customized method can be developed to create accurate perspective illustrations. This combination ideally occurs with image-editing software that supports layering and transparency, and modeling software that allows images to be rendered or exported with embedded alpha channel information for attributes such as transparency, z-depth, materials, and shadows.

The process of combining layers of three-dimensional renderings, film, and illustrations is defined as *compositing*. Most people are familiar with the use of *green* or *blue screen filming* that allows foreground elements/actors to be separated from the background and new background plates to be inserted. Architects and landscape architects can also take advantage of compositing by using three-dimensional models as a base for more complex illustrations.

Figure 25.2. Composite layer extraction.

Composition

When a base is being created for any perspective image, it is important to first carefully consider the composition that is being created. *Composition* refers to the arrangement of elements within the camera's frame. For visual artists, the *rule of thirds* is a common method that attempts to keep the subject and horizon from bisecting the image. The rule of thirds refers to the process of splitting the image plane vertically into three parts (thirds) and placing the focus of the image on one of the vertical splits. In most three-dimensional modeling applications, a virtual camera is used to frame the view or create the composition. This requires careful consideration of camera position and field of view.

Figure 25.3. A green screen is used to film and composite figures in the environment.

Figure 25.4. Rule of thirds grid. *Charlie Pruitt, BLA 2012, Louisiana State University Robert Reich School of Landscape Architecture*

Virtual Cameras

The position of the camera is typically controlled in two ways. The first is directly in the viewport using controls that orbit, roll, pan, and dolly the camera. This method requires viewing the scene directly through the camera and interactively adjusting the view. This allows for instant one-to-one feedback and can be a quick way to position a view. All three-dimensional modeling software allows the user to manipulate their view in this manner; but while intuitive, it doesn't allow the precision that is sometimes necessary when creating compositions. Tremble SketchUp provides a slightly different mechanism to position your view that allows the user to adjust the point of view by controlling the camera direction as though it is the viewer's eyes.

Figure 25.5. Three-dimensional camera controls.

The second method for camera control is through the positioning of the *camera body* and the *camera target*. The camera body and target are points in space that typically define the start and end vectors of a view. Each point, the body and the target, can be transformed independently with an interactive *gizmo* or by specifying coordinates within the Cartesian grid.

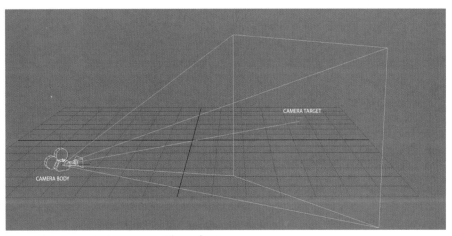

Figure 25.6. Camera body and target with transforms.

The height of the camera is an important consideration that allows the viewer to surmise specific experiential qualities of the space. For example, a camera that is placed at 3.5 feet would portray a child's view, where a height of 5 feet to 6 feet would portray an adult's. A worm's eye view of 1 foot above the ground plane would abstract the image and dramatize the subject, and an aerial view of 30 feet to 100 feet would create a separation between the viewer and the site. Where the camera is placed within the site and the height of that location also defines the view—for example, a view at ground level along an interpretive trail has different qualities than a view from a lookout tower. Both views are from a human-scale perspective, but there are different landscape experiences in each view.

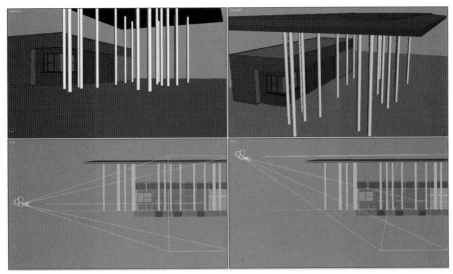

Figure 25.7. Camera height diagrams.

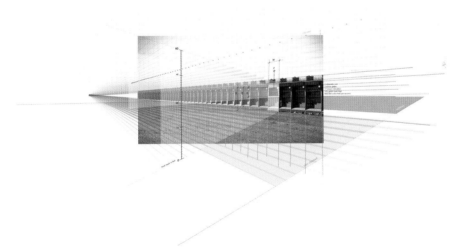

Figure 25.8. Example view angles.

How the frame is filled with elements in an illustration is also an important way to convey proposed or existing site experiences. Vegetation or overhead structures in the foreground that "cover" the viewer can provide a sense of refuge, a virtual vantage point from which to view the surroundings. Conversely, opening up the foreground allows the viewer's eye to travel to the edge and off the page, implying a site that is expansive and sprawling. The concepts of circulation, program, and occupation can also be expressed through the framing and viewpoint location.

Figure 25.9. Foreground vegetation and shadow. *Spackman Mossop+Michaels*

Figure 25.10. Expansive views. *Fletcher Studio*

Figure 25.11. Photoshop drawing over image from Google Street View. *Spackman Mossop+Michaels*

Figure 25.12. Example of program. *Prentiss Darden and Silvia Cox, MLA 2014, Louisiana State University Robert Reich School of Landscape Architecture*

Figure 25.13. Example of circulation. *Abram Ebersohn, BLA 2015, Louisiana State University Robert Reich School of Landscape Architecture*

In conjunction with camera placement, it is also important to use field of view in an efficient manner. The *field of view* can be described as the angular extents of the observable world. Typically, the human eye has a field of view that is approximately 180 degrees;

most illustrations are created in a range of 40 to 100 degrees (50mm to 15mm camera lens). A wide-angle lens will distort geometries, exaggerating object forms that move between the foreground and background. The choice of lens is an important method that can create motion and drama in an illustration.

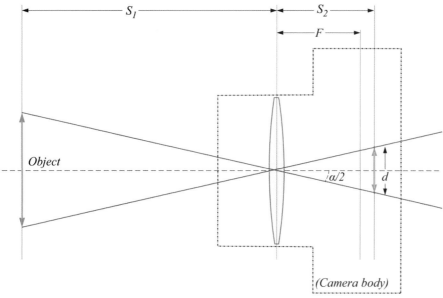

Figure 25.14. Field of view.

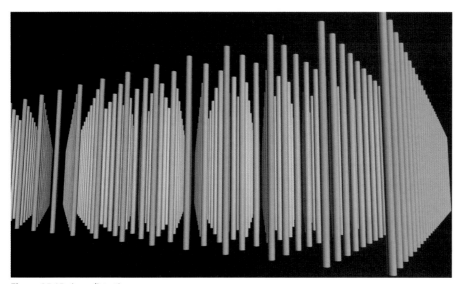

Figure 25.15. Lens distortion.

Exporting and Rendering

In order for a composition created with a camera in three-dimensional modeling software to be used, the view must be exported or rendered in a file format that can be used in image-editing software. Depending on the software, files can be created that are either raster- or vector-based. When raster files are created, the final illustration size will be limited by the pixel resolution of the exported imagery. Two things need to be considered when determining the export or rendering resolution: the final output or printed size of the illustration and the limitations of the hardware exporting the file.

The issues related to hardware limitations are stickier points and are often not defined by simple formulas. In simple terms, there is an exponential relationship between image pixel size and the memory that is required to render or export the image. The complexity of the three-dimensional scene—which is a product of geometry, materials, and effects—also contributes to the memory needs when rendering or exporting. If lack of memory (RAM) is an issue and resolution is not a negotiable factor, it may become necessary to export scene elements separately in order to overcome hardware limits. This often involves rendering the foreground, middleground, and background as separate layers to minimize the model complexity. It is also possible to render effect elements such as fog, lighting volumes, and so forth as separate passes, which will also separate the complexities of that process and put less strain on the hardware. In order to render illustration components separately, most three-dimensional modeling software that *renders* an image allows the user to save image formats with alpha channels to define transparency or other attributes. The most common formats that support alpha channels are Targa, TIFF, and Photoshop files.

It is important to devote time to the composition of a perspective drawing. Many factors contribute to an interesting and meaningful perspective illustration, including composition and viewer location. When used properly, they are powerful tools to convey complex landscape images.

In landscape, the location of objects in space is perceived through the veil of atmospheric perspective. *Atmospheric perspective* refers to how an object's appearance is affected by layers of moisture and particulate matter in the air. As the distance between the object and the viewer increases, more layers of air affect the object's appearance. Generally, this manifests as haze, shifting the appearance of objects in the distance toward a bluish hue and less saturated colors.

Traditionally, landscape representation, painting, and drawing have used basic techniques to simulate the effect of layers of air between the viewer and objects within the environment. The simplest means is the *desaturation* and gray-blue haze applied to objects that are farther away from the camera. Other methods involve rendering less detail and using a variety of thinner, lighter linework in the distance.

Figure 25.16. Saturation and detail diminish with distance. *Keely Rizzato, MLA 2014, Louisiana State University Robert Reich School of Landscape Architecture*

All of these traditional techniques for creating depth in the landscape are essential when developing digital representations. Atmospheric perspective can be used in two-dimensional collages as well as full three-dimensional renderings in order to heighten perceived depth. When representing the landscape, atmospheric perspective is expressed in several ways but always with these basic characteristics.

Detail

Objects closer to the viewer will be rendered with more detail. As objects recede toward the horizon, they begin to lose their definition. This can be observed in the rendering of trees in the landscape, where trees close to the viewer appear completely detailed. As trees are rendered toward the horizon, they become less detailed until they finally blend into the hillsides in the distance.

Color

Color tends to shift from saturated in the foreground to less saturated near the horizon. This shift represents the scattering of light through the atmosphere, particularly water vapor and particulate matter. During daylight, color tends to shift toward blue due to shorter wavelengths of light within scattered skylight. At night, there is virtually no skylight; therefore, objects tend to shift toward a reddish hue.

Figure 25.17. Detail diminishes with distance. *Keely Rizzato, MLA 2014, Louisiana State University Robert Reich School of Landscape Architecture*

Figure 25.18. Trees lose saturation as they get farther away from the viewer.

Contrast

The veil or haze of the atmosphere also affects an object's contrast; contrast decreases as elements recede from the viewer. Objects in the distance have smaller shifts in value, making them appear less detailed or less crisp than objects in the foreground. This effect can sometimes be confused as a lack of focus, but it is simply a side effect of low contrast. As long as it is subtle, a blurring effect can be used to heighten the lack of contrast.

Brightness

Brightness is the subtlest effect that helps to create atmospheric perspective. If all lighting conditions are equal, objects near the viewer are typically brighter than objects near the horizon. This can change though, based on the location of the viewer in relation to lighting quality within the landscape.

Figure 25.19. Contrast decreases as distance from the viewer increases.

Figure 25.20. Lack of brightness is relative to distance from the viewer.

The tools used for creating atmospheric perspective come in two categories: two-dimensional layering (or compositing techniques) and three-dimensional, environmental techniques. Both types of techniques overlap one another and share the same basic assumptions discussed earlier.

Two-Dimensional Photoshop Adjustment Layers, Opacity, and Screening

In most cases, atmospheric perspective is accomplished in an image-editing program such as Photoshop, using a large array of tools. In most cases, this is achieved using adjustment layers, layer opacity, and screening.

Photoshop provides advanced two-dimensional tools to create the illusion of atmospheric perspective. Adjustment layers provide a robust method for applying brightness/contrast and hue/saturation adjustments directly within the layer stack. You can experiment with this method by creating three shape layers consisting of consecutively smaller rectangles falling back in space.

1. Select the middle layer (the largest rectangle) and apply a hue/saturation adjustment layer.

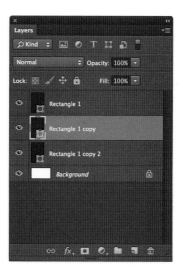

Figure 25.21. Rectangle shape layers in Photoshop.

2. Decrease the saturation and push the hue toward blue. Then click OK. This creates an adjustment layer below the top layer that applies to all of the layers below. Now the two smaller rectangles are adjusted similarly: the color is less saturated and the color is bluer.

3. Copy the same adjustment layer by selecting the layer and Alt+dragging the layer above the bottom layer—this doubles the effect of the adjustment layers.

Figure 25.22. Apply an adjustment layer.

Figure 25.23. Copy the adjustment layer.

The rectangle exercise gives us a very simple scenario to illustrate the application of adjustment layers. In more complicated renderings, a variety of techniques are employed to create this same illusion.

Layer opacity is another method to create the effect of atmospheric perspective. This method works well when placing entourage elements within a perspective image. Atmospheric perspective works in conjunction with all other aspects of creating perspective renderings and, therefore, must be based on a well-constructed and believable image. When placing entourage elements, such as scale figures, within a perspective rendering, it is essential that the head of each figure is near the horizon line if the view is at eye level and that they are properly adjusted to fit the overall color scheme.

A typical process for adding scale figures is shown in the following figures. It is important to note that each figure is quickly placed within the perspective rendering and transformed to the correct size. A guide is commonly set to determine the horizon line for the tops of the scale figures' heads. Scale figures are then arranged in the layer stack with foreground figures near the top and background figures near the bottom. Opacities can then be adjusted. Even foreground figures should have some transparency, typically starting at 90% opacity and working down to 25% opacity for figures in the background.

Figure 25.24. Placing and transforming scale figures.

Figure 25.25. Adjusting the opacity of scale figures.

In conjunction with adjusting the opacity, it is also possible to add hue/saturation adjustments similar to how they were added in the rectangle exercise earlier. *Layer clipping* uses the pixels of one layer to constrain the pixels or effect of another layer. Because the adjustment layer should affect only the entourage element, layer clipping is used. To apply layer clipping in Photoshop:

1. Hold down the Alt key, place the cursor between the layers, and then click between the layers.
2. The top layer will be clipped by the pixels on the layer below it, constraining the effect.

Other methods are possible to create similar effects and can be used with similar outcomes. In Photoshop, the Color Overlay layer effect can be utilized to give a layer a bluish hue; this method works particularly well when combined with layer opacity.

Figure 25.26. Layer clipping and adjustment layers.

Figure 25.27. Layer effects.

On larger areas, such as the ground plane, it is often necessary to apply an adjustment layer differently across the entire layer. If elements on the layer move through three-dimensional space from the foreground to the background, it is necessary to specify how the adjustment layer affects areas differently than other areas. Typically, this can be specified within the adjustment layer mask using a gradient that goes from black to white (no adjustment in the foreground to full adjustment in the background). This allows the adjustment effect to be applied smoothly across the gradient, creating the illusion of depth.

Some image-editing programs, such as GIMP, do not provide the ability to apply adjustments or layer effects. Therefore, it is necessary to use alternative methods. A common method is to organize your layers from foreground to background within the layer hierarchy. It is then possible to create layers in the hierarchy that are used as haze—this can simply be a layer filled with a light-bluish gray. Using the Opacity layer, it is then possible to adjust the opacity of the Haze layer to get the desired effect. Copying the layer down in the layer hierarchy allows the layers to build on one another, making the foreground elements brightest and the background elements obscured.

Figure 25.28. The Adjustment layer gradient mask.

Figure 25.29. Haze layers.

Two-Dimensional/Three-Dimensional Z-Depth

Most three-dimensional modeling and animation software, such as 3ds Max and Maya, provide options to generate a z-depth channel. The *z-depth channel* uses shades of gray to designate how far objects are from the camera. In most cases, the z-depth channel generates white for elements closer to the viewer and black for elements farther from the viewer.

Figure 25.30. Typical z-depth.

A typical method to generate a z-depth buffer involves generating render elements, or a g-buffer. Using Autodesk Maya, you must first open the **Render Settings > Render Able Camera** and turn on the depth channel (z-depth). You then must navigate to the camera's attributes using the **Attribute Editor > Output Settings**, where you can enable the z-depth type. Maya allows you to embed a z-depth channel into an .iff or .rla file, or you can specify another file type, such as .tif; and the z-depth information will be rendered to a separate RGBA file.

Figure 25.31. Maya z-depth settings.

Once a z-depth channel has been rendered, it is possible to use the information in any image-editing or compositing program to simulate depth. Because the z-depth is created using shades of gray, it can be used to generate a mask to control the effect of an adjustment layer. Depending on how the z-depth layer was generated, it may be necessary to invert the values to make foreground values black and background values white. This will apply the adjustment layer in a manner similar to the gradient used earlier. As you can see, this is a much more refined method of applying atmospheric perspective, but it requires that the majority of the image be created within a three-dimensional modeling package.

Figure 25.32. Full landscape z-depth.

Three-Dimensional Atmosphere/Environment

Haze or atmosphere can also be created directly within your three-dimensional model-ing software. This is often a good solution, especially when creating animations, because it allows all of the steps to be rolled into one package. Nearly every three-dimensional modeling package offers some method to generate environmental fog—even Google SketchUp incorporates this effect. More advanced three-dimensional modeling software usually has multiple methods for generating atmosphere or environmental fog. Typi-cally, they can be categorized as simple fog and physical fog. The latter is generally more accurate, with better options to control how the fog behaves with other elements in the environment; but normally, it takes much longer to calculate and render.

Typically, fog is generated as an environmental attribute and is enabled and controlled through two planes and the gradient between the two planes. In software such as Maya or 3ds Max, additional shaders or maps can be used to generate animated fog or to designate areas where fog is heavier than in other areas.

A typical application of fog in 3ds Max involves adding fog in the **Render** > **Environment** menu. Once the fog has been added, two settings (Near and Far) control the amount of fog present in the environment. Both settings are a percentage, with 0% being no fog and 100% being completely opaque fog. Typically, the Near setting is set to 0 to 5 % and the Far setting is set to 5 to 15%, creating a gradient of fog between the Near and Far. It is also possible to set a color for the environmental fog, as well as adjust settings for Noise and Phase in order to animate the fog.

Figure 25.33. Environmental fog.

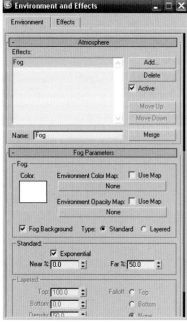

Figure 25.34. Environmental fog in 3ds Max.

Understanding Level of Detail

Level of detail, often referred to as LoD, is the use of more detailed models in the foreground and less detailed models in the background or context. LoD algorithms come from a specific area of computer graphics that focuses on optimizing real-time graphics. It is important to understand how level of detail modeling (although not a specific technique) can make your workflow more efficient.

With traditional mediums, designers illustrated what was in the frame of the camera; but with digital media, it is possible to model and create portions of the model that are outside our frame of view. Understanding the concept of LoD allows us to concentrate on elements of the model or environment that will be seen by the viewer while also adding detail to only the foreground models or elements, allowing the rest of the model to have fewer details. Not only does this follow the principles of atmospheric perspective, it also creates more efficient illustrations.

There are many ways to generate atmospheric perspective when representing the landscape with digital tools. Any singular or combinatory effect can be used to alter the four attributes affected by atmospheric perspective: detail, color, contrast, and brightness. Understanding how to alter these attributes allows us to develop techniques that are purely two-dimensional, hybrid two-dimensional/three-dimensional, or purely three-dimensional.

Chapter 26
Camera Match Three-Dimensional Object to Site Photo

The term *camera matching* traditionally refers to the process of aligning a virtual view or scene with a photograph or film sequence. Many different techniques exist for camera matching and, therefore, many terms exist for both still imagery and film sequences. *Match moving* is the process of tracking a sequence of images and aligning a virtual camera with camera view in the sequence. This alignment allows virtual elements to be composited with the live action in a shot that may have complex camera movements. This technique is similar to camera matching for still shots, but it uses the change in tracking points to determine camera positions. Rather than matching a site model to a photo, *photogrammetry* is a term that refers to the process of extracting three-dimensional information from two-dimensional photographs.

Figure 26.1. Wireframe model over photo.

A camera match requires a series of points that can be "matched" between the existing photograph and virtual model. Most camera matching occurs through this method and requires two dimensions and typically five or more match points. The five points should exist with four points on one plane or dimension and another point on the second dimension. This will provide the software sufficient information to correctly calculate the desired view.

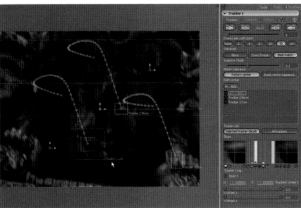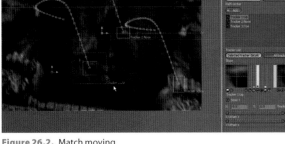

Figure 26.2. Match moving.

Figure 26.3. Planes with identified reference points.

A successful camera match allows for many possibilities in design representation. The most common use is to create reference models that can be rendered and used as layers in Photoshop. These layers provide a structure to collage additional textures and entourage.

We will examine two methods for camera alignment used to create a camera match. The first method uses CamPoints in 3ds Max Design 2014, and the second method uses perspective grid alignment in SketchUp.

Camera Match with 3ds Max 2014

Camera matching in 3ds Max requires a minimum of five points dispersed across two dimensions. For a successful match to be created, the distances between each point need to be known. The distance can be determined through site measurements or by using known points on a CAD survey. 3ds Max also requires synchronization between the rendering resolution, viewport background, and the resolution of the photo used for the camera match. This can be achieved by setting the rendering resolution in render setup to the same resolution as your photo.

1. To import the photo into 3ds Max, press Alt+B or select **Views > Viewport Background**.
2. Click the File button, and browse to the file location in the window. A wide range of image and movie formats are supported. 3ds Max allows more complicated matches using a video segment, allowing live action footage to be matched, or using an animated sequence as background footage.
3. Once the photo is imported, select Display Background and Lock Zoom Pan. Under Aspect Ratio, select Match Bitmap.

Figure 26.4. Rendering resolution in 3ds Max and Image Resolution in Photoshop.

Figure 26.5. The Viewport Background dialog box in 3ds Max.

The image will be displayed in the Active viewport. The rendering of 3ds Max viewports is dependent on the performance of your computer's video card. You can adjust the display resolution of the background image by selecting **Customize > Preferences**, and clicking the Viewport tab and choosing Configure Driver. You can select to have the graphics card match the resolution, which can lead to computer slowdowns for large images, or choose up to 1024 pixels. For camera matching, using a higher resolution is useful for viewing the details in the background image.

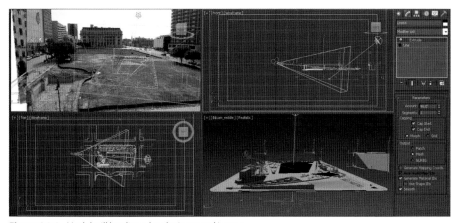

Figure 26.6. Model will be aligned to the imported image.

In order to match the scene to the background image, CamPoints need to be created. These *CamPoints* are placed in the environment and can be referenced to points on the image. In order to use the CamPoints, geometry must be created in the three-dimensional environment with the correct dimensions to match elements in the photograph. It is also possible to simply use coordinates, if they are known, rather than actual geometry. CamPoints should represent real-world positions that correspond to the image being displayed—otherwise, the camera match will not be able to resolve itself.

1. To create a CamPoint, use the Create panel, select Helpers, select Camera Match from the drop-down menu, and then click the CamPoint button. You can snap the CamPoint to geometry using 3D Snaps, or you can place the CamPoint and reposition it with the Transform Type-in dialog.

Figure 26.7. Model in relation to the image. Alignment points will be based on surrounding context.

2. Place each CamPoint at the correct location within the model until a minimum of five CamPoints are positioned within two dimensions.

Figure 26.8. Camera match markers are placed on modeled geometry.

3. After the CamPoints are positioned, a relationship needs to be established between each CamPoint and a position on the background image. On the Command panel, select the Utilities tab and then choose Camera Match, which will open the Camera Match dialog box within the Command panel.
4. This dialog box will have a list of the currently created CamPoints. Highlight the first CamPoint in the list and then click the Assign Position button.
5. Using your cursor, select the position on the photograph to which the current Cam-Point belongs—or enter two-dimensional coordinates to place or adjust the CamPoint.
6. Repeat this process for each of the five (or more) CamPoints in order to create a relationship in the three-dimensional environment with the image.

Figure 26.9. Camera match markers are associated with areas of the image.

Figure 26.10. Camera view derived from camera match.

After assigning a position on the image to each CamPoint, click the Create Camera button. Your new camera will align itself with the image based on the position of the CamPoints. If you need to make adjustments to the camera, you can select a CamPoint in the list, make the adjustments, and then press the Modify Camera button.

After a successful camera match is created, it is usually prudent to lock the camera to preserve its position. It is very easy to accidentally move the camera with an errant selection or by navigating in the camera viewport.

Match Photo with Tremble SketchUp

Tremble SketchUp introduces a utility called Match Photo that facilitates the synchronization of a background photo with the three-dimensional environment. SketchUp's method of synchronization is based on the perspective grid and requires an origin point, horizon line, and four vanishing point lines—two on the *x*-axis and two on the *y*-axis. For each of the vanishing point lines, it is desirable to use distances that exist across the image and exist perpendicular to one another (*x* and *y*). In order to scale the model correctly, it is also necessary to have a known dimension on the image. In order to provide an accurate scale, it is best to use a dimension that is as long as possible—so rather than using the height of a curb edge, it would be better to use the width of a street or plaza.

1. To access the Match Photo features, use **Window > Match Photo** to bring up the Match Photo palette.

Figure 26.11. Image with defined vanishing points.

2. The first step is to create a new Match Photo by pressing the Create New Matched Photo button in the upper-left corner of the palette. Browse to the location of the photo and select the file. TrembleSketchUp allows JPEG, TIFF, Targa, BMP, and PNG files to be used for a Match Photo.

3. This will create a new scene titled with the file's name. If you navigate away from your Match Photo, you can always click the Scene button at the top of the window to navigate back.

After creating the new Match Photo, the view will show an origin (yellow box), a horizon line (yellow line), two red vanishing point lines, and two green vanishing point lines.

1. The first step is to reposition the origin to define 0,0 on the photo. This can be accomplished by clicking and dragging the origin point and moving it to the desired location. The location of the origin is important because this will be where you start modeling in the newly matched photo.

2. When working in the Match Photo, it is possible to pan and zoom. It is important to zoom in order to accurately position each reference point, because small inaccuracies will be magnified across the Match Photo.

Figure 26.12. The Match Photo palette and the Create New Matched Photo button.

Figure 26.13. Reference points placed over background image.

3. After moving the origin point, you can begin aligning each of the vanishing points in the *x*- and *y*-axes. Ideally, an object or landscape element that has two known perpendicular sides will be used as reference axes. Click and drag each endpoint to align

the virtual vanishing points with the vanishing points on the image. The grid may look wrong until you have all four vanishing points aligned. Remember to use your pan and zoom in order to make the alignment as accurate as possible. When all four vanishing point axes are aligned, click and drag the horizon line until it is aligned with the horizon in the image.

4. When you are done placing the reference points, right-click in the viewport and select Done.

Figure 26.14. Aligned Match Photo with geometry.

If you need to make adjustments, you can edit the Photo Match and refine the placement of the vanishing points. The Match Photo also provides options to adjust the opacity of the photo as well as change the display style of the grid and planes that define the perspective. It is also possible to generate textures from the Photo Match, which can be useful when creating context geometry for models.

Figure 26.15. The textures from the photo will be matched to the new model geometry.

Chapter 27
Create a Photoshop Perspective Collage

Some perspective images can be created completely from Photoshop images without using any three-dimensional modeling program as a base. Often these images are similar to *ideograms* or are experimental images used to show programming ideas or material relationships. Perspective images created from scratch within Photoshop can be incredibly evocative images using multiple layers and transparencies.

The source material for perspectives is usually created from images of the site itself or existing entourage from other projects. The technique should be fluid and quick, especially at the beginning of the drawing until the final layout is determined. The first part of the drawing should be done with this in mind and an eye toward finding good combinations of different images, compositions, and overall tone of the image. It is rare that drawings like these start off with a predefined idea of exactly what the finished image will look like. Rather, the process is similar to sketching to find how the image might look and then refining that image once the groundwork has been laid.

Methods

These drawings typically start by creating the background, and then the general composition of the image is built up as the drawing progresses. Consider the following example to understand the anatomy of one of these perspectives:

1. The drawing starts with a section of the forest background. This section does not need to be finely drawn. Especially at the beginning, do not spend too much time trying to refine the drawing. The beauty of digital media is the ability to edit and rework a drawing over and over. Start by roughing out an overall idea of how the image will look, where the horizon line will be, where the vanishing points might go, and so forth.

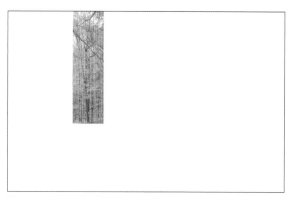

Figure 27.1. Start building the background with sections of an existing photograph. At this point in the drawing, speed is key. Do not spend too much time on any one image as the drawing is being built.

2. Add several more layers of images to build the background. This is the time to begin to figure out where the horizon line should be and experiment with the overall composition of the drawing.
3. Continue to build the image until most of the background is established.

Figure 27.2. Continue to build the background while experimenting with the overall composition of the image.

Figure 27.3. The background is built from a variety of elements.

4. The ground plane is built with several different types of small images. For this application, the edges of the ground plane images are roughed up using the Eraser tool. These small images are the building blocks of the entire forest floor.
5. Duplicate the building blocks to create the forest floor. Notice that the copies of the images are altered. On the left side of the image, the copy of the meadow grass has the saturation lowered. On the right side of the image, the copies of the image that are closer to the viewer are more saturated in color. This is how the illusion of depth is created in the drawing. As objects get farther away, they become less saturated, lighter, and bluer. As these images are copied, each copy should be altered to reflect its spatial position in the image.

Figure 27.4. The ground plane starts with several small elements that are copied around the drawing. This figure shows two of these elements.

Figure 27.5. As the elements are copied, the saturation and lightness of the images are altered. As the ground plane moves away from the viewer, it becomes less saturated. The images also become smaller.

6. More of the ground plane is built up. It is important to establish the mid-ground elements in the ground plane first. This allows all of the images that are closer or farther away to be either less or more saturated than the mid-range elements. It also helps hold the drawing in place by creating a mid-ground plane that is different from the foreground or background.
7. Other ground plane elements can be added to create the base. Continue to copy these elements around the ground plane, changing the size and saturation of each image.
8. Fill in any missing areas of the image until the basic composition is established.
9. Begin to add foreground elements to the drawing. These elements typically come from the entourage collection. The foreground elements should be darker and more saturated than the background.

Figure 27.6. Creating the mid-ground is important. This should be established first. It helps give a texture reference for creating the foreground and background. The scale of the foreground and background (i.e., the size of the little images used to create the ground plane) should be relative to this mid-ground image.

Figure 27.7. Additional ground plane elements can be added to the drawing.

Figure 27.8. Continue to build the ground plane.

Figure 27.9. Ground plane and background are complete.

10. Continue to add foreground elements to the drawing. The foreground elements that are farther away are usually made to be more transparent and less saturated, similar to the ground plane textures.
11. The pathway is created from a standard section of pathway from a photograph.
12. The pathway image is copied into the rendering.
13. The pathway needs to be altered to fit the drawing. Select **Edit > Transform > Distort**, and use the Distort tool to change the shape of the pathway.
14. Copy the image and use the Distort tool to place it at the end of the first image. Do this a few more times to build the basis for the path. Once a base for the path has been built, merge the layers.
15. Select and erase any part of the image that does not line up.
16. Adjust the path to create the base path. In this example, copy any parts of the path that need to be altered.
17. Move the combined pathway to the correct area in the composition. Copy and alter the path to set the correct orientation.

Figure 27.10. Add foreground elements. These elements should be more saturated and less transparent than the background images.

Figure 27.11. Continue to fill in with foreground images. The farther away the image, the less saturated and more transparent it becomes.

Figure 27.12. Source image for pathway.

Figure 27.13. Copy the image into the drawing.

Figure 27.14. Use the Distort tool to alter the shape of the pathway.

Figure 27.15. Copy the image to build the pathway.

Figure 27.16. Continue to build a base for the path. Once the base has been built, merge the layers.

Figure 27.17. Select one side of the path.

Figure 27.18. Erase any areas on the path that are not lined up.

Figure 27.19. To copy the white border to the other side of the path, select the border using the Lasso tool.

18. Use the Hue/Saturation adjustment to alter the color of the pathway to fit the composition.
19. Add people, wildflowers, and shadows to create the final image. The text on the pathway is created by using the Text tool to write the words. Their position is adjusted using the Distort tool in a similar way to the methods used to compose the path.

Figure 27.20. Using the Move tool, hold Alt and drag the selection. This will make a copy of the white border.

Figure 27.21. Select **Edit > Transform > Distort**, and use the Distort function to bend the shape to fit the other side of the path. Erase any areas outside the white border with the Eraser tool.

Figure 27.22. Move the path to the proper place in the composition.

Figure 27.23. Copy and alter the shape of the path to set it in place.

Figure 27.24. Adjust the color and transparency to finalize the place of the path in the composition.

Figure 27.25. Add people and other details to create the final image. *Spackman Mossop+Michaels*

Chapter 28
Developing a Perspective Image in Photoshop from a Three-Dimensional Model

Creating a perspective rendering with a three-dimensional model as a base is a common method of illustration. The three-dimensional model serves as the perspective grid, creating a reference to add context, texturing, vegetation, and entourage. This technique was originally used for analog renderings; a composition was created and the view was exported to be traced and rendered using pen, graphite, and/or colored pencil. This is the basic technique that will be followed here, except the rendering will be accomplished digitally.

Base Model

The view for the base model will be either rendered or exported from a three-dimensional modeling application such as 3ds Max or SketchUp. Both applications have two different options for exporting, and it is worthwhile to quickly touch on each of them. In 3ds Max, an image can be rendered with an *alpha mask*. This mask will create an image with *only* the pixels that represent the model and the rest of the image will be transparent. In order to use this alpha mask, the model view must be rendered and then saved as either a TIFF or PSD file with the alpha mask enabled. This is typically an option when saving the file. The resulting image will have a channel called alpha that can be used to select the pixels or to invert the selection and delete the background if it is not already transparent.

If the view will be exported from SketchUp, an alpha channel is not an option. The best option is to create a style that maximizes the contrast between the model surfaces and the background. This will create an image where the background can be selected in Photoshop using the Color Range selection or Magic Wand tool. The default "engineering" style in SketchUp will provide crisp linework, and a completely white background and ground plane, making selections very simple with the Magic Wand tool.

The image that will be used for the following example was generated from a model in 3ds Max; the background is transparent. For more information on making selections, see

Chapter 7: Source Imagery/Entourage. For more information on creating camera compositions, see Chapter 26: Camera Match Three-Dimensional Object to Site Photo.

1. The first step is to create a series of reference lines over the base image. Create a new layer group and name it **construction**. Make the layer group Active.

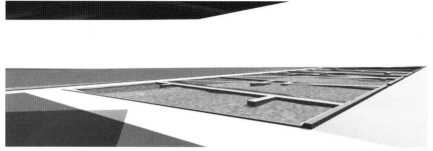

Figure 28.1. The base model is rendered and used as the framework for the Photoshop rendering.

2. Select a bright garish color; for this example, hot pink will work. Select the Line tool and begin tracing the site infrastructure back toward the vanishing points.
3. Trace the major elements such as the water edge, pathways, vertical elements, and so forth. This will serve as the framework as content is added to the rendering.
4. Flatten the group by selecting it and merge the group (Ctrl+E).

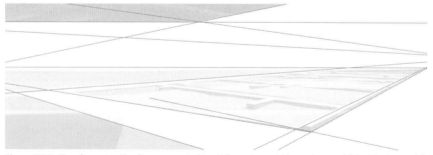

Figure 28.2. Rough construction lines are created to reinforce the vanishing points established by the model.

Adding Site Context

In most cases, the digital model will have been a study, used to determine scale and massing—and it requires Photoshop to create an experiential image that evokes the designer's sense of place. Creating that sense of place should start with the site context. A perspective view needs to have *context,* a site where the design resides. When composing views for a rendering, consider what aspects of the context will be visible. If they are identifiable monuments, they should be incorporated. This will create an identifiable marker in the landscape that will orient the viewer.

The first step will be to determine which parts of the existing site photos to use when creating the context. The following two photographs contain the elements needed to create the context; one has a good view of the railway bridge and the second has a strongly defined water's edge. In order to use the images, it will be necessary to select out the bridge and water's edge from the original source imagery. This can be accomplished using two different methods, the first of which will be used to capture the water's edge.

Figure 28.3. The source imagery that will be used to create the context.

1. Using the Lasso tool, simply trace a rough selection around the area of the water's edge that needs to be selected. The tracing does not need to be accurate; it merely needs to encompass the area to be extracted.

Figure 28.4. Select the edge that will be used in the rendering.

2. Copy the selected area using Cmd/Ctrl+C (or select **Edit > Copy**) and switch back to the model base image and paste the water's edge into the image. Create a new layer group, name it **far context**, and drop the pasted artwork into the group.

3. Position the artwork into the area where it will be used, in this instance the artwork is warped. Use the Free Transform tool (Cmd/Ctrl+T) and then right-click within the bounding box on the canvas and choose Warp. Adjust the edges and rectangles of the warp to straighten the image. Press Enter or double-click within the bounding box when done.

Figure 28.5. Transforming the edge with the Warp tool.

4. Position the image and use the Free Transform tool (Cmd/Ctrl +T) to scale the image into the location. Using the Warp, Skew, and Perspective transforms, finish transforming the image.

5. It is easier to delete the background from the context artwork now as opposed to doing it in the source image. This can be done using the Magic Wand tool to select the sky and then deleting it using the Eraser tool to remove a portion of the water. If a soft edge is used to delete the water, it will blend better into the water from the model.

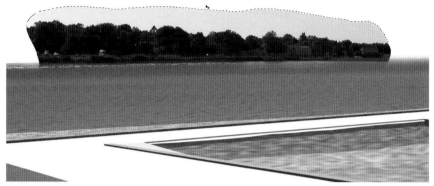

Figure 28.6. Select the sky with the Magic Wand and delete.

The second image is the bridge that must be extracted from the blue sky. This can be accomplished using Select by Color Range.

1. Before using Select by Color Range, convert the background layer of the source image to a normal layer, double-click on the layer, and then click OK when the dialog box appears.
2. Using the Crop tool (C), crop the image down to the edges of the bridge. Leave a small amount of room, 5 to 10 pixels.
3. Instead of selecting the bridge directly, it will be easier to select the sky because it has a continuous and similar range of colors. Selecting the bridge would require increasing the color range across several colors, creating a selection with excess selections across the image. Go to **Select > Color Range**. In the dialog box, make sure that Select is set to Sampled Colors, Fuzziness is around 30 to 40, and that the radio button for Selection is activated. The color range to be selected will be colors that are sampled from the image. The Eyedropper is used to specify the colors to be selected. The Fuzziness controls how far beyond the selected color range the selection will go. The Selection radio button simply creates a preview in the window of what the selection will be, rather than a preview of the image.

Figure 28.7. Crop the source image to the edges of the bridge before selecting.

4. To make the selection, use the Eyedropper to select a blue in the sky. The selection preview will appear in the window. Hold down the Ctrl or Cmd key and select another blue in the sky; this will add to the selection. Continue selecting blue pixels until the entire sky is selected in the preview window. Press OK to apply the selection.

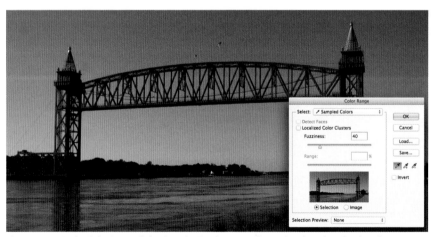

Figure 28.8. In the Color Range dialog box, the Eyedropper will sample color values for the selection.

5. The sky is now selected. If selected areas need to be kept, those areas can be deselected using the Selection tool. Because the layer is not a background layer, the pixels can simply be deleted. If there are more areas to select, Select Color Range can be used again.

Figure 28.9. The sky is selected for deletion.

6. After everything has been deleted, drag the layer into the base image and use the Transform tool to align the context image.

The last step is to add the sky, blend the context, and organize the context layers.

1. Create a new layer group and pull it below the model base. Place both context layers into this new context folder.

2. Create a new layer and call it **sky**. Switch to the Gradient tool and make sure it is set to a linear gradient. Change the foreground color to white, and then switch the foreground and background by pressing X. Double-click the new foreground swatch and use the Eyedropper to select a blue from the water. The color of water is usually just a reflection of the sky and, therefore, it will look right if the blue comes from the water.

Figure 28.10. The bridge is placed into the rendering and transformed.

3. Make the sky layer Active. Using the Gradient tool, drag from the top of the image down to the bottom while holding down the Shift key; this will keep the gradient straight. This will create a gradient that goes from blue (foreground color) to white (background color). The white should be on the horizon line, and it should then go up to the blue sky.

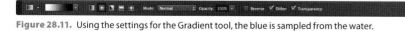

Figure 28.11. Using the settings for the Gradient tool, the blue is sampled from the water.

4. Select the other context layers (the bridge and water's edge) and adjust the opacity to approximately 70%. This will blend the context layers with the sky.

The context will instantly ground the image in a recognizable landscape. This provides a sense of scale and orientation for the model base.

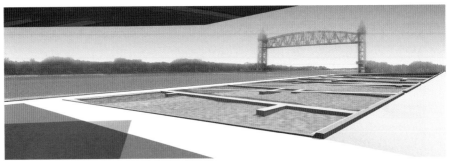

Figure 28.12. Using the settings for the Gradient tool, the blue is sampled from the water.

Textures

The next steps will be to add texture to the model using source imagery. The wetland area near the front of the image needs to have texture added.

1. The source image is a view of a marsh area from an elevated perspective. In order to use the image, simply drag it into the perspective rendering and align the bottom edge with the bottom of the wetland area.

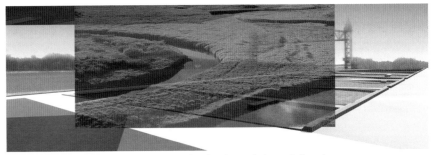

Figure 28.13. The wetland texture image is placed in the rendering and aligned.

2. Using the Free Transform tool (Cmd/Ctrl+T), scale the image down so that the perspective changes. Press Enter after the image has been transformed to set the transformation. Rename the current layer to **wetland texture** and then turn off the layer.
3. Using the Polygon Lasso, make sure the feather is set to 0. Trace around the edge of the wetland area, and zoom in if necessary. As the cursor gets near the edge of the canvas, it will scroll. If a mistake is made, use the Backspace or Delete key to undo one step.

Figure 28.14. The image is scaled down vertically to change the perspective and to fit within the space.

Figure 28.15. The Polygon Lasso is used to select around the edges.

4. Turn the wetland texture layer back on, and make it Active. Then create a layer mask. It will use the current selection to mask the image. Adjust the layer opacity on the image to blend it with the model below.

5. The color of the texture can be adjusted by adding a hue and saturation adjustment layer above the wetland texture layer. Adjust the color; this will affect all of the layers below the wetland texture layer. Hold down the Alt key and hover the cursor over the area between the adjustment layer and the wetland texture layer in the Layers palette. When the Clip icon appears, click the mouse button. This will apply the adjustment only to the pixels on the wetland texture layer.

Figure 28.16. A layer mask crops the image, and an adjustment layer is clipped to the image in order to change the hue/saturation.

Because masks and adjustment layers are being used, it is possible to reposition the texture or adjust the color at any point during the rendering process.

Adding Vegetation

This example will highlight how to add two types of vegetation to the perspective. Grasses in the wetland area will be added first, and then trees will be added as smart objects to the walkway near the water's edge.

1. For grasses to be added to the wetland area, a source image that contains the grasses is needed. The following image will work for this rendering. The grass edges and background are much too complicated to cut out by hand. Not only would it take many hours to accomplish, but it would never look convincing. In this case, just use the Polygon Lasso tool (L), select a portion of the grasses to be used in the rendering, and copy them (Cmd/Ctr+C).

2. Create a layer group at the top of the layer stack in the perspective rendering, and paste the grasses into the group. Select the layer and make it Active.

Figure 28.17. Quickly select a portion of the grass area to be used within the rendering.

3. Use the Move tool (V) to position the grasses. Using the Free Transform tool (Cmd/Ctrl+T), scale, skew, and transform the grasses within the wetland area until they match the perspective.

4. Instead of selecting the background away from the grasses, it is much faster to use a brush tip with custom settings to erase away the edge. In this instance, the Grass Brush

tip shape (rotated upside down, and with scatter dynamics applied) will create a per-fect eraser to create the top edge of the grasses. If possible, it is better to use brushes to create complex edges when Color Range or the Magic Wand can't be used.

Figure 28.18. Use the Scale, Skew, and Perspective transforms to adjust the image.

Figure 28.19. A dynamic brush can be used to erase the top edge of the grasses.

5. Rename the layer to **grass texture** and adjust the opacity to approximately 75 to 80%. This will blend the grasses with the rendering. Create a new layer group, put the grass texture in it, and copy the grasses around the wetland area using the Move tool while holding down the Alt key. Use the Eraser brush previously created to alter each of the grasses so that they are not identical.

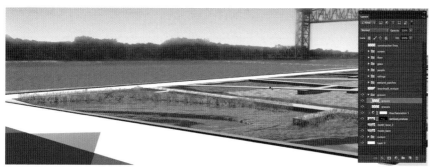

Figure 28.20. The grass image is copied and transformed throughout the desired area.

6. When adding collage elements, such as the grass, shading needs to be added to ground the element into the rendering. Create a new layer and place it under the grass texture layer. Switch to the Brush tool and choose a soft brush. Hold down the Alt key; this will switch to Eyedropper. Pick a dark color near the base of the grasses. Go into the color swatch and make the color much darker.

7. Paint around the base of the grasses on the new layer. The color will be much darker than needed. Switch the layer screening mode to Multiply, and adjust the opacity to 15 to 35%. This shading provides shadows at the base of the grasses and grounds the image in the rendering.

Figure 28.21. Shading is applied to the base of the grasses to create shadow.

This method can be used to add any collage element that has random edges. The shading helps to solve the cut-and-paste effect that occurs when combining elements from different images. For some images, it may also be necessary to use adjustments such as Hue and Saturation, or Brightness and Contrast, to blend the images with the rendering.

The next step will be to add trees using smart objects. The trees will be added using an existing entourage file.

1. Drag the tree into the rendering and rename the layer to **park tree**. Right-click on the layer and choose Convert to Smart Object. Place the smart object into a new layer group called **trees**.

2. Position the tree within the rendering. Go into Free Transform mode (Cmd/Ctrl+T). Move the origin point to the base of the tree. While holding down Alt+Shift, scale the tree to the correct size. Shift will keep the scaling proportional, and Alt will scale the image around the origin point, which is at the bottom of the tree image.

3. Copy and scale the tree images into position within the rendering. Reorder the layers so that trees in the background are behind trees in the foreground.

4. Adjust the layer opacity of the trees. The trees in the foreground should be at 95% opacity, and the trees in the background should be at approximately 60%. The trees in the middleground should have an opacity that is somewhere between 60 and 90%.

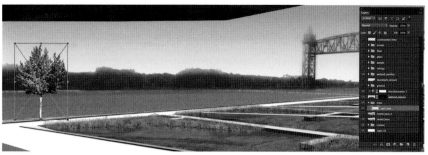

Figure 28.22. The tree image is inserted, positioned, and scaled.

Figure 28.23. The trees are copied and adjusted to blend within the perspective.

Adding Scale Figures

Scale figures help define the spatial quality of a rendering. Figures can also convey the program of a given space. Whenever possible, use the activity of figures to illustrate what people may experience within the various spaces. The scale figures will be added using an existing entourage file.

1. Drag the layer into the rendering and rename the layer to **people standing**. Create a new layer group entitled **entourage** and place the layer in the group. Transform and position the file within the rendering using the Transform tool.
2. Depending on the rendering style, the entourage can be rendered as black and white. Simply go to Image > Adjust > Black and White.
3. To add a shadow for the people, create a new layer under the People Standing layer. Hold down Ctrl and click the People Standing Layer thumbnail to select the pixels on that layer. Make the new layer Active, and fill the selection with black.

Figure 28.24. The scale figures are inserted and transformed.

This will create a black silhouette of the people. For some renderings, silhouettes can be used instead of the actual images of the people.

4. In this case, Free Transform (Cmd/Ctrl+T) the silhouette, right-click, and flip it vertically. Position the silhouette at the base of the people and scale it vertically. Skew the shadow in the direction of the light.

5. Rename the silhouette layer to **people standing shadow**. Adjust the opacity to 50% and change the screening mode to Multiply. Adjust the People Standing layer to approximately 80%. This will blend the shadow and the entourage with the rendering.

Figure 28.25. The figures are selected, and a new layer is filled with black to create a silhouette.

Figure 28.26. The silhouette is flipped vertically, scaled, and skewed to create a shadow that aligns with light cast in the perspective.

Figure 28.27. The figures are blended with the perspective by lowering the opacity.

The same techniques described previously can be used to finish the texturing, add vegetation, and create depth in the final rendering. It is important to realize that it is not always necessary to create complex selections in order to add complex imagery to a rendering. If possible, use Photoshop's brush dynamics to create complex edges. It is also important to use adjustments and opacity to blend the elements within the illustration.

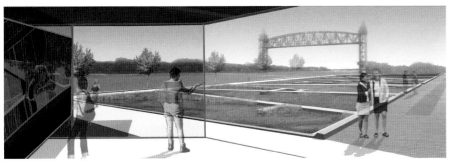

Figure 28.28. The final rendering was created using a combination of the previously mentioned techniques. *Bradley Cantrell and Kenneth Wes Michaels*

Bibliography

As, Imdat, and Daniel Schodek. *Dynamic Digital Representations in Architecture.* New York: Taylor and Francis, 2008.

Belofsy, Harold. "Engineering Drawing—A Universal Language in Two Dialects." *Technology and Culture*, Vol. 32, No. 1 (Jan. 1991): 23–46.

Booker, Peter Jeffrey. *A History of Engineering Drawing.* London: Chatto and Windus, 1963.

Corner, James. *Recovering Landscape: Essays in Contemporary Landscape Theory.* New York: Princeton Architectural Press, 1999.

Dilnot, Clive. "The State of Design History, Part I: Mapping the Field" and "The State of Design History, Part II: Problems and Possibilities." *Design Issues*, Vol. 1, Nos. 1 and 2 (Spring and Autumn 1984).

Dittmar, Gunter, Kenneth Rogers, and Emmanuel Ginis. "Architecture and Depiction." *Design Quarterly*, No. 113/114, City Segments (1980): 4–7.

Doyle, Michael E. *Color Drawing: Design Drawing Skills and Techniques for Architects, Landscape Architects, and Interior Designers.* Hoboken, NJ: Wiley, 2006.

Jones, Peter Lloyd. "Drawing for Designing." *Leonardo*, Vol. 17, No. 4 (1984): 269–276.

Leggitt, Jim. *Drawing Shortcuts: Developing Quick Drawing Skills Using Today's Technology.* New York: Wiley, 2002.

Meggs, Philip B. *A History of Graphic Design.* New York: Van Nostrand Reinhold, 1983 and 1992.

Reid, Grant. *Landscape Graphics.* London: Watson-Guptill, 2002.

Sullivan, Chip. *Drawing the Landscape.* Hoboken, NJ: Wiley, 2004.

Theory in Landscape Architecture: A Reader (Penn Studies in Landscape Architecture). Philadelphia: University of Pennsylvania Press, 2002.

Thiel, Philip. "Unique Profession, Unique Preparation." *Journal of Architectural Education*, Vol. 17, No. 1 (Oct. 1962): 8–13.

Treib, Marc. *Representing Landscape Architecture.* New York: Routledge, 2008.

Tufte, Edward R. *Envisioning Information.* New York: Graphics Press, Cheshire, 1992.

Tufte, Edward R. *The Visual Display of Quantitative Information*, 2d ed. New York: Graphics Press, 1992.

Waldheim, Charles. *The Landscape Urbanism Reader.* New York: Princeton Architectural Press, 2006.

White, Jan V. *Using Charts and Graphs: One Thousand Ideas for Getting Attention Using Charts and Graphs.* Englewood, CO: Libraries Unlimited, 1984.

Woodward, David. "Cartography and Design History: A Commentary." *Design Issues*, Vol. 2, No. 2 (Autumn 1985): 69–71.

INDEX